Disability

Disability

Challenges for Social

Insurance, Health Care

Financing, and Labor

Market Policy

Edited by
Virginia P. Reno
Jerry L. Mashaw
Bill Gradison

NATIONAL ACADEMY OF SOCIAL INSURANCE
Washington, D.C.

Copyright © 1997
National Academy of Social Insurance
1776 Massachusetts Avenue, N.W., Washington, D.C. 20036
Distributed worldwide by Brookings Institution Press
1775 Massachusetts Avenue, N.W., Washington, D.C. 20036-2188, U.S.A.

Library of Congress Cataloging-in-Publication Data

Disability : challenges for social insurance, health care financing, and labor market
  policy / edited by Virginia P. Reno, Jerry L. Mashaw, Bill Gradison.
    p. cm.
  Papers presented at the Eighth Annual Conference of the National Academy of
    Social Insurance, held in Washington, D.C., Jan. 25-26, 1996.
  Includes bibliographical references and index.
  ISBN 0-8157-7405-2
  1. Insurance, Disability—Government policy—United States—Congresses.
  2. Vocational rehabilitation—Government policy—United States—Congresses.
  3. Handicapped—Employment—Government policy—United States—
  Congresses.   4. Health care reform—United States—Congresses.
  5. Social security—United States—Congresses.   I. Reno, Virginia P.
  II. Mashaw, Jerry L.   III. Gradison, Willis D., 1928- .   IV. National
  Academy of Social Insurance (U.S.). Conference (8th : 1996 : Washington, D.C.)
HD7105.25.U6D574   1997   96-45847
362.4′0973—dc21   CIP

9 8 7 6 5 4 3 2 1

Typeset in Times Roman

Composition by AlphaWebTech
  Mechanicsville, Maryland

Printed by R. R. Donnelley and Sons Co.
  Harrisonburg, Virginia

Preface

The National Academy of Social Insurance is a nonprofit, nonpartisan organization devoted to furthering knowledge and understanding of social insurance programs and principles. It conducts research and serves as a forum for discussion and debate on important developments in the field of social insurance.

This book is based on papers delivered at the Academy's eighth annual conference, held January 25-26, 1996. The conference featured findings and recommendations of the Academy's Disability Policy Panel, which was convened in response to a request from the Chairman of the Ways and Means Committee in the 102nd Congress.

The Academy received financial support for its Disability Policy Project, including the dissemination activities of the conference, from The Pew Charitable Trusts, The Robert Wood Johnson Foundation, and corporate members of the Health Insurance Association of America that offer long-term disability insurance. UNUM Life Insurance Company also contributed to the conference. The Commonwealth Fund provided support for the paper by Stanley B. Jones, who also thanks Lynn Etheredge for his assistance.

As with all activities organized under its auspices, the Academy takes responsibility for ensuring the independence of this book. Participants in the conference were chosen for their recognized expertise and with due consideration of the balance of disciplines appropriate to the program. The resulting chapters are the views of the presenters and are not necessarily the views of the officers, board, or members of the Academy.

The editors would like to thank all of the conference participants for sparking a lively discussion and debate. We also commend the Academy staff for facilitating the smooth running of the conference, in particular, Pamela Larson, Terry Nixon, Kathryn Olson, Suzanne Payne, and Cynthia Spiller-Goodman.

We appreciate the efforts of all those who made this book possible: the authors for their attention to the task of turning their presentations into chapters; the Academy staff who organized the process, Kathryn Olson and Allison Watts; the manuscript editor, Colleen McGuiness; the indexer, Max Franke; and the staff of the Brookings Institution Press.

VIRGINIA P. RENO
JERRY L. MASHAW
BILL GRADISON

Contents

1

Introduction

Virginia P. Reno

THE EIGHTH ANNUAL CONFERENCE of the National Academy of Social Insurance, held January 25–26, 1996,
drew more than three hundred participants to discuss findings of the
Academy's Disability Policy Panel and to explore how trends in Medicare and
Medicaid and in twenty-four-hour coverage in workers' compensation affect
working-age Americans with chronic health conditions or disabilities. The
conference also examined an often-neglected side of disability policy, namely
how labor market developments affect employment opportunities for disadvantaged workers in general and workers with disabilities in particular.

Conference cochair Bill Gradison, president of the Health Insurance Association of America and former U.S. representative (R-Ohio, 1975–93), opened
the conference by acknowledging the backdrop of federal budget debate on
Medicare and Medicaid. Drawing on his ten years' experience serving on the
House Budget Committee, he noted that social policy decisionmaking is often
budget-driven, not policy-driven. Social insurance issues are at the center of
political debate today, he added, and new thinking must be done about the
relative responsibilities of various sectors and payers; how to define the functions of the federal government and state governments; what responsibilities, if
any, should rest with employers; and what individuals and their families ought
to do for themselves. He concluded that, despite highly charged policy debates,
this conference is dedicated to the proposition that there is still room for
rational discourse on social insurance issues and that through such efforts
public policies can be affected in a positive way.

In introducing the first session, "Disability Benefits Policy: Is There a
Crisis?" Susan Daniels, associate commissioner for disability in the Social
Security Administration (SSA), observed that advances in treatment for people
with physical disabilities, mental illness, and mental retardation have brought
enormous changes and opportunities for them. Technology—both assistive

1

technology and general technology available to everyone—has dramatically changed the potential of people with disabilities, and American social values of equity and fairness have brought about changes in law in relation to people with disabilities. Consequently, rethinking social policy is appropriate, natural, and beneficial to Americans with disabilities and to those without.

Jerry L. Mashaw, Sterling professor of law at Yale University and chair of the Academy's Disability Policy Panel, reported on the Panel's findings and recommendations after nearly three years of study. The Panel's charge was to answer three basic questions: (1) Do Social Security disability benefits provide a strong disincentive for people to work? (2) How can an emphasis on rehabilitation and work be built into the cash benefit programs without greatly increasing costs or weakening the right to benefits for those who cannot work? (3) Are there ways to restructure disability income policy that would encourage beneficiaries to use their residual work capacity?

In answer to the first question, the Panel concluded that current benefits are not a strong deterrent to work. While any income support can be viewed as some degree of work disincentive, the Panel's conclusion derives from the strict and frugal design of the Social Security disability insurance (DI) and Supplemental Security Income (SSI) programs, the circumstances of persons who receive these benefits, and cross-national comparisons of spending on disability benefits. U.S. spending on public disability benefits, at 0.7 percent of gross domestic product (GDP) in 1991, is relatively low compared with other industrialized countries. It is less than half the share spent in the United Kingdom (1.9 percent) or in Germany (2.0 percent), which is often a model for its emphasis on rehabilitation before pensions. And U.S. spending is less than one-fourth the spending in Sweden (3.3 percent), which also emphasizes rehabilitation and public sector employment, if needed, for workers with disabilities.

In contrast with disability benefits in the public systems of other countries or in the private sector in the United States, Social Security replacement rates are modest. They fall far short of enough to maintain a disabled worker's earlier standard of living. The modest replacement rates reflect an expectation that Social Security benefits will be supplemented by pensions or insurance and savings. But disabled workers are much less likely than retirees to have these supplemental sources of income. The vastly smaller amount of asset holdings of disabled workers is particularly striking and reflects two realities about the onset of disability. First, it occurs unexpectedly, before workers have accumulated their hoped-for retirement savings. Second, new costs at the onset of disability—health care, medications, and living expenses during waiting periods for cash benefits—can deplete retirement savings.

While neither DI nor SSI pose strong work disincentives, the Panel concluded that constraints on access to health care can be a significant barrier to work. Lack of health care can result in unnecessary losses in employment when workers fail to get the care they need. Further, the high cost of health care for people with chronic conditions is likely to influence hiring decisions of employers. And fear of losing coverage through Medicare or Medicaid can be a significant barrier to employment for disability beneficiaries. Lack of health care coverage is a much more important structural impediment than are disability cash benefits.

Drawing on national statistics and interviews with beneficiaries, Mashaw pointed out that, within the broad population of persons with disabilities, those who receive Social Security or SSI are the subset with the most significant and persistent impediments to work. Only a fraction have prospects for returning to work. Nonetheless, the Panel believes there is room for improvement.

On the question of linking beneficiaries with rehabilitation, the Panel recommends a radical new approach of issuing return-to-work (RTW) vouchers to beneficiaries. On the question of promoting work through changes in income policy, the Panel recommends a disabled worker tax credit (DWTC), modeled after the earned income tax credit (EITC). Other Panel proposals to promote return to work among beneficiaries include a simplified and affordable way for former DI beneficiaries to purchase Medicare coverage after they return to work; a tax credit under the federal income tax for part of the cost of personal assistance services that disabled individuals need to work; and improvements in the implementation of work-incentive provisions in the DI and SSI programs.

Mashaw noted that, in its review, the Panel emphasized that work disability is a relational concept and is distinct from an impairment. While a chronic health condition or impairment is an important element of disability, work disability occurs only when an impairment, in conjunction with the person's other abilities, the demands of work, and the broader environment, make him or her unable to perform the tasks of work. In the Panel's analysis, changes in the broader environment are important in understanding causes of the growth in the disability rolls in the early 1990s. Such changes included a growing eligible population, the shock of an economic recession, declining demand for workers doubly disadvantaged by chronic health conditions and limited skills, and retrenchment in other parts of the support system for persons whose capacity to work is severely limited.

The Panel concluded that, in addition to its legislative proposals to promote work, matching policy commitments with adequate resources to administer them is essential. In cash benefit programs, low administrative costs can too quickly translate into high program costs. The recession of the early 1990s came on the heels of a 25 percent reduction in staffing at the Social Security Administration. The Panel emphasized that, to maintain proper stewardship and public confidence in cash benefit programs, administrative resources must be sufficient to promptly and accurately decide claims, provide essential services to beneficiaries, and conduct timely reviews of the continuing eligibility of those receiving benefits.

Mashaw concluded that, while some changes are warranted, a crisis does not exist in disability policy. Talk of crisis is counterproductive and has precipitated radical swings in disability policy in the past. Too often corrective action came after problems were already being attended, thereby fostering overreaction in the opposite direction. In the final analysis, disability income policy will be judged by the balance it achieves between the twin goals of providing a decent level of income support to those who are unable to work and offering realistic opportunities and supports for those who have the capacity to work.

Bringing a cross-national perspective, Philip R. de Jong, professor of economics at Erasmus University, Rotterdam, and fellow at the Leiden University Institute for Law and Public Policy in the Netherlands, noted that European disability pension systems differ from those in the United States in several important respects. First, they coexist with more comprehensive systems of national health insurance, unemployment insurance, short-term sickness and temporary disability benefits, and universal assistance for the poor. Second, by U.S. standards, long-term disability benefits in European countries are relatively generous, with replacement rates of 60 to 70 percent, and some have generous benefits for partial disability. Holland, in particular, has high spending on long-term disability benefits and has introduced retrenchment initiatives to reduce that spending.

The Dutch reforms seek to strengthen incentives and shift some of the cost of disability from public programs to private individuals, employers, and insurers. Reforms affecting workers would reduce replacement rates—albeit to levels that still look generous in the United States—and tighten eligibility criteria to more closely resemble American standards. Reforms affecting employers would privatize short-term sickness benefits by requiring employers to provide them directly to their own workers instead of through a universal public system. Holland is also considering privatizing long-term disability benefits, perhaps using the American workers' compensation system as a model. De Jong concludes that both demographic pressures and fiscal constraints are pushing European systems in the direction of American disability income policies.

Dallas Salisbury, president of the Employee Benefit Research Institute, brought a private sector view of recent trends in employer-financed benefits in the United States. A new focus on the total cost of disability to employers—including the direct cost of employees' health and disability benefits and the indirect cost of lost time from work, replacement workers, and productivity losses—has led employers to look at aggressive disability management as a way to control costs. At the same time, the availability of both health and disability insurance coverage is declining among private and public sector employees. Coverage under employment-based health insurance declined by another 2.8 million individuals in 1994, he noted, while the dramatic move toward managed care continues. Of those with employment-based health coverage, those enrolled in managed care plans rose from about 26 percent in 1988 to an estimated 65 percent in 1995. Employee cost sharing is becoming the rule, not the exception, in employment-based health insurance.

Private long-term disability benefits cover a minority of employees today, according to Salisbury, and the number of insurance companies willing to offer these policies is declining. As the work force ages and the baby boomers enter the disability-prone years, these policies and their premiums are less attractive to insurers and employers. One consequence of recent trends is that work-based benefits are moving toward greater flexibility that allows employees to opt out of health and disability coverage and receive cash compensation instead. This flexibility is appealing to younger employees who, Salisbury notes, are confident they will not face sickness or long-term disability.

In opening the second session, "Encouraging Work through Cash Benefit Policy: New Proposals," Susan Suter, president of the World Institute on Disability and a member of the Academy's Panel, emphasized two recurring themes in disability policy: People with disabilities prefer work to benefits; and facilitating work often means dealing with the interaction between the individual's abilities and the environment. Building on those themes, professor emeritus of economics at Rutgers University Monroe Berkowitz provocatively defended the Panel's proposal for return-to-work (RTW) vouchers.

Under that plan, beneficiaries would receive an RTW ticket that they could use to shop among providers of rehabilitation or RTW services in either the public or private sector. Once a beneficiary deposited the ticket with a service provider, the Social Security Administration would have an obligation to pay the provider, but only after the beneficiary returns to work and leaves the benefit rolls. Providers whose clients successfully return to work would, each year, receive in payment a fraction of the benefit savings that accrue to the Social Security trust funds because the former beneficiary is at work and not receiving benefits.

Berkowitz emphasized the many appealing features of the plan. First, it incorporates the principle in existing law that the purpose of paying for rehabilitation services out of Social Security trust funds is to reduce long-run trust fund expenditures. Second, it gives beneficiaries a choice of the service providers. This contrasts with past policies, when only state vocational rehabilitation agencies were paid from trust funds for serving beneficiaries. Third, it fosters competition among service providers—both public and private—and could expand access to rehabilitation services for beneficiaries. Fourth, it rewards service providers for their results, not for the cost of their inputs. Consequently, providers who are effective would make a profit. At the same time, the incentive-based payments would be cost-effective for the Social Security trust funds. Finally, it is administrable by the Social Security Administration.

The RTW ticket proposal is also appealing for what it does not do, according to Berkowitz. First, it does not attempt to define in federal rules who should be selected for services, what services they should be offered, or what fee is reasonable for those services. These kinds of decisions are best made on a case-by-case basis between service providers and individual beneficiaries. As Berkowitz explained, "For whatever reason, SSA has not proven to be an effective rehabilitation agency. (That is a bit like saying that the Internal Revenue Service has not done a good job of improving the mental health of the taxpayers.) Rehabilitation has never been defined as SSA's responsibility." Second, the plan does not spend trust fund monies for services that are not effective. Because payments to providers are made only after trust fund savings accrue, providers would be paid only when they are successful. Payments might well exceed the cost of the providers' services. But they would be only a fraction of the savings to the trust funds.

In commenting on the proposal, Tony Young of the American Rehabilitation Association supported the incentive-based approach but urged that it be modified to allow interim payments to providers as certain milestones are achieved on the road toward the client's return to work. Without milestone payments, he argued, small-scale service providers could not afford to participate. Consequently, the plan would not achieve the desired level of consumer choice and ultimate success in promoting work and yielding benefit savings. Young also expressed disappointment in the modest expectations of success, indicating that higher return-to-work rates are needed.

William G. Johnson, professor of economics at Arizona State University, expressed skepticism about the proposal's chances for success, likening it to Samuel Johnson's definition of a second marriage as "a triumph of hope over experience." He attributed his low expectations to the poor record of past efforts to rehabilitate beneficiaries, the strict eligibility criteria that beneficiaries have already met, and his recent research on return-to-work outcomes for workers with partial disabilities in Ontario. That study found that many who did return to work ultimately left the work force because of the long-term effect of their disabling conditions and others had multiple repeated episodes of work incapacity.

Berkowitz, nonetheless, urged that the RTW proposal is worth a try, arguing that, to the extent that effective service providers are linked with highly motivated beneficiaries through the market-based approach, a chance remains to make some individuals better off, without making others worse off, and to yield trust fund savings in the process.

Richard V. Burkhauser, professor of economics at Syracuse University, made the case for a second innovative proposal from the Disability Policy Panel. The disabled worker tax credit (DWTC) would be a wage subsidy for low-income workers with disabilities that would be separate from the Social Security disability benefit programs. The wage subsidy would be paid to low-income persons not because they are unable to work, but because they work despite their impairments. Patterned after the existing earned income tax credit (EITC), it would reward work for low earners with disabilities without increasing reliance on disability benefit programs that are designed primarily for persons who are unable to work.

The DWTC is designed for three groups in particular. First, older workers would be encouraged to remain at work even though they experience a decline in hours of work or wage rates as a result of progressive impairments. In his research, Burkhauser found that many people spend a long time—three to five years—from the onset of a health problem until they ultimately leave work. The wage subsidy would help some of them avoid or delay turning to disability benefits. Second, the transition would be eased from school to work for young people with developmental disabilities whose earnings capacity is doubly limited by their youth and their impairments. By subsidizing their earnings, it encourages work even part-time or at low pay that over the long run can improve young workers' human capital through on-the-job experience. Finally, transition would be facilitated off the DI and SSI rolls for beneficiaries who return to work. The wage subsidy would compensate for some of the loss of benefits that occurs when beneficiaries work.

The exact parameters for a DWTC will determine its cost and impact. Under the illustrative proposal the Panel developed, about 3.1 million low-income working people with disabilities are estimated to receive the credit, at a total cost of about $3 billion, in 1996. The recipients would be mainly working disabled individuals with incomes below twice the poverty threshold.

William Johnson commended the careful design of the DWTC proposal but cautioned that, unless problems of access to health care for working people with disabilities are addressed, a wage subsidy alone may not have the hope-for effect of increasing employment.

In his commentary, Michael J. Graetz, law professor at Yale University, pointed to issues that have been raised about the earned income tax credit on which the DWTC is based. Those issues involve the complexity of the EITC, issues of inclusion and compliance, the delivery of the credit, work incentives, and potential marriage penalties. As alternatives, he suggested two other kinds of tax proposals: One would exempt low-income workers from the Social Security tax altogether; a second, modeled after the targeted jobs tax credit, would subsidize employers directly for employing workers with disabilities. Burkhauser, in response, noted that the existing EITC for childless workers is about equivalent to an exemption from Social Security taxes. The purpose of the Panel's DWTC proposal is to build on that to provide a positive subsidy for low-wage workers with disabilities. Furthermore, while the targeted jobs tax credit has been available to low-income disabled workers as well as other disadvantaged workers, it has had a limited effect. Studies have questioned whether the jobs credit increases long-term employment or simply subsidizes employment that would have occurred anyway. The DWTC is a more effective way to make work pay for low-income workers with disabilities.

"Challenges in Medicare and Medicaid for Persons with Disabilities" was the topic of session three, introduced by Robert Reischauer of the Brookings Institution and chair of the Academy's Steering Committee on the Future of Medicare. Bruce C. Vladeck, administrator of the Health Care Financing Administration, acknowledged that disability policy, and the relationship of Medicare and Medicaid to it, is in a state of evolutionary flux. Here as everywhere, he noted, the definition of the problem is the first critical challenge. What various groups—the public, the press, and policymakers—perceive as problems, or solutions, relates to their conceptions of disability. These conceptions underlie the programmatic responses to disability that they advocate and also provide the perspective from which they evaluate success or failure.

The traditional priorities of public, as well as private, health insurance center on acute care, not long-term care, Vladeck added. Consequently, the health policy debate tends to be about the payments made, instead of not made. This focus leaves gaps in Medicare and Medicaid coverage of services that persons with disabilities would use. For example, the programs give short shrift to mental health services; institutional long-term care services still outweigh community-based services; and access to assistive technology is limited. As a result, individuals with disabilities generally find that they do not get enough help, or at least not enough of the kind of help they prefer, from Medicare and Medicaid.

Stanley B. Jones of George Washington University explored the challenges faced by large payers for health care coverage—such as Medicare, Medicaid, and large employers—as they attempt to establish incentives for managed care plans to offer quality care to chronically ill persons. In the market of competing health care plans, the threat of adverse selection encouraged plans to be ambivalent, at best, about investing in care for the chronically ill. On a societal level, such investments offer great potential for reducing costs and improving value. But for an individual plan in a competitive market, to do better than its competitors in delivering value to people with chronic conditions runs the risk of attracting more chronically ill subscribers, thereby driving up its costs and premiums in comparison with its competitors. Consequently, health plans have an incentive to de-market their plans among chronically ill consumers.

Patricia Riley, of the National Academy for State Health Policy, focused her analysis on the special problems faced by states and by disability beneficiaries when they are dually eligible for both Medicare and Medicaid. According to Riley, about one-third of all persons with disabilities who are under age sixty-five and covered by Medicaid are dually eligible for Medicare. That happens when persons qualify for the federal Medicare program through their entitlement to Social Security disability benefits, but because they have low income and limited assets, they also qualify for means-tested Medicaid coverage that is determined by state rules. Differences between the two programs make dual coverage problematic for states that are seeking to manage care and control the costs of their Medicaid programs, she notes. For example, while the federal Medicare program offers beneficiaries a choice of whether or not to participate in managed care, states can require Medicaid beneficiaries to enroll in managed care plans. While Medicare charges beneficiaries premiums and imposes cost-sharing, the means-tested Medicaid program for low-income persons generally does not. And while Medicare covers mainly acute care, Medicaid also covers long-term care.

R. Alexander Vachon, professional staff member of the Senate Finance Committee, brought a contemporary legislative perspective to issues of disability policy. He argues that a "new age of reform" is precipitated by three events. First, the end of the cold war has weakened the rationale for providing domestic spending on national security grounds. Second, the expansion of federal authority that began during the economic emergency of the Great Depression has stopped. He cites the enactment of welfare reform legislation in August 1996 as clear evidence of this change. Finally, federal budget deficits continue to place enormous pressure on discretionary domestic spending. He argues that the welfare reform cuts in cash benefits for adults with addiction disorders and for low-income children with disabilities do not represent a return to the punitive dark days of disability policy, as feared by Vladeck. Instead, the cuts were based on the belief that treatment and services are more effective than cash support, according to Vachon. He criticizes two recent studies of the SSI childhood disability program for failing to address whether cash benefits or services yield better outcomes for children. Those studies concluded that both adequate family income and in-kind services are needed by low-income children with disabilities.

In opening the fourth session on "Workers' Compensation, Twenty-Four-Hour Coverage, and Disability Management," Patricia Owens of UNUM Life Insurance Company of America observed that, without national health insurance, the workplace remains at the center of health care coverage and employers are now rethinking how various programs—voluntary health insurance, mandatory workers' compensation, and short-term and long-term disability benefits—should fit together as part of their overall human resource strategy.

John F. Burton, Jr., of Rutgers University, reviewed the varied methods by which states, employers, and insurers are seeking to control the growth in workers' compensation benefits for both medical care and cash compensation paid to workers injured on the job. After a period of rapidly escalating costs in the 1980s, when expenditures rose at an average rate of more than 13 percent a year, spending growth slowed to less than 3 percent a year in the early 1990s. The medical component of compensation continues to grow more rapidly than cash benefits and until recently had grown more rapidly than medical expenditures in the general health care system. According to Burton, the only good news, at least from the perspective of workers' compensation, is that, after 1990, medical benefits in compensation grew more slowly than in the general health care system (4.9 percent compared with 8.3 percent).

The recent move to introduce managed care in workers' compensation is driven by concerns that the rapid growth in compensation costs was caused, in part, by cost-shifting from the rest of the health care system, which has already moved rapidly into managed care arrangements. Traditional approaches to control costs in workers' compensation, such as medical fee schedules, utilization review, hospital prospective payment systems, and limiting employees' choice of treating physician, have not been particularly successful according to Burton's review of the research literature. Employee cost-sharing is increasingly common in employment-based health insurance and is rare and highly controversial in workers' compensation.

Burton concluded that the limited success of traditional cost-containment approaches has prompted consideration of reforms that integrate workers' compensation with other components of the health care system. "Twenty-four-hour coverage" is the term used to describe various efforts to reduce or eliminate distinctions between the benefits and services provided for work-related injuries and those provided in the general health care and disability benefit system.

Burton distinguished among four different approaches to twenty-four-hour coverage, offered examples of these approaches, and analyzed the legal and regulatory issues that arise under each. He concluded that careful studies are needed of the effects of these new initiatives, both in terms of the the cost of medical and cash benefits and the quality of care provided to injured workers. The rapid move toward managed care has preceded hard evidence of its effectiveness. While he is encouraged by current efforts, Burton worries that this may be another area in which workers' compensation reform is based more on fad than fact.

Bruce Barge summarized key elements of sound disability management from his book *The Executive's Guide to Disability Management.* He emphasized that twenty-four-hour management is distinct from twenty-four-hour coverage. Total management involves a focus on employers' total costs, not just premium cost for a particular benefit; an emphasis on the customer, who in the case of disability management is the injured worker; redesign of internal systems to promote effective service to the ill or injured worker; and operations management, which ingrains the objectives of disability management at all levels and functions of the organization.

James N. Ellenberger of the AFL/CIO provided a labor perspective on the tensions in workers' compensation between cost containment and adequate protection for workers. While current discussions focus on reducing costs to employers, he argued that workers pay for job injuries and illness, not only through foregone wages, but also in the loss of their health and reduced well-being of their families. While twenty-four-hour coverage is being sold to employers as a way to control costs, it is less an issue of controlling costs than of retaining or gaining market shares among insurers, dictating choice of physician, and shifting costs onto the backs of workers, he argued.

Ellenberger took particular exception to cost-containment policies related to choice of physician and introduction of copayments in workers' compensation. He observed that introduction of managed care shifts the issue of choice of physician in favor of the insurer or employer. While proponents of managed care traditionally argue that it improves quality and controls unnecessary use of medical care, Ellenberger noted that physicians fill additional roles in workers' compensation. Doctors' views are critical in determining the amount of compensation the insurer or employer owes the employee, because their findings influence determinations about whether the impairment is work-related, the degree of impairment, and under what circumstances the individual can return to work. These are not questions of quality, but of control.

Ellenberger also took exception to the notion of introducing employee copayments into workers' compensation. Shifting costs to workers through copayments or deductibles would alter the historic trade-off between labor and management when workers' compensation schemes were adopted. Under that trade-off, employers accepted full financial responsibility for workers' compensation and, in return, received immunity from tort suits filed by employees for harm caused on the job.

Lex Frieden, vice president of the Institute for Rehabilitation and Research and one of the national leaders credited with passage of the Americans with Disabilities Act of 1990, gave his perspective on the fit between civil rights, social insurance, and jobs. Civil rights do not guarantee work, and social insurance does not guarantee work. As long as discrimination exists, then civil rights protection must be in place. As long as people cannot provide for themselves and their families, a comprehensive social welfare strategy must exist to support people who cannot work, either because of their personal characteristics, the absence of work, or the absence of infrastructure and environmental support in the community.

In the final session, "Alternatives to Income Support: Where Are the Jobs?," economists Alan B. Krueger, of Princeton University, and Van Doorn Ooms, director of research for the Committee for Economic Development (CED), drew similar conclusions from slightly different perspectives. Krueger spent a year as chief economist for the Labor Department in the Clinton administration. Ooms's research is sponsored by corporate leaders who are trustees of the CED. Both highlighted the clear labor market trend in favor of highly skilled workers and against less skilled workers, whose wages have fallen further and further behind.

The change in real wages at the bottom of the wage distribution has been extraordinary, noted Ooms. The drop in real earnings for full-time workers in the lowest 5 to 10 percent of the distribution over the last twenty years has been on the order of 25 to 30 percent, an enormous drop. And wage declines are not just at the bottom. The disparity is growing wider between high school graduates, who comprise a large share of the work force, and college graduates, according to Krueger.

The changes fit with economic theory, which says that an excess supply of less skilled workers relative to the demand for their services will bring a decline in either their employment or their wages, or both. Both have occurred, but the decline in wages is more pronounced. That unemployment is no higher than it is suggests that the labor market is adjusting, according to both Krueger and Ooms. At the same time, noted Ooms, a fundamental problem emerges for society. Historically, education has been the great leveler in American society between people who began life with considerable opportunity and assets and those who did not. But unless the investment in people is changed, education may have the opposite effects: Those who have will get more, and those who start off with little will get less.

Krueger and Ooms agreed that the two leading causes of declining demand for less skilled workers are technological change and rising competitive pressures on employers. The proliferation of computers at work lends support to the technology explanation, according to Krueger. Between 1984 and 1993, the proportion of workers who use computers at work rose from nearly a quarter to nearly half. Ooms added that technology alters demand for workers in two ways. First, workers are displaced by machines—such as automatic teller machines (ATMs) for bank tellers, computer graphics for graphic artists, computer software packages for insurance agents, and the disappearance of telephone operators and gas station attendants. Second, demand increases for highly skilled workers who develop and use the new technology.

Drawing on experience of corporate leaders, Ooms found support for the competitiveness explanation as well as the technology explanation. When he first studied economics, the term "satisficing" described the behavior of managers who did not have to maximize profits or minimize costs. When employers were protected from an extremely competitive environment—by regulatory barriers, economies of scale, or other barriers to entry—a greater margin of benevolence toward their workers was evident. But today, cost-efficiency and productivity improvements are imperative.

The good news, according to Ooms, is that productivity gains bring higher incomes, on average, over the long term. The bad news is that the work place is much less forgiving. These changes fall enormously hard on people without skills at the bottom of the labor market.

Katherine S. Newman, professor of public policy at Harvard University, documented the experience of unskilled workers in her research on rejected applicants for service sector jobs in Harlem. Building on her earlier research on middle-class downward mobility, in *Declining Fortunes* and *Fall from Grace,* her new study found that well-qualified applicants for unskilled jobs in low-income neighborhoods were often unsuccessful. Furthermore, hiring practices disadvantaged particular categories of applicants for minimum-wage jobs. Least likely to be hired were local residents in depressed communities, young people, the native-born, African Americans, high school dropouts, and those who lacked contacts with someone already employed by that particular employer. It is general knowledge that in high-skill occupations, a person must know someone to find a job, Newman explained. This same principle holds at the bottom of the low-wage labor market. Many restaurants in New York City, including the most profitable, had never advertized or hired from walk-in applicants, she found. All recruiting was done through the work force in place.

Newman emphasized the vital importance of recognizing the realities of low-wage labor markets. Qualified job seekers are left feeling desperate when they are turned down for employment despite their best efforts. Believing that less qualified recipients of public benefits are going to do much better is folly. For inner-city minorities and low-skilled persons with disabilities, the problem is not values; it is jobs. There are not enough to go around, Newman concluded.

On the specific question of jobs for persons with disabilities, Krueger and Ooms found some hopeful signs—as well as the need for caution. In a recent study of workers with spinal cord injuries that he conducted with David Kruse of Rutgers University, Krueger found that having a college degree and having used computers at work before the injury greatly increased prospects for post-injury employment. Workers with spinal cord injuries who used computers in their post-injury jobs had earnings comparable to other computer users. However, most injured workers did not have college degrees, and most were not employed after their injuries.

To estimate future job prospects, Krueger compared the occupations of current workers who report work disabilities with Labor Department projections of occupational growth over the next decade. He concluded that job growth is shifting away from the occupations that disabled workers tend to hold. Furthermore, the growing occupations tend to require more education, while workers who report disabilities have fewer years of education, on average, than other workers.

Ooms found a double-edged sword in labor market trends for persons with disabilities. The good news is that highly skilled workers with disabilities will have better prospects for employment and accommodation. And employers who have highly skilled workers (with or without disabilities) will try to keep them, by instituting safety and wellness programs, employee assistance programs, rehabilitation, and return-to-work policies. The bad news is at the other end of the labor market. The cost of accommodating the growing number of contingent, temporary, and low-paid workers is high in relation to their wages and tenure. The double-edged sword means better job prospects for highly skilled workers and an especially harsh labor market for individuals who have both significant skill deficits and disability. Ooms confirmed Newman's finding that limited skills, low income, and disability often occur together and that their combined disadvantages are greater than the sum of their individual effects.

Elaborating on Ooms's theme of the unforgiving work place, Leslie J. Scallet, director of the Mental Health Policy Resource Center, brought her dual perspective as a lawyer and advocate for persons with mental illness and as an employer in a small nonprofit organization. According to Scallet, downsizing and streamlining means employees have to be highly flexible; instead of having two or three employees to do different activities, one employee might be expected to do all kinds of activities. Workers who have mental disabilities will have a harder time being flexible in this kind of environment. Second, the new emphasis on speed and productivity is particularly difficult for workers who have mental disabilities. Third, policies that reduce welfare or other sources of income support bring added competition for low-skill jobs that will make finding and keeping a job more difficult for some workers with disabilities. Finally, many mentally ill people who have found a niche in the work force have done so in a semi-sheltered environment of public or nonprofit agencies. Reduced funding and downsizing in these agencies jeopardizes some of the success that has occurred to date. The ultimate question, according to Scallet, is who should pay the price for shifting demands in the labor market. Without policy intervention, people who have the least power will pay, she concluded.

In his wrap-up of the conference, Jerry Mashaw highlighted the unfinished business of disability policy in three broad domains—in the demand side of the labor market, in health care, and in income policy. In the realm of income policy, he noted that workers' compensation, unemployment insurance, and retirement benefits are, in some cases, alternatives to DI and SSI. But retrenchment or gaps in these programs will increase demands placed on disability income benefits.

He observed that demands on disability policy will not decline through a strategy of benign neglect. The unfinished business of disability policy confronts two major challenges. First, pervasive cost constraints deter investment in human capital and in the administrative resources necessary to make programs work well. The tendency is to promote short-term savings at the risk of long-term losses. In this regard, Frieden urged conferees to meet the cost challenge head-on by figuring out the cost of doing nothing, as well as the cost of any particular policy proposal. A second risk is that political ideology, in either extreme, will triumph over hard facts and prudent judgment. Bill Gradison, however, reminded conferees that political debates have not always been so fractious and need not remain so indefinitely. Many times in the past, bipartisan efforts have forged difficult compromises when they were needed to maintain social insurance programs on a sound and prudent course. In concluding, Mashaw said he was heartened that the Academy offers an independent forum where people of different persuasions can be informed by solid analysis and civilly debate serious issues of public policy, as they did in this conference.

2

Disability Benefits Policy:
Is There a Crisis?

IN ASSESSING EXISTING DISABILITY cash benefits policies, the papers in this chapter report on the findings of the Disability Policy Panel, compare the U.S. and European social welfare programs, and discuss what is happening to disability benefits that go beyond the basic social insurance protection of Social Security.

Findings of the Disability Policy Panel
Jerry L. Mashaw

THE NATIONAL ACADEMY of Social Insurance formed the Disability Policy Panel nearly three years ago in response to a request from the chairmen of the House Ways and Means Committee and its Social Security Subcommittee. To conduct the study, the Academy convened an eighteen-member group from among the nation's leading experts on disability policy. Members came from divergent perspectives and backgrounds, including people from the private sector; public administrators; persons from the disability community; and scholars from a variety of academic disciplines, including economics, law, medicine, rehabilitation, and sociology.

The Panel's charge from the Academy was to respond to three basic questions:

(1) Do disability cash benefits provide a strong disincentive for people to work?

(2) Can an emphasis on rehabilitation and work be incorporated into the disability cash benefit programs without greatly expanding costs or weakening the right to benefits for those who cannot work?

(3) Can disability income policy be restructured to encourage beneficiaries to use their residual work capacity?

Benefits and Work

The Panel concluded that current benefits are not a strong deterrent to work.[1] Anyone who has studied cash benefits policy recognizes that income support can, to some degree, be viewed as a work disincentive, because the purpose of income support is to provide income to substitute for earnings.

—In the case of social insurance—old-age, survivors and disability insurance, and unemployment insurance—benefits make up for part of earnings when workers lose their jobs, lose their capacity to work, or are no longer expected to work. This is the basic purpose of social insurance.

—In the case of social assistance, such as Supplemental Security Income (SSI), benefits provide a basic minimum level of income for people who are poor and are severely limited in their ability to support themselves through work.

The conclusion that benefits are not a strong deterrent to work is based on a review of the strict and frugal design of existing programs, an understanding of the attributes and circumstances of their beneficiaries, and a comparison between U.S. spending on disability benefits and that in other industrialized countries.

Program Design

Social Security disability insurance (DI) and SSI use a test of disability that is the strictest of any disability program in the United States, public or private. Under the law, benefits are paid only when a person has a medically determinable impairment of such severity that, given one's age, education, and work experience, he or she cannot perform substantial gainful work (currently defined as earning more than $500 a month) in any job that exists in significant numbers in the national economy, regardless of whether or not the person would be hired for such a job. Benefits are payable only if the impairment is expected to last twelve months or result in death within a year.

A five-month waiting period is imposed after the onset of a disability before DI benefits are paid and another twenty-four-month waiting period must elapse before Medicare coverage begins.

The modest level of DI benefits can be appreciated by looking at their replacement rates (the level at which benefits replace prior earnings). Studies find that 75 to 80 percent of workers' prior earnings are needed to maintain their standard of living. DI provides much lower replacement rates than these.

1. Mashaw and Reno (1996).

At average earnings and above, replacement rates range from 43 percent for a person earning $25,000 to about 26 percent for one earning $60,000.[2] At lower earnings levels, say $15,000, benefits replace half the worker's prior earnings but are nonetheless below the poverty threshold.

Beneficiary Circumstances

The modest replacement rates reflect an expectation that Social Security benefits will be supplemented by pensions or savings for retired or disabled workers. When the economic status of DI beneficiaries is compared with that of retirees, disabled workers, on average, have lower incomes and are less likely to have pensions, insurance, or savings to supplement their Social Security benefits. The vastly smaller asset holdings of disabled workers is particularly striking. They are less likely to own their homes (and have smaller home equity when they do), and they have far less in savings. This reflects the fact that disability occurs unexpectedly, before workers have accumulated the savings they hoped to have by retirement. Further, they are likely to have drawn on their savings to meet living expenses during the waiting period for DI benefits or to cover disability-related costs, such as health care and medications.

SSI benefits are even more modest. They are paid subject to the same stringent standard of disability and a strict means test. In 1996, the maximum federal SSI benefit is $470 a month. While some states supplement the federal benefits, the federal guarantee alone amounts to about 70 percent of the poverty threshold.

Foreign Comparisons

When U.S. disability benefits are compared with public programs in other countries, U.S. expenditures are relatively low. U.S. spending for DI and SSI combined amounted to 0.7 percent of the gross domestic product (GDP) in 1991, less than half the share spent in the United Kingdom (1.9 percent) and less than a fourth of the spending in Sweden (3.3 percent).

Even Germany, which has a reputation for disability policies that are highly oriented toward work, spends far more than the United States on long-term disability benefits (2.0 percent). This is despite the Germans' emphasis on rehabilitation before pensions and provisions for quotas, tax penalties, and subsidies for job accommodations to encourage private employers to hire

---

2. Replacement rates can be up to 50 percent higher for the one in five beneficiaries who receive an allowance for dependents.

disabled workers. That Germany spends more is not a criticism of the German emphasis on rehabilitation and employment. The point is only this: While these interventions may produce desirable outcomes for persons with disabilities, they do not produce lower public expenditures for long-term disability benefits than found in the United States.

Health Care Coverage and Work

While neither DI nor SSI, in and of themselves, pose strong incentives to claim benefits in lieu of working, constraints on access to health care can be a significant barrier to employment.

Persons with chronic health conditions, or disabilities, are at risk of high health care costs. They often cannot gain coverage in the private insurance market, and even when they do have private coverage, it often does not provide the range of services and long-term supports needed to live independently. Medicare or Medicaid, therefore, are crucial supports.

Furthermore, health care coverage has declined in recent years and the number of uninsured has grown, both among the entire nonelderly population and among working-age adults who have disabilities. Between 1988 and 1993, the proportion of the total nonelderly population that is covered by employment-based health insurance declined from 67 percent to 61 percent. During the same period, Medicaid coverage grew from 9 percent to 13 percent. However, the total number of persons without coverage from any source rose from 34 million to 41 million, or by roughly 1 million a year. Adults with work disabilities also experienced a decline in employment-based coverage and an increase in Medicaid coverage between 1989 and 1993. The net result is an increase in the number of uninsured persons with work disabilities from 2.3 million to 2.9 million.[3]

Gaps in health care coverage limit employment among ill or disabled workers in three ways. First, gaps in coverage result in unnecessary losses in employment when uninsured people fail to get the care they need to treat, cure, or ameliorate the disabling consequences of their conditions. Second, from the employer's perspective, firms may be reluctant to hire persons who are at risk of high health care costs if the employer's health plan would bear that cost. Finally, from the perspective of individuals with disabilities, work may not be economically feasible if health care coverage is not available. The Panel has

3. Tabulations of the March 1994 *Current Population Survey* provided by the Employee Benefit Research Institute, Washington, D.C.

heard repeatedly that fear of losing Medicaid or Medicare is a major barrier to work.

Assurance of universal health care coverage would break down this barrier. In the absence of such reforms, the Panel is recommending a way to make Medicare coverage more affordable for DI beneficiaries who return to work. It recognizes that this modest reform would not alter the crucial point that lack of access to health care coverage seems to present a much more important impediment to work for persons with disabilities than is the availability of cash benefits.

Beneficiaries and the Broader Population with Disabilities

The Panel's review was also informed by a look at the prevalence of disability in the United States and how beneficiaries fit into that broader population. This reality check is important when thinking about proposals to promote work among beneficiaries.

—According to the Survey of Income and Program Participation, nearly 30 million working-age Americans have some type of functional impairment, which may or may not limit their ability to work.[4]

—According to the March 1994 *Current Population Survey,* nearly 17 million working-age Americans report having a work disability; that is, they have impairments that limit the kind or amount of work they can do.

—Working-age adults who receive Social Security or SSI disability benefits—7.1 million at the end of 1994—are a subset of those who have a work disability. They have the most significant and persistent work disabilities.

Many in the broader population are employed despite their impairments.

—About half the 30 million who have some sort of impairment are employed.

—About one-third of those who report work disabilities are in the labor force, either working or looking for work.

Work is far less common among those who meet the strict eligibility requirements for Social Security or SSI benefits.

—About 4 million persons receive disabled worker benefits from Social Security. They tend to be older workers. More than half (56 percent) are age fifty or older, while just 4 percent are under age thirty. Many have impairments

---

4. They include persons age fifteen to sixty-four who report that they have difficulty seeing, hearing, speaking, walking, lifting, or climbing stairs; who report a limitation in performing work or housework; who use mobility aids such as wheelchairs, canes, or walkers; and who report limitations in activities of daily living or instrumental activities of daily living. See McNeil (1993).

associated with aging, such as arthritis or other musculoskeletal disorders. Others have life-threatening diseases, such as acquired immune deficiency syndrome (AIDS), neoplasms, or circulatory or respiratory diseases. Mental illness is an important cause of disability for younger workers.

—About 618,000 persons age eighteen to sixty-four receive Social Security as adults disabled since childhood who are dependents of a parent who is retired, disabled, or deceased. Mental retardation is by far their most common impairment, with nearly two in three recipients having that as their primary diagnosis.[5]

—Some 2.4 million disabled, working-age adults lack insured status for Social Security benefits and receive only SSI benefits.[6] Many SSI recipients have disabilities that began in childhood or early adulthood. Nearly a quarter (24 percent) have mental retardation and another 34 percent have other mental disorders. Others have sensory disorders, such as blindness, or neurological or musculoskeletal disorders. Because many have conditions that began in childhood or early adulthood, SSI recipients tend to be younger than DI beneficiaries. About 35 percent of working-age SSI beneficiaries are age fifty to sixty-four, while about 19 percent are under age thirty.

To get beneficiaries' perspectives on their prospects for work, the Academy sponsored interviews with Social Security and SSI beneficiaries in four sites around the country. A brief summary of findings for four beneficiary groups follows.

Adults with cardiac, respiratory, and other health conditions often were very ill with life-threatening conditions. They had conditions such as brain tumors, human immunodeficiency virus (HIV) infection, respiratory obstruction, cancer, lupus, emphysema, multiple sclerosis, and cardiac conditions. They came from a range of occupations—accountant, clerk, day care center worker, insurance representative, management secretary, nurse manager, school teacher, and switchboard operator. Many had remained on the job months or years after the onset of their conditions, determined to beat the odds of their diagnosis. By the time they turned to Social Security, they had experienced the loss of their health, their livelihood, and their hopes for ending their work lives with a comfortable retirement. Their emphasis was on preserving their health, and often their lives, and finding meaning in activities without the rewards of paid employment.

---

5. Another 161,000 persons age fifty to sixty-four are not insured for disabled worker benefits but receive Social Security as disabled widows or widowers on their deceased spouse's work record. Their impairments are similar to those of older disabled worker beneficiaries.

6. Another 1 million receive SSI that supplements their Social Security disability benefits.

Adults with musculoskeletal impairments often had back injuries and chronic pain. They reported difficulty with a broad range of physical functions: walking, standing, stooping, lifting, sitting, and sleeping. Some had difficulty with concentration resulting from pain or the medications used to ease it. They were disproportionately from physically demanding blue-collar jobs (custodian, meatpacker, construction contractor) but included white-collar workers from the service sector as well (sales person, restaurant manager, hospital transcriber, hospital information analyst). They typically had remained on the job after the onset of their injuries before they or their employers determined they could no longer carry out their responsibilities, even with accommodations. Some had aggressively sought training or other work and were still looking. They reported that their limited functional capacity and the cost to employers for health care and workers' compensation coverage made them less attractive than younger, healthy job applicants. They typically qualified for Social Security disability benefits only after lengthy appeals. The long hiatus between earnings and benefits often had wiped out their savings.

Adults with mental disorders included persons with cognitive impairments and mental illness, such as clinical depression or schizophrenia. Many were in treatment with costly prescription medications financed by Medicaid. If they were able to earn enough to leave the benefit rolls, continued coverage of their medication would be essential. They had held jobs as a home shopping club worker, musician and piano teacher, graphic illustrator, and in sheltered employment. Some were working part time, others looked forward to returning to work, although with some trepidation. Having an advocate—whether a family member, therapist, or community mental health clinic—was a key link in getting support in their communities.

Young adults ages eighteen to twenty-five were a diverse beneficiary group. Some who had high aptitude and solid support from their families or public agencies—such as the state commission for the blind—viewed SSI as a temporary support while they attended college to prepare for professional careers. Some beneficiaries with mental retardation had part-time jobs bagging groceries or busing tables and typically had a social worker to help cope with problems at work or in managing their affairs. Other young beneficiaries had impairments involving head injuries and physical trauma from automobile accidents and were still recuperating. Some were completing their high school graduate equivalency degree. Many young beneficiaries hoped to work but had not yet found a job they could do with their impairments. Interviews with parents of young adult beneficiaries included some whose children had significant cognitive or multiple impairments that precluded competitive work or participation in group interviews. They wanted their adult children to be treated with dignity and respect and to live with as much independence as possible.

In developing policy proposals to promote return to work among beneficiaries, the Panel recognizes that Social Security and SSI disability benefits are paid to persons who have met a very strict test of work disability, only a fraction of whom have prospects for returning to work. Nonetheless, the Panel believes there is room for improvement.

Rehabilitation and Cash Benefits

To strengthen the linkage between beneficiaries and rehabilitation services, the Panel is recommending a radical new approach. Beneficiaries would receive a return-to-work (RTW) ticket, similar to a voucher, that they could use to shop among providers of rehabilitation or RTW services in either the public or private sector. Once a beneficiary deposits the ticket with a service provider, the Social Security Administration would have an obligation to pay the provider, but only after the beneficiary returns to work and leaves the benefit rolls. Each year, providers whose clients successfully return to work would receive a payment representing a fraction of the benefit savings that accrue to the Social Security trust funds because the former beneficiary is at work and not receiving benefits. The merits of this approach are presented in Monroe Berkowitz's paper.

Cash Benefit Policies to Promote Work

The Panel has several recommendations for changes in cash benefit policies that would promote work: a wage subsidy, an improved Medicare buy-in, a tax credit for personal assistance services, and improvements in the implementation of existing work incentives.

Wage Subsidy for Low-Income Workers with Disabilities

The disabled worker tax credit (DWTC) would be separate from Social Security disability benefit programs. The wage subsidy would be paid to low-income persons not because they are unable to work, but because they work despite their impairments. Patterned after the existing earned income tax credit, it would reward work for low earners with disabilities without increasing reliance on disability benefit programs that are designed primarily for persons who are unable to work. Richard V. Burkhauser discusses this proposal in his paper.

Improved Medicare Buy-in

Fear of losing health care coverage reportedly is a major impediment to leaving the disability benefit rolls. The Panel recommends an improved Medicare buy-in for DI beneficiaries who return to work. Under current law, DI beneficiaries are eligible to purchase Medicare coverage after they leave the benefits rolls because they have returned to work despite the continuation of their impairments. But the eligibility criteria are complex, the coverage is expensive to purchase, beneficiaries appear not to know about it, and few former beneficiaries buy it. The Panel is proposing a simplified Medicare buy-in with premiums charged on a sliding scale related to the former beneficiary's earnings.

Personal Assistance Tax Credit

The Panel recommends a personal assistance tax credit to compensate working people for part of the cost of personal assistance services they need to work. Some persons require personal assistance services to live independently and, with those services, are able to work in the competitive labor market. Personal assistance services, however, can be expensive. They are financed by public programs in some states, but generally only for low-income persons. As such, those who need personal assistance services face a dilemma when they go to work. Their income may disqualify them from receiving publicly financed services, yet they may not earn enough to pay for the services on their own.

Administering DI and SSI Work Incentives

The Panel believes that the most important enhancement needed in existing work incentives in DI and SSI is to improve the way in which they are implemented. Such improvements would involve both service providers who assist beneficiaries and the Social Security Administration. After in-depth analysis and extensive field research, the Panel concluded that:

—Work incentive provisions are inherently complex. Efforts to simplify them by redesign are not particularly promising. Therefore, beneficiaries need help to understand the rules and comply with them when they work.

—Some help could be offered by service providers who assist beneficiaries in returning to work, such as those who accept the RTW tickets, state vocational rehabilitation counselors, state or local mental health or developmental disabilities agencies, independent living centers, job coaches, providers of supported employment services, or those who work with recipients of private disability benefits. Such service providers would need to understand the rules and reporting requirements of the work incentive provisions and consider it part of their job to assist their clients in complying with them.

—Some tasks necessary to make work incentives successful can be performed only by the Social Security Administration or an entity it employs. These tasks include prompt processing of earnings and other reports from beneficiaries so that benefits can be adjusted as their circumstances change. If benefits are not adjusted promptly, working beneficiaries are at risk of being charged with large overpayments or of being without either earnings or benefits should their work attempt falter. If returning to work is to be a priority, personnel and systems support for these functions are essential.

Work Disability, the Environment, and Program Participation

In its analyses, the Panel emphasized that work disability is distinct from an impairment (such as blindness, hearing loss, or spinal cord injury). A chronic health condition, or impairment, is an essential element of work disability. But work disability exists only when an impairment, in conjunction with the person's other abilities, the demands of work, and the broader environment, make her or him unable to perform the tasks of work. Consequently, changes in the broader environment affect the prevalence of work disability and the demands placed on disability benefit programs.

The general environment of work disability is important in understanding causes of the growth of disability benefit programs in the early 1990s. That growth did not reflect a flaw in the basic structure of the DI or SSI programs or in the people who turn to them. While some program criteria were modified in the 1980s, many causes of growth lie elsewhere: a growing working population, the shock of an economic recession, declining demand for workers doubly disadvantaged by chronic health conditions and limited skills, and retrenchment in other parts of the support system for persons whose capacity to work is severely limited.

—The working-age population is larger and the baby boomers are entering the disability-prone years. Consequently, some growth in the programs is to be expected.

—Job losses during the recession of 1990–91 brought a wave of new benefit allowances. Disability incidence rates—new benefit awards as a percentage of the insured population—peaked in 1992 and have flattened out since then.

—Under competitive pressure to downsize and streamline their organizations, firms are less able to accommodate workers, particularly if they are doubly disadvantaged by limited skills and physical or mental impairments.

—Cutbacks in state assistance programs, constraints on access to health care, and cost controls in other wage-replacement programs increase demands on these federal programs.

Given this interpretation, what should be done? Several points stand out.

First, the rapid growth in the early 1990s appears to be a temporary phenomenon tied to the economic recession of 1990–91. Talk of crisis and radical remedies are not necessary. A review of the history of the disability programs over the last twenty-five years finds wide swings in policy responses to changes in the disability rolls. Too often corrective action came after problems were already being attended to, thereby fostering overreaction in the opposite direction. This is a long-term program, which is large, complex, and fragile. Adjustments must be made carefully and cautiously at the margins. Thought must be give to ripple effects over a long period of time.

A number of careful changes should be made. First, the Panel's proposals are judiciously designed to promote work: the RTW tickets, the DWTC, an improved Medicare buy-in, the tax credit for personal assistance service, and improved implementation of work incentives.

Second, policy commitments must be matched with adequate resources to administer them. In cash benefit programs, for example, low administrative costs can translate quickly into higher program costs. This is penny-wise and pound-foolish policymaking. The 1990–91 recession that brought rapid growth in disability workloads came on the heels of a 25 percent reduction in Social Security Administration staff during the 1980s.

Administrative resources must be set at a level that ensures stable, effective management of the disability programs. Resources must be adequate to provide:

—Fair, accurate, and prompt decisions on disability claims;

—Individualized service to beneficiaries that is contemplated under the law, including accurate information and prompt action to implement benefit adjustments when beneficiaries work; and

—Timely and predictable review of the continuing eligibility of those receiving disability benefits.

All of these activities are essential to secure the integrity of and public confidence in the disability benefit system.

Third, determinations of work disability are inherently complex, and the conditions that result in work disability change as medical technology evolves and as the demands of work change. The definition of disability in the Social Security Act, while very strict, is a valid statement of the nature of severe work disability. Its specific implementation is spelled out in regulations, which need to be periodically updated through expert professional review so that eligibility criteria are kept current with new research and professional knowledge. These updates should be undertaken at the administrative level, through regulations, and do not require changes in the law.

In closing, two themes of the Panel's report should be emphasized. First, many of the most promising interventions to promote employment among persons with disabilities lie outside of cash benefit programs. Thought needs to be given to changing the environment, increasing demand for workers, reengineering work tasks so that they can be performed by persons with physical or mental impairments, educating future workers so they have the skills to work despite the onset of various limitations in physical functioning, and providing basic health care. All these remedies for work disability lie outside of cash benefit policies and are likely to require substantial investment of new resources.

Disability income policy must strive for balance—a balance between providing a decent and dignified level of income to workers whose careers are interrupted by disabling illness and functional loss, on the one hand, and a realistic set of opportunities and supports for those who have the capacity to work, on the other. In the final analysis, the success of U.S. disability income policy will be judged by how it achieves this balance.

U.S. Disability from a European Perspective
Philip R. de Jong

EUROPEAN WELFARE STATES are facing hard times. They are considered wasteful and inefficient. To indicate the elements ripe for change is relatively easy. But to reach political agreement on the appropriate changes, and to get sufficient social support for any proposal to curtail existing entitlements, proves difficult. The constituency of the welfare state includes not only current beneficiaries, but also older workers, small-scale businesses, and all those who are well insured by collective arrangements at prices that do not reflect the full social cost of income transfers.

Disability policies should be judged in a broader social welfare context.[7] What are the main differences between Europe and the United States in terms of social welfare programs? Why do European welfare states need to be reformed? And what reforms have been implemented, or are being contemplated, and what do they imply for workers with disabilities?

7. This presentation is based on de Jong (1995); Aarts and de Jong (1996); and Aarts, Burkhauser, and de Jong (1996).

Transatlantic Differences

Social welfare programs germinated from ideas in the Atlantic Charter, drafted by British prime minister Winston Churchill and U.S. president Franklin D. Roosevelt in 1941. This document offered a blueprint for the postwar Keynesian welfare state, which rested on the twin principles of "freedom from want" and "freedom from idleness." For the United Kingdom, this blueprint was elaborated by British economist William Henry Beveridge, who proposed a national safety net to protect every citizen against poverty.

Despite the common origin, the general approach to social welfare in the United States differs from that in Europe. Universal programs in the United States are based on employment; that is, on a private market version of the freedom-from-idleness principle. For example, full coverage under Social Security is only obtained through a sufficiently long work history. Workers' compensation insures all those who are employed, but only against work-related injuries and diseases.

The freedom-from-want principle—the responsibility of the state to protect all of its residents from poverty—never found an American majority. Consequently, several major differences between U.S. and European welfare systems emerged. First, while the United States has no universal safety net provision for those below the poverty line, west European countries have a constitutionally established responsibility to guarantee their citizens a social minimum. Second, contrary to European systems, in the United States temporary sickness is not covered by a statutory sick pay plan that encompasses all those in paid employment and all medical contingencies, whether work-related or not. Third, Americans are not universally (or federally) insured against loss of earnings as a result of unemployment. And, fourth, despite the existence of two federal programs that cover health costs for target groups (Medicare and Medicaid), a statutory, universal health insurance program does not exist.

Advantages of Broad Coverage

European-style broad coverage has major advantages compared with the American mean-and-lean welfare state. First, comprehensive welfare states are less adversarial, less litigious, and, given proper involvement of business and labor, more consensus building. Statutory programs run by public insurance monopolies reduce the transaction costs that go along with private insurance markets or with the delivery of statutory benefits by private insurers. Such transaction costs stem from the intransparency of insurance markets and the subjectivity of risks that are defined in medical terms (sickness, disability, health costs) or socioeconomic terms (poverty, involuntary unemployment).

Second, a broad set of legal entitlements allows the legislator to appeal to the responsibilities of those covered. In Germany, for instance, workers with disabilities are routinely referred to mandatory rehabilitation programs, which are supported by employment quota regulations that mandate firms to fill 6 percent of their job slots with persons with disabilities. In Norway and Sweden, disabled workers can also be obliged to undergo rehabilitation and to accept jobs in the public sector at large or in special sheltered workshops. Likewise, universal accessibility of European health care systems, at cost levels that are low in comparison with the United States, is achieved by compulsory insurance, detailed regulation of capacity planning, medical salaries, and prices of drugs and medical services.

Disadvantages of Broad Coverage

The design of the postwar welfare state in Europe reflects a focus on equity. The political climate around 1970 was to create generous, pay-as-you-go financed programs. The designers of these programs had fairness in mind, not manageability or efficiency. They were not fully aware that incentives matter, that these programs can only survive cyclical and other shocks when they contain appropriate checks and balances.

European experience with generous and easily accessible social insurance programs that cover wage loss as a result of unemployment, sickness, disability, or early retirement shows that such welfare states are structurally unstable. Their instability stems from a macroeconomic relationship that is called "the social security trap" (see figure 2-1).[8] This mechanism is set into motion by an exogenous shock—for instance, a steep rise in labor supply caused by baby boomers entering the labor market in the early 1970s or a reduction in employment precipitated by the oil crisis of 1973. As a result, growth is seen in both official unemployment and redundancies among older workers hidden under the labels of disability and early retirement.[9]

Swollen beneficiary rolls require higher contribution rates. When these higher rates add to employers' costs for labor compensation, employers, in turn, seek higher productivity per worker. When productivity standards rise,

8. See Van Praag and Halberstadt (1980).

9. The data in table 3-1 in Richard V. Burkhauser's paper demonstrate how the disability rolls swelled in the Netherlands and Sweden as well as the United States in response to the threat of massive (official) unemployment between 1970 and 1975.

Figure 2-1. The Social Security Trap

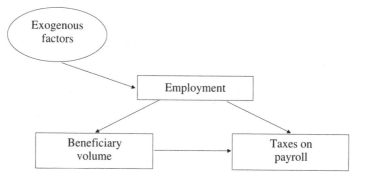

the number of marginally unemployable workers increases. They will seek shelter under unemployment and disability insurance schemes and increase the beneficiary rolls, fueling a new round of rises in contribution rates, labor cost, and productivity standards.

Other exogenous forces, economic or institutional, may also ignite this trap. For example, employment growth may be reduced by cyclical up-swings and down-swings as well as by structural technological trends or increased international competition. More important, the harmful effects of this mechanism may be reinforced if the beneficiary rolls rise as a result of increases in program generosity or accessibility.

Since the early 1970s, the social security trap has plagued European welfare states. During the deep recession of 1982, politicians became aware of its undermining effects. But by then, the welfare state had turned into an entitlement state in which citizens had strongly vested interests. Among the European Community (EC) countries, only the United Kingdom under Prime Minister Margaret Thatcher was able to break out of the spiral. Political leaders in the other EC countries could cut back only on the fringes of their welfare states unless they were willing to risk losing their constituency.

The effects have been devastating: Taxes on wages made gainful employment of low-productivity workers increasingly difficult; their jobs were shifted to the informal market or to low-wage countries. And market employment for workers with disabilities became virtually inaccessible. In Holland, for instance, a host of employment promoting measures—partial benefits, wage subsidies, job protection, and Americans with Disabilities Act-type regulation—all explicitly targeted at disabled workers proved ineffective. To the extent that an excess supply of healthy, well-trained replacements existed, employers were not interested in using these subsidies. Likewise, redundant employees who could easily qualify for full disability benefits generally preferred early retirement on disability benefits over the hazards of labor force participation. The improper use of disability pensions as generous unemployment or early retirement benefits was facilitated by allowing representatives of business and labor to run the social insurance programs. But the managerial autonomy of business and labor was not matched by financial responsibilities, because they could shift the financial consequences of their liberal policies to central funds, also run by business and labor, which calculated uniform, pay-as-you-go contribution rates.

The result was massive long-term unemployment, partly hidden as disability or early retirement.[10] Despite cuts in statutory benefit levels or replacement rates, which were in most cases repaired by collectively bargained supplements, effective benefits were kept at relatively high levels for lack of politically viable alternatives. And, despite changes in the direction of stricter eligibility criteria, administrative practices to award benefits leniently continued.

In sum, until the 1990s, attempts to eliminate the social security trap in Europe failed. The prospect of further growth of disability and old-age benefit rolls resulting from an aging population, combined with a fiscal need to reduce budget deficits and increasing global competition, made policymakers acutely aware that the welfare state was in crisis and that more drastic measures had to be taken.

The crisis also has a sociological dimension: The solidarity between workers and beneficiaries and between successive generations, on which welfare state programs are based, eroded because people increasingly felt that the allocation of disability benefits was arbitrary and mainly served the interests of individual employees and firms. In other words, individual rationality led to irrationality in the aggregate.

The Reforms

Every aspect of the European welfare state is now under review. The simple theory behind the reforms is that incentives matter. The social security trap can be eliminated only if the three parties involved in the use and management of disability insurance—employees, employers, and program administrators—are confronted with the financial consequences of their risk behavior and award policies.

---

10. In 1994, the regular Organization for Economic Cooperation and Development (OECD) unemployment rate for the Netherlands was 7 percent. According to the OECD definition of broad unemployment, the Dutch unemployment rate including disability and early retirement was 27 percent. See Organization for Economic Cooperation and Development (1994, p. 63).

The general tendency is to shift the public-private mix in bearing the disability risk in the direction of private individuals, private enterprises, and private insurers. Statutory replacement rates have been lowered, albeit to levels that still look generous to the American public. In Holland, for instance, statutory disability insurance benefits have been made dependent on age, such that a forty-year-old average wage earner, if fully disabled, would be entitled to a 53 percent replacement rate instead of the uniform 70 percent that prevailed until 1994. In Sweden, replacement rates under the sickness benefit scheme were cut from 90 to 75 percent in 1996.

The leniency that pervaded the Dutch disability insurance program is reflected by the distribution of new beneficiaries across diagnostic groups. In 1994, the two diagnostic groups that are likely to contain the largest segment of subjective symptoms—psychological (35 percent) and musculoskeletal disorders (25 percent)—accounted for 60 percent of all entries.[11] In 1994, the Swedish share of these diagnoses among new disability beneficiaries was 65 percent, but with a much smaller share (19 percent) of psychological problems.[12]

These data indicate that the allocation of disability benefits in the Dutch and Swedish welfare states is wasteful. To improve on efficient allocation, eligibility standards have been made stricter. In Holland, for instance, disability is now measured in relation to all jobs in the economy, where it used to be commensurate with one's training and work history. Moreover, the medical cause of the inability to perform gainful activities must be objectively assessable. And finally, while only few benefit recipients' disability statuses were reconsidered after entering the rolls, they are now being reviewed regularly.

In countries with high rates of work absence, such as Holland and Sweden, the financial responsibility of employers to pay sickness benefits has been reinforced. Before a 1992 reform that required Swedish employers to pay the first two weeks of sickness, there was neither an incentive for employers to alleviate work-related causes of their employees' poor health nor an incentive to curb long-term absenteeism. A similar measure was taken in Holland in 1994, which required that employers with more than fifteen employees had to cover 70 percent of lost wages during the first six weeks of sickness, while smaller employers had to cover the first two weeks. As of March 1996, Dutch employers bear the financial responsibility for the full duration of sickness benefits up to twelve months. They are legally obliged to pay 70 percent of one's usual earnings and to contract a private Occupational Health Service for

11. Ctsv (1996, p. 94).
12. Aarts, Burkhauser, and de Jong (1996, p. 143).

the assessment of a sick worker's health status, a recovery plan if needed, and the quality of the firm's work environment.

According to European standards, the degree of privatization that prevails under the Dutch sickness benefit program is novel and experimental. Employers may choose to have their sickness benefit liabilities covered by a private insurer, but they are in no way required to do so. Contrary to the workers' compensation regulation that covers a much more narrowly defined risk, Dutch employers are self-insured unless they choose not to be.

The current Dutch government has proposed to privatize, in a similar way, the disability insurance scheme, which covers earnings loss after sick pay has run out. At a minimum, it wants to do away with the existing uniform contribution rates for disability insurance and introduce some form of experience rating. This can be done within a public, pay-as-you-go financed social insurance system. A further step that would bring Dutch disability insurance in line with the Dutch privatized sickness benefits would have legally mandated coverage delivered by private insurers. Several versions of a privatized disability insurance system are under study and will be debated by parliament before the end of 1996.

Conclusion

Whether the Dutch model of privatized social insurance will be followed by other European welfare states remains to be seen. One of the great advantages of private delivery of social insurance in Holland is that it would replace bureaucratic administrators who have no incentive to contain damages with self-insured employers or private insurers who face competitive pressures. But along with increased efficiency comes a number of potential disadvantages. First, given the conflicting interests of employees and of employers, whether self-insured or experience-rated, a privatized system will be more adversarial. The U.S. workers' compensation experience reveals how wasteful litigation can be. But that same experience also shows that some amount of litigation is necessary to manage an insurance system that covers a risk as elusive as disability.

A second, related point is the involvement of business and labor to produce consensus. The involvement of the social partners in the administration of Dutch disability insurance was such that it led to consensus but at very high cost. In a privatized system, new structures for this involvement have to be found.

And, third, a privatized system involves higher operation (administration and transaction) costs than a bureaucratic monopoly. This implies that privatization can lead only to lower premium rates if the beneficiary rolls decrease more than operation costs increase. The gains of privatization, then, fully depend on increased efforts of employers to prevent or reduce absenteeism and disability. These efforts may be focused on prevention of illness and injury and at recovery through managed care that could benefit both employees and employers. But they also may bring recruitment strategies and employment policies that emphasize stringent health checks that discriminate against workers with disabilities.

However divergent disability policies may have been recently, convergence may be the result of a learning process that evolves from the mistakes made in the past. Convergence in Europe is promoted by fiscal urgency, fueled by demographic pressure, in the direction of a more American style of disability income policies.

For the American disability and health programs to converge to a European-type welfare state, another political mindset and a more homogeneous society are required.

New Developments in Private Health and Disability Benefits
Dallas Salisbury

IN BOTH THE PUBLIC AND PRIVATE SECTORS, the direct cost to employers of disability insurance and disability benefits are estimated at about 3 percent to 4 percent of total payroll.[13]

Indirect costs for employers that have disabled employees have been estimated to range from between 1 dollar to 5 dollars per dollar of that direct cost, according to an article on the new move in private disability and employer disability toward aggressive disability management, which is similar to the twenty-four-hour coverage approach that is common in European countries.[14] The trend is motivated largely by the recent growth in workers' compensation and projections that such costs may double by the year 2000.[15] As a result, in overall health insurance provision, including disability and workers' compensation, a push is seen toward integration, a greater attention to rehabilitation and training, and far less focus on simply writing a check and hoping that the individual some day can go back to work.

13. Tortarolo and Polakoff (1995, p. 49).
14. Tortarolo and Polakoff (1995, p. 49).
15. Tortarolo and Polakoff (1995, p. 49).

A further result of these costs is a decline in the availability of both health and disability coverage among private and public sector employees. The health insurance marketplace has experienced an additional decline of about 2.8 million individuals covered by employment-based health insurance in 1995 and a dramatic movement toward the managed care approach.[16] Only 26 percent of those with employment-based health insurance were in managed care in 1988, while fully 53 percent were in managed care arrangements in 1993. Estimates now are that the figure was closer to 65 percent in 1995.[17]

The move to cost-sharing is a secondary aspect of this change. In 1980, 26 percent of full-time private sector employees were asked to pay part of their health insurance expenses. That is now up to 61 percent of those with single coverage and exceeds 76 percent of those with family coverage. Meanwhile, 72 percent of those employees in the public sector provide payment of some portion of their insurance costs.[18]

Another aspect of this change is that cost-sharing has led to flexibility. More and more employers are beginning to give individuals the option of not having employment-based health insurance coverage or disability insurance coverage and instead receiving direct cash compensation. Increasingly, employees are asking for this flexibility, particularly younger employees who believe that they will never face sickness and for whom the notion of disability is inconceivable. Thus, they do not state a large preference for mandatory coverage.

The medical savings account (MSA) that is part of the 104th Congress budget debate would go beyond the one step that has grown dramatically in the employer setting: flexible compensation vis á vis so-called medical reimbursement accounts. Today, approximately 50 percent of full-time employees in private medium and large firms, 40 percent of those in small firms, and close to 50 percent of those in public sector state and local establishments are able to put aside tax-free dollars to finance copay deductibles and other expenses under relatively generous medical insurance programs.[19] Essentially, the MSA would move this arrangement to catastrophic medical care protection only, and these front-end dollars, instead of being used for dental work or an extra pair of designer sunglasses, would be used for basic medical care expenditures.

The MSA is an example of this further movement by some employers, but mainly in the public policy debate, to build in additional levels of incentive for individuals to take care whether or not they use their insurance coverage.

16. Fronstin and Rheem (1996).
17. U.S. Bureau of Labor Statistics (1981 and 1994).
18. U.S. Bureau of Labor Statistics (1981, 1993b, and 1994).
19. U.S. Bureau of Labor Statistics (1993a, 1993b, and 1994).

Essentially, unnecessary use of medical services may not be such a big problem. However, fear is often expressed concerning how much people spend that they would not spend if they were paying themselves. It is still in the behavioral model and seems to be extensive.

Employers, as a result, have generally not added disability coverage to their medical insurance across the board. Articles on the front pages of the *New York Times* or the *Wall Street Journal* tend to report on surveys of the very largest employers, including the federal government, and to suggest that most workers have this type of protection. More accurate data from a generalized perspective can be drawn from the Bureau of Labor Statistics surveys of employers of all sizes.

These surveys conclude that, among full-time employees in private sector medium and large firms (those with 250 or more employees) today, 44 percent have some form of employment-based long-term disability insurance. That drops to 22 percent of the 75 percent of all full-time workers who work for businesses with fewer than 250 employees and to 26 percent of full-time workers in the state and local sector.[20]

The number of sellers of these insurance policies to public and private sector employers indicate that the marketplace is consolidating. The number of insurers willing to write these policies has been declining because of a number of factors, including a consensus that, with the aging of the American work force and of the baby boomers, the good risks are going to be fewer and the bad risks (those who are likely to file claims) probably will grow significantly, putting pressure both on policies in force and on premiums.

This demographic pressure and the dramatic increase in the number of claims being filed are leading to a movement toward integration and management of disability programs in the context of workers compensation insurance and health care insurance generally. An excellent article released in the 1995 third quarter edition of *Benefits Quarterly* reports on three major corporations that are at the cutting edge of this movement.[21] California Edison, General Electric, and L. L. Bean are attempting to adopt this type of integrated approach. However, the authors note that none of these companies has moved the experimentation to the point of being satisfied with the results in spite of the high objectives established for the programs.

In addition, as a result of these demographic changes, coverage reductions are evident in most policies. Particularly in the individual marketplace, it is growing increasingly difficult for any individual who seeks disability coverage

20. U.S. Bureau of Labor Statistics (1993a, 1993b, and 1994).
21. Tortarolo and Polakoff (1995).

outside of employment-defined policies, with guaranteed premiums and guaranteed renewability, which as recently as two years ago were standard design features of individually purchased policies.

Cost is the reason that few individuals purchase individual disability insurance coverage relative to the group marketplace. Moreover, small group policies are much more expensive than large group policies and their cost is closer to that of individual coverage.

One insurer provided two estimates of disability insurance costs for a group of twenty-five employees and for a single individual, assuming that the person is thirty years old and that the annual benefit that he or she would wish through this disability policy would be $12,000 per year in income as a result of a disability. A small employer buying a group policy to cover all of its workers would pay a premium of $200 per year per employee for that $12,000 per year benefit. That is two-and-one-half times the cost that would be obtainable by a company the size of General Motors or the federal government. The individual going into the private disability market would generally be quoted an annual premium of $1,000 per year per $12,000 per year.

Therefore, the cost issue, as it affects this marketplace, is one that hits home. It is predominant in the private sector. The move by government employers toward integration and management and toward long-term redesign underlines the relatively low rates of employee group disability coverage. Far fewer individuals in the American workplace today have disability coverage than have health insurance coverage. Far fewer without employer coverage, given the option of buying personal disability coverage, buy disability coverage, compared with the number who purchase private health insurance coverage.

From the perspective of the individual, the crisis is the growing inability to obtain disability coverage on an individual basis, most particularly a policy with a guaranteed premium rate and guaranteed renewability. From the employer perspective, the crisis is that costs are now, depending on the employer, between 6 percent and 12 percent of total payroll (an average of 9 percent among firms studied), and the demographics imply that that number can only go up and that this is a growing challenge in terms of total cost management.[22] From the underwriters' perspective, given the massive number of previously issued guaranteed renewable fixed premium policies that are in the marketplace, the crisis stems from not having understood the types of changes in America that, if foreseen, would have caused them to write different policies. One can go back to what is happening in the health insurance marketplace as the most dramatic example of this challenge.

22. Tortarolo and Polakoff (1995), citing Chelius, Berkowitz, and Owens (1992).

In California, some individuals were about to consult with two of their clients who are surgeons. In 1993, the income of these two doctors net of all expenses was a total of $1.2 million. In 1995, having essentially been required to move to a world of managed care, the net income was down to $200,000. These two doctors have personal guaranteed premium, guaranteed renewability disability income policies, ensuring them an income of $522,000 per year should they become disabled.

One might suggest that they have an incentive to break a finger of their right hand, which, under the liberal distinitions in the old policies, would entitle them to the full benefit. The downside of managed care and the challenges of disability management point to the reason that the number of doctors moving into disabled status has gone up dramatically since 1991.

This example suggests that insurers who are moving away from guaranteed premiums and guaranteed renewability are not doing so for purely draconian reasons. For those who are involved with disability and similar programs, whether in public social programs or in employment-based programs, it is an extraordinarily difficult challenge to foresee demographic trends and to simultaneously predict training, job, and other work force and health managed care issues that could dramatically affect the long-term costs and the long-term effectiveness of program design. These are trends that previously even the most proficient seer of the future could never conceivably, with the best actuarial talents, have built into the estimates in advance.

References

Aarts, Leo J. M., Richard V. Burkhauser, and Philip R. de Jong. 1996. *Curing the Dutch Disease: An International Perspective on Disability Policy Reform.* Aldershot, U.K.: Avebury.

Aarts, Leo J. M., and Philip R. de Jong. 1996. "European Experiences with Disability Policy." In *Disability, Work, and Cash Benefits,* edited by J. L. Mashaw and V. P. Reno. Kalamazoo, Mich.: W. E. Upjohn Institute for Employment Research.

Chelius, J., M. Berkowitz, and P. Owens. 1992. *The Total Cost of Disability.* UNUM Corporation.

Ctsv (Commissie toezicht sociale verzekeringen). 1996. *Ontwikkeling arbeidsongeschiktheid. Jaaroverzicht AAW/WAO 1994.* Zoetermeer, Netherlands.

de Jong, Philip R. 1995. "Unemployment and Disability." In *Working Policies? Facts, Analyses, and Policies Concerning Employment and Nonparticipation in the Netherlands,* edited by Teun Jaspers and others, 81–104. Groningen, Netherlands: Wolters-Noordhoff.

Fronstin, Paul, and Edina Rheem. 1996. "Sources of Health Insurance and Characteristics of the Uninsured." *EBRI Issue Brief* 170 (February).

McNeil, John M. 1993. *Americans with Disabilities: 1991–92: Data from the Survey of Income and Program Participation.* Current Population Reports, Household Economic Studies, P70-33. U.S. Department of Commerce: Government Printing Office.

Mashaw, Jerry L., and Virginia P. Reno, eds. 1996. *Balancing Security and Opportunity: The Challenge of Disability Income Policy.* Final Report of the Disability Policy Panel. Washington, D.C.: National Academy of Social Insurance.

Organization for Economic Cooperation and Development. 1994. *Economic Surveys: The Netherlands.* Paris.

Tortarolo, John S., and Phillip L. Polakoff. 1995. "The Future of Disability Management Is . . . Integration." *Benefits Quarterly* (third quarter): 49.

U.S. Bureau of Labor Statistics. 1981. *Employee Benefits in Medium and Large Private Establishments, 1980.* Government Printing Office.

———. 1993a. *Employee Benefits in Small Private Establishments, 1992.* Government Printing Office.

———. 1993b. *Employee Benefits in State and Local Governments, 1992.* Government Printing Office.

———. 1994. *Employee Benefits in Medium and Large Private Establishments, 1993.* Government Printing Office.

Van Praag, Bernard M. S., and Victor Halberstadt. 1980. "Towards an Economic Theory of Nonemployability: A First Approach." In *Public Choice and Public Finance,* edited by Karl W. Roskamp. Paris.

3

Encouraging Work through Cash Benefits Policy: New Proposals

TWO RECOMMENDATIONS OF THE Disability Policy Panel are considered in this chapter: return-to-work vouchers and the disabled worker tax credit.

Linking Beneficiaries with Return-to-Work Services
Monroe Berkowitz

A NEW SCHEME TO IMPROVE the rate at which people leave the disability rolls and return to work attracts two groups of players. One group consists of some people who are already on disability rolls and receiving Social Security disability insurance (DI) or Supplemental Security Income (SSI) benefits. The other group consists of a wide variety of private and public sector providers of services designed to return beneficiaries to work.

The idea of the basic scheme is simple. Select beneficiaries would be given return-to-work tickets. Because the scheme is voluntary, the beneficiaries need not do anything with the tickets. However, if they choose, a person on the rolls may deposit the ticket with a provider from the public or private sector. Once the ticket is deposited and accepted by the provider, it becomes a contract between the Social Security Administration (SSA) and that provider. Under the contract, the SSA agrees to pay the provider a percentage of the savings to the trust fund if the person leaves the rolls.

The objective of this scheme is to improve the rate at which beneficiaries leave the rolls to return to work. The scheme is not designed to cure all of the problems of the disability benefits system. The scheme will be successful if return-to-work rates improve.

SSA actuaries estimate that about seven thousand DI benefit terminations each year result from return to work, which is about 0.18 of 1 percent of those on the rolls. The number who leave because of medical recovery or return to work has always been small—about 1.5 percent to as much as 2.5 percent of those on the rolls. The numbers look better if a cohort of people are followed through their experience with the program. The numbers even look better if attention is confined to younger persons. However, progress should be more substantial.

Once a person gets on the disability beneficiary rolls, he or she likely remains there until age sixty-five or death. The number who come off the rolls for other reasons is negligible. The objective in proposing a new scheme is to increase the number of persons who leave the rolls by returning to work.

The new scheme accepts the world as it is. Whether a mistake was made in 1956 when it was decided to give cash benefits to disabled workers without first requiring them to undergo rehabilitation in one form or another is unclear. Perhaps the SSA should have concentrated on rehabilitation instead of the issuance of cash benefits. For whatever reason, SSA has not proven to be an effective rehabilitation agency. (That is a bit like saying that the Internal Revenue Service has not done a good job of improving the mental health of the taxpayers.) Rehabilitation has never been defined as SSA's responsibility. SSA has many strong suits, but providing rehabilitation services and returning people to work is not one of them. SSA is not equipped to negotiate with providers, to decide on the services that ought to be provided, to determine the amount of such services, and to set the prices that ought to be paid for them.

The return-to-work scheme that the Disability Policy Panel has endorsed takes the Social Security Administration out of the business of having to make decisions in this area. Under this scheme, providers are given incentives to participate, and then they are paid according to results, not costs, or the extent of their efforts.

If the objective is to pay providers according to results, what results are being sought? The answer is simple: getting and keeping people off the benefit rolls and into jobs. Therefore, providers should be paid only when that happens.

What should they be paid? The proposal is designed to simplify SSA's administrative tasks. The SSA should not be involved in judging the quality of the services provided or be working out utilization procedures and fee schedules. To the maximum extent possible, this scheme is designed to be regulation-free.

When the result is known and when a person is off the rolls and working at a job, the proposal calls for paying the provider a percentage of the savings that accrue to the Social Security trust funds. Such payments are to be made only after these savings have been accrued by the trust fund.

What are the objections to this scheme? The question arises of whether legislators will agree to a scheme that pays according to results. Under the proposal, some providers are going to get a windfall, possible large annual payments without having done a good deal of work. Other providers who have done considerable amounts of work will receive nothing in return. One or two good newspaper stories about either of these cases may be sufficient to kill the legislature's enthusiasm for the scheme. At the same time, providers will be unhappy if they bear all of the risks. Providers would prefer to be paid something up front or along the way, perhaps at the occurrence of specific events called milestones.

Providers will have financial problems, but how these milestone payments can be incorporated is unclear. Such payments involve SSA in all the problems that the scheme seeks to avoid. How can a milestone be defined? When is it achieved? How much should be paid? Possibly these kinds of problems could be worked out, but someone in the bureaucracy likely would have to make these judgment calls.

Furthermore, payments up front or at milestones are payments for steps in the process. They are for interim results that may or may not contribute to the desired result—return to work.

The experience of employers under private benefit programs and under workers' compensation is that whatever is paid for will be supplied by providers. Should work evaluations be mandated? If a work hardening program that is designed to prepare persons for the rigors of a job becomes part of a scheme, it will be supplied. Providers are good at providing such services, especially those that are ill defined and whose quality is not easily ascertainable. Social Security reportedly will overcome these problems by a rigorous evaluation. But the first of these rigorous evaluations remains to be seen.

The proposed scheme calls for payment according to results, and only after those results are achieved. If no providers are willing to play this game, the situation is no worse off than it is now.

Who should get tickets? Tickets ought to be given only to persons who are not expected to leave the rolls without services, and that means that some difficult decisions must be made. SSA or its Disability Determination Services units in the several states would be called upon to select persons who would not be eligible to receive these tickets.

The first group of excluded persons would be those who are expected to medically recover and those who are expected to leave the rolls on their own steam. Persons scheduled for continuing disability reviews (CDRs) might receive tickets at the time of the CDR, if they are going to be continued on the rolls.

Under this scheme, administrators must identify the persons who would be expected to leave the rolls without services. The procedure is the only protection that the scheme has against the charges of creaming, if creaming means that providers are getting credit for performing what are essentially unnecessary services.

Another group of persons that might be denied tickets are those who are terminally ill or over a particular age. The exclusion of this group is not crucial. They could be issued tickets were it deemed politic to do so. Providers probably would not take up these tickets or invest a great deal of money in the rehabilitation of these beneficiaries. The reality is that these people—and there will be a good many of them—are older and will not be attractive to providers who are to be paid by results.

One objection is that providers will seek out those beneficiaries who are most likely candidates for return to work and ignore others who may be older, sicker, or otherwise disadvantaged in the labor market. If providers are rational and possess the requisite information, they will first seek out the persons who have the highest probability of success.

It is difficult to see how these considerations raise meaningful equity issues. A particularly disadvantaged group may be farther back in the queue, but these persons are not now being served. Instituting the scheme will not make them worse off. If the scheme makes some persons better off without making any persons worse off, it would appear to deserve societal support.

The scheme is based on the notion that a market will develop that will have all the advantages of a free and open competitive system. Of most value is the freedom of choice that it gives beneficiaries. They will have in their possession a ticket that is potentially a valuable commodity to the providers. They can pick and choose among providers who will offer them visions of what can be done.

There are dangers , but is it not time that persons who advocate empowerment of consumers, who agitate for freedom of choice, and who want to make the consumer—not the bureaucrat—the arbiter of services be given their day in court? Here is a marvelous opportunity to do just that.

This scheme means what it says about consumer empowerment. The beneficiary need do nothing, but, if the choice is to become involved, then the consumer chooses the provider and decides when to leave the provider if dissatisfied. The degrees of freedom are so much greater than in any program that depends on consumer sign-off on some toothless Individualized Written Rehabilitation Program.

Some people worry about how such a scheme would be publicized. This scheme does not requires a great deal of, if any, information dissemination. These beneficiaries have in their hands a piece of paper that may be worth $15,000 to $50,000 or more to a provider. That should be attractive to clients. However, considering whatever kind of apparatus is necessary to publicize this scheme should not be dismissed out of hand.

If market mechanisms are allowed to work, each beneficiary should have several providers competing for the business. If all does not go as planned, no harm has been done. No trust funds have been lost. No one is worse off, and the present system will continue.

An important issue arises about who can qualify to be a provider. The market should be open to the widest variety of providers possible. Providers ought to be drawn from the ranks of job developers, placement specialists, as well as those who are certified in the traditional rehabilitation areas. Persons with credentials should compete with others as would be characteristic of a free, open, competitive market. One reason to let a wide variety of providers to compete is the belief that numerous ways exist to return persons to work. Not much empirical evidence is available that any one method works better than another.

A foolproof test of success exists—whether or not a person returns to work, leaves the rolls, and stays off the rolls. Payments are made to providers only after persons have left the rolls.

Issues can be raised about changing providers. If consumer choice and the characteristics of a free market are to be preserved, some provision must be made for a change in providers. Beneficiaries may become disillusioned with their provider, or the provider may despair of the ability to return the person to a job. In the latter case, the provider might return the ticket or attempt to sell it to another provider. A market should develop along those lines.

If the person decides that cooperation with the provider is no longer possible, it is not likely that that person is going to return to work. The relationship thus should be broken. As much as possible, the market ought to have a free reign. If the provider can sell the ticket, the sale has to be to a provider who would be suitable to the beneficiary.

A private mechanism could be set up to settle disputes, an arbitration system or something of that nature.

The whole system is based on the voluntary cooperation of the beneficiary. No compulsion is introduced in any aspect of the scheme. If the provider cannot persuade the beneficiary to cooperate, the provider will lose whatever investment that has been made to date. The only alternative would be to try and sell the ticket to some other provider.

Can beneficiaries be their own provider? Could some close relative be the provider? Preferably not. Some minimal showing should be made that the provider is in the business of supplying services designed to return beneficiaries to work. But this is not an open-and-shut issue. Consideration and thought might be given to the possibility that beneficiaries be their own provider.

The one fundamental cost problem stems from induced demand. Would this scheme be so attractive that people would get on the rolls so they could get off? The true cost of the DI program is not the benefits paid; it is the lost productivity of idle workers. If people are attracted to the program because of the money they would receive to get off the program, at least these people will be working. On the one hand, such a cost could be factored in because it may induce behavioral changes. On the other hand, it might have a contagious effect with additional people running off the rolls.

Can the scheme apply to SSI beneficiaries? There does not seem to be any reason why not. Some adjustments must be made to the percentages of benefits paid to providers. SSI beneficiaries leave the rolls for any number of reasons, and the reimbursement ought to be conditioned on return to work. But a great potential exists, especially for young people who come onto the rolls after having been through schooling.

Can a scheme be devised for applicants who are denied beneficiaries? It is possible but, undoubtedly, more complicated. A loan fund could be tapped by denied beneficiaries or applicants. This area must be approached separately. Denied beneficiaries do not draw benefits from the trust fund. Payments are not made from the trust fund until a person has been accepted as a beneficiary.

This scheme deserves a trial on the theory that there is nothing to lose. The current situation—less than one quarter of 1 percent of people are leaving the rolls—can be bested. At risk is the possibility that some persons will be attracted to the program, and, in that case, little harm will be done if they are attracted to the benefits only to leave them.

A political consensus to advocate for this program must be sought. The base for such a consensus likely will come from disability advocates. Providers are not going to buy into this program. Why should they if they can get something up front and something along the way?

The bureaucrats will not necessarily endorse a scheme that deprives them of power. Basic support must come from those people who have the interest of the disability community at heart and label themselves as disability advocates. They should join with those who believe in maximum freedom to choose for persons with disabilities. The scheme is worth trying, and, given the low number of beneficiaries who now return to work, there is little to lose.

The Disabled Worker Tax Credit
Richard V. Burkhauser, Andrew J. Glenn, and David C. Wittenburg

CHANGES OVER THE LAST QUARTER century in the population receiving disability benefits have as much to do with economic and political forces as with changes in the underlying health of American citizens. The explosion in the population of young disability benefit recipients since 1989 is a major new and less-than-optimal outcome of a disability policy dominated by income transfers. A work-based alternative to disability benefits—the disabled worker tax credit (DWTC)—offers some hope of reducing the dramatic movement of younger persons onto the Supplemental Security Income (SSI) rolls. The DWTC is one of a series of work-based initiatives recommended by the Disability Policy Panel of the National Academy of Social Insurance.[1]

The American Disability Benefit System in International Perspective

Economic and political forces play an important role in determining the relative size of the population receiving disability benefits and how it changes over time, as seen in table 3-1, which shows the ratio of disability benefit recipients per thousand workers by age over the past quarter century in the United States, the Netherlands, Sweden, and Germany. All four countries experienced growth in this ratio over the period, but initial starting points and patterns of growth are different for each. These cross-national differences cannot be explained by differences in underlying health conditions.[2]

In the United States, the 52 percent increase in the relative disability rolls in the 1970s was the result of both substantial increases in real social security benefits and the easing of eligibility standards for older workers. The ratio grew most rapidly among those aged forty-five and over.[3] During this decade,

---

1. For a more complete discussion of the DWTC and all other initiatives of the Disability Policy Panel, see Mashaw and Reno (1996).

2. For a more complete discussion of table 3-1 and disability policy in the four countries, see Aarts, Burkhauser, and de Jong (1996). For an analysis of the importance of macroeconomic factors on the disability rolls, see Stapleton and others (forthcoming). For a perspective on the political factors that influence the size of the disability rolls, see Berkowitz and Burkhauser (1996).

3. See Burkhauser and Haveman (1982) for a discussion of this period of disability policy history.

Table 3-1. Disability Benefit Recipients per Thousand Workers by Age, in the United States, the Netherlands, Sweden, and Germany, 1970–94

Age and country	Recipients per 1,000 workers						Percent change		
	1970	1975	1980	1985	1990	1994	1970–80	1980–90	1990–94
15 to 64									
United States	27	42	41	41	43	62	52	5	44
Netherlands	55	84	138	142	152	151	51	10	–1
Sweden	49	67	68	74	78	97	39	15	24
Germany[a]	51	54	59	72	55	54[b]	16	7	–2
15 to 44									
United States	11	17	16	20	23	38	45	44	65
Netherlands	17	32	57	58	62	66	235	9	6
Sweden	18	20	19	20	21	27	6	11	29
Germany[a]	7	6	7	8	5	5[b]	0	–28	0
45 to 59									
United States	33	68	83	71	72	96	151	–13	33
Netherlands	113	179	294	305	339	289	160	15	–15
Sweden	66	95	99	108	116	143	50	17	23
Germany[a]	75	64	84	103	75	80[b]	12	–11	7
60 to 64									
United States	154	265	285	254	250	294	85	–12	18
Netherlands	299	437	1,033	1,283	1,987	1,911	245	92	–4
Sweden	229	382	382	512	577	658	67	51	14
Germany[a]	419	688	1,348	1,291	1,109	1,064[b]	222	–18	–4

Source: Derived from Aarts, Burkhauser, and de Jong (1996, table 1–1).
a. German data refer to the population in the western states of the Federal Republic of Germany.
b. Figure refers to 1993.

the United States joined Sweden, Germany, and the Netherlands in using its disability benefit system to provide early retirement benefits for workers not old enough to be eligible for benefits through the traditional Social Security retirement system. The use of disability payments as a bridge to early retirement is consistent with the origin of Social Security disability insurance (DI) in the 1950s as a program limited to older workers. With the exception of the Netherlands, growth in the relative disability rolls in all countries in the 1970s was primarily among older workers.

Retrenchment in disability policy in the early part of the 1980s, together with a strong economy in the remainder of the decade, led to a mere 5 percent increase in the relative disability benefit population in the United States during the 1980s. This was the smallest growth among the four countries. This small increase in overall growth, however, concealed a 44 percent increase in the relative disability population aged fifteen through forty-four, an increase that far exceeded that of younger workers in the other countries.

When the economic recession of the early 1990s hit, the relative disability benefit population aged fifteen to forty-four rose by 65 percent and the overall relative disability population rose by 44 percent. Three changes in disability policy rules before the recession contributed to this upsurge. First, the definition of mental impairment necessary to receive benefits was loosened. Second, the requirement that the federal government show proof of medical improvements in a beneficiary's condition before benefits could be terminated were put into place in the mid–1980s. Finally, the SSI eligibility criteria for children were dramatically loosened as a result of the 1990 Supreme Court decision in *Sullivan* v. *Zebley*.[4] Growth of the disability population ratios in the United States between 1990 and 1994 far outstripped growth in the other countries, especially among younger persons.

These administrative and court-enforced changes in U.S. Social Security regulations have dramatically altered the beneficiary population and the disability system's traditional role as a bridge to early retirement benefits for older workers. The massive increase in the numbers of children receiving SSI benefits and the sharp increase in the number of younger adult beneficiaries on both SSI and DI are new and extremely worrisome phenomena for those who would like to see people with disabilities of working age integrated into mainstream employment. A lifetime of disability benefits is not the appropriate policy option for younger people with disabilities either from a social point of view or from their own perspective.

---

4. For recent discussions of the influences of policy changes on the SSI rolls, see U.S. General Accounting Office (1994 and 1995); U.S. Department of Health and Human Services (1994).

Growth in the Disability Benefit Population

While a consensus is building on the causes of the recent growth in the U.S. disability benefit population, the appropriateness of this policy outcome remains debatable. For instance, disability rights advocates see the growth in mental disorder awards as the expected consequence of a society finally reaching out to an underserved population, while those concerned with the solvency of the disability system see it as an unwarranted lowering of the eligibility criteria for disability benefits.[5] Likewise, the outreach successes of state agencies, which have also been a factor in increasing the disability rolls, are seen either as an appropriate attempt to provide disability benefits to people unaware of their rights or as further evidence of a concerted effort to shift the burden of general welfare assistance from the states to the federal government.[6]

Whatever one's view on the current situation, however, it is important to understand that it is not the result of a series of policy accidents. Poverty policy experts advocated and laid the groundwork for the existing system. Supporters of a universal negative income tax (NIT) in the 1970s argued that all Americans have a right to some minimum benefit with no quid pro quo. The NIT would have provided a guaranteed minimum benefit to all families, which would be taxed away as they received income from other sources. While a popular idea in the 1970s, it never achieved political success because even then the majority of voting Americans were uncomfortable with the notion of providing benefits to those who are expected to work. For those not expected to work, an NIT was more politically popular and in 1972 became the SSI program. Since 1974, this federal program has provided a guaranteed income to those over age sixty-five and those under age sixty-five considered unable to work because of disability. But commonly heard in policy circles in the 1970s were whispers that the passage of SSI effectively provided an NIT not only for older people but also, with a sufficiently flexible definition of disability, for younger people. Today many policy experts and most advocates for the poor see the expansion of SSI as the best practical method of ensuring a universal federal government-financed minimum income floor under all Americans.

But the political mood in the 1990s is much less supportive of federal guaranteed minimum income programs than it was in the 1970s. The enactment of welfare reform legislation that among other things ended the federal guaran-

---

5. For a lively debate about the appropriateness of the increase in the disability benefit population, see Goldman (forthcoming) and Weaver (forthcoming).

6. For a view of this outreach strategy, see Bound, Kossoudji, and Ricart-Moes (forthcoming). For a warning of its financial consequences, see U.S. General Accounting Office (1995).

tee of Aid to Families with Dependent Children (AFDC) by a Republican Congress and a Democratic president just before the 1996 elections provides ample evidence of this change in political mood. To the degree that SSI or DI are seen as mechanisms for supporting those who could work, their survival is also threatened. The voting majority is less willing to tax itself to pay for such benefits, and thirty years of War on Poverty programs have raised serious concerns about the dangers to the human spirit that a life of permanent dependence brings.

While the voting majority has lost faith in the value of payments to those who do not work, what is more in keeping with traditional American values and what a majority of Americans will support are government programs that subsidize work, not welfare, or, to borrow a phrase from a current political leader—programs that make work pay. The tension that disability administrators face is that as general benefit programs such as General Assistance and AFDC are cut to shift people into the work force, increasing efforts will be made to place these former beneficiaries on SSI as their benefits expire.[7]

Even the defenders of the current system of disability payments should pause in light of the new political realities of the 1990s. Welfare rights advocates argue that, while SSI is not a generous program, at least it provides a safe haven against the uncertainty of the labor market. Advocates for people with disabilities have labored tirelessly in the halls of Congress to ensure that most people on SSI will never have to leave that program. The history of congressional reaction to rising disability rolls, however, suggests that SSI is not a permanently safe harbor.

Today government is being reinvented, and the idea of increasing the economic well-being of welfare recipients appears to have little support from the two major political parties. For young people with disabilities who are on the verge of moving either toward work or welfare, the future value of a lifetime of SSI benefits is uncertain. Perhaps the advocates of people with disabilities should shift their focus from defending programs that subsidize nonwork to programs that enable and encourage work.

The Americans with Disabilities Act of 1990, with its emphasis on accommodation and the view that the majority of people with disabilities can work, should be at the center of a set of policies that begin to shift the collective energies from nonwork to work subsidies. If people with disabilities are able to work, then public policies should be built around this expectation and not around a lifetime of welfare benefits.

---

7. For some evidence that this is already happening, see Burkhauser and Daly (1995).

A Pro–Work Disability Policy: A Disabled Worker Tax Credit

Severe disabilities, especially when accompanied by poor work skills, limit labor market opportunities. But, using data from the Panel Study of Income Dynamics to trace the work, labor earnings, and economic well-being of men and women following the onset of a disability, Richard V. Burkhauser and Mary C. Daly find work is still common among people with disabilities.[8] Hence, the onset of a disability need not, and for the majority of people with disabilities does not, lead inevitably to the disability transfer rolls.

In addition, some evidence is available that early intervention helps keep people with disabilities in the work force. Richard V. Burkhauser, J. S. Butler, and Yang Woo Kim find that 75 percent of those workers who were not accommodated by their employer following the onset of a disability were gone after three years.[9] But it was nine years before 75 percent of workers who were accommodated left their employer.

However, once people are on the DI or SSI rolls, they rarely return to work. Thus far efforts to encourage disability beneficiaries off the rolls via extending Medicaid benefits or lowering the implicit tax on SSI benefits have not been successful. Hillary W. Hoynes and Robert Moffitt argue that people on the benefit rolls are not sensitive to tax rate changes and that making eligibility easier for those with disabilities who do work is likely to increase program participation, because a large share of people with disabilities work and might become eligible for benefits with a relaxed work test.[10] Hence, the current back-to-work incentives are not likely to be effective.

If inducing beneficiaries off the disability rolls is unlikely to have much success, do better ways exist to reduce the rolls and further increase work among people with disabilities? What follows is a sketch of the disabled worker tax credit, one of a number of pro-work initiatives recommended by the Disability Policy Panel that offer some hope of increasing the employment of people with disabilities.

Remedies provided by the Americans with Disabilities Act—banning discrimination, requiring reasonable accommodation, and breaking down architectural barriers—are likely to be most effective for skilled workers who have faced these barriers in the past.[11] But workers with physical or mental impairments who have low skills and limited training are doubly disadvantaged in

---

8. Burkhauser and Daly (1996a).
9. Burkhauser, Butler, and Kim (1995).
10. Hoynes and Moffitt (1996).
11. Burkhauser and Daly (1996b).

today's labor market. This type of worker has swelled the disability benefit rolls since 1989. The DWTC provides a work-based alternative for such workers.

A DWTC pays those who live in low-income families, not because they are unable to work, but because they do work, albeit at low income levels despite their impairments. As such, the DWTC rewards work for wage earners with disabilities who live in low-income families without increasing reliance on disability benefit programs.

The DWTC provides wage earners with disabilities an alternative to entering disability benefit programs. While available to DI or SSI beneficiaries who leave the benefit rolls, it would also be provided to workers with significant disabilities who work and do not receive DI or SSI benefits. As such, it is designed to:

—Ease the transition off the DI and SSI benefit rolls for those who return to work. The wage subsidy would compensate for some of the loss of benefits that takes place when beneficiaries return to work.

—Ease the transition from school to work for young people currently in the SSI–childhood disability program whose earnings capacity is doubly limited by their youth and their impairments. By subsidizing their labor earnings, it encourages work—even part time or at low pay—that over the long run can improve young workers' human capital through on-the-job experience.

—Encourage older workers to remain at work even though they experience a decline in hours of work or wage rates as a result of progressive impairments. By subsidizing labor earnings, it encourages older workers who live in low-income families to delay the point at which they turn to the benefit system.

The exact parameters for a DWTC would determine how much it costs and who it benefits. The illustrative proposal here would provide a refundable credit to persons with significant disabilities who work. Under the proposal, an estimated 3.1 million working people with disabilities would receive the new credit, at an additional cost of about $3 billion, in 1996. The average subsidy would be about $1,000 per year over any subsidy the individual might receive from the existing earned income tax credit (EITC).[12] The credit targets low-income people who work despite their disabilities. According to data from the *Current Population Survey,* about one in three recipients of the DWTC would

12. These estimates were prepared using data from the 1990 *Current Population Survey* to estimate the size of the eligible population with disabilities and the impact of different credit options on income. The estimate is based on 1996 EITC parameters established by the Omnibus Budget Reconciliation Act of 1993.

be persons with disabilities with tax-unit income below the poverty line, and three in four would have incomes below twice the poverty line.

Criteria for Developing an Illustrative Proposal

The specific design of the DWTC could take a number of forms. Its cost, impact on the incomes of workers with disabilities, work incentive effects, and administrative issues will vary depending on the specific design features. The proposal illustrated here reflects one set of choices about defining eligibility for the credit and balancing the particular goals to be achieved in deciding the size and shape of the DWTC.

Eligibility for the DWTC

Low-income people whose disabilities represent a significant impediment to work—but who nonetheless have some capacity to work—are the target group for the credit. Implementation must also be administratively feasible, which has two aspects: making a determination of disability for eligibility purposes and paying the credit to beneficiaries. The credit would be paid through the existing income tax system, which already provides a wage credit for low-income workers—the EITC. The task of determining eligibility, however, is no easy matter. Although the Internal Revenue Service (IRS) has a definition of disability that is used for purposes of making a deduction from taxable income, the agency does not have the capacity to make disability determinations.[13]

The IRS disability determination should be based on assessments already being made by other agencies. The most obvious group to target for the DWTC are current DI and SSI beneficiaries, although this group is least likely to make use of such a credit, because presumably they are the most severely disabled and are currently receiving benefits. A group more likely to be influenced by a DWTC is new applicants for DI or SSI who have been denied benefits. For instance, persons denied at step five have been determined to have a severe impairment and are unable to do their past work, but they have been found able to do other work that exists in the national economy. For both DI and SSI

13. Income tax rules allow a deduction from income for impairment-related work expenses for persons with a disability, defined as "a physical or mental disability that limits your being employed, or substantially limits one or more of your major life activities, such as performing manual tasks, walking, speaking, breathing, learning, and working." U.S. Internal Revenue Service (1994, p. 233).

beneficiaries and applicants denied at step five, information from SSA could be used to certify eligibility for the DWTC.

Additional groups who might pass the disability eligibility test for a DWTC include persons certified by state vocational rehabilitation agencies as having met the first part of the eligibility test for services; they have "a physical or mental impairment which for such individual constitutes or results in a substantial impediment to employment." State vocational rehabilitation agencies could be responsible for certifying individuals who meet this eligibility test.

The Size and Shape of the DWTC

The DWTC mirrors the earned income tax credit in design and builds upon it. Under the DWTC, workers living in low-income tax units would receive a credit equal to a certain percentage of their labor income. As labor earnings rose from zero, so would the amount of the credit up to a maximum credit amount. Once the maximum was reached, the credit would plateau over a range of labor earnings and then would begin to decrease as adjusted gross income continued to rise until it was fully phased out. Only persons with labor earnings would be eligible for the credit.

The size and shape of the DWTC as earnings rise would depend on the following parameters:

—During the phase-in range of the DWTC, each additional dollar of labor earnings would increase the amount of the credit by a specified percentage of the additional earnings. This percentage is referred to as the phase-in rate of the credit.

—The DWTC would continue to phase in as labor earnings rise until a maximum credit amount is reached.

—When the maximum credit amount is reached, the credit would plateau over a fixed range of labor earnings. The worker would receive the maximum credit amount on labor earnings within the plateau range.

—When income rises above the maximum income for the plateau range, the credit would begin to phase out. The maximum credit amount would be decreased by a specified percentage of the excess of adjusted gross income (or, if greater, labor income) over the ending income of the plateau range.[14] This percentage is referred to as the phase-out rate of the credit.

14. Like the EITC, the phase-in of the DWTC is based on labor earnings of the person with a disability while the credit phase-out is based on adjusted gross income (AGI) of the tax unit unless labor earnings exceed AGI. Basing the credit phase-out on AGI is designed to ensure that workers who live in families with significant income do not benefit from the credit.

—The tax credit would continue to phase out as income rises until it is fully phased out. This point is referred to as the break-even point.

In designing its illustrative DWTC proposal, the Academy's Disability Policy Panel considered the following goals in setting these parameters:

1. Work subsidies for disabled workers, with or without children, that are larger than those provided through the existing EITC. Many people with disabilities experience special impediments and added costs when they go to work. The DWTC is designed, in part, to lessen these burdens. Workers with disabilities should, therefore, receive larger work subsidies through the DWTC than nondisabled workers of the same family size receive through the EITC.

2. A high phase-in rate at the front end of the credit to provide strong work incentives for those with very low earnings. A high phase-in rate for the DWTC provides strong incentives for persons to work even part time or at low pay, such as young workers who are making the transition from school to work. The support provided through the DWTC may make it possible for some low earners to enter or remain in the work force instead of turning to the disability benefit system.

3. A plateau range coordinated with the DI and SSI work incentives. The DWTC is intended, in part, to ease the transition off the DI and SSI rolls for beneficiaries who have the capacity to do so. DI beneficiaries would be eligible for the credit after benefits stop because of a return to work. The credit would soften the impact of the loss of DI benefits by providing an increasing marginal return to work as labor earnings rise. As long as the DWTC is designed so that the DI beneficiary is in the phase-in range of the credit when benefits stop, the worker continues to experience an increasing marginal return to work as earnings rise.

To coordinate the DWTC with the SSI work incentives, the plateau range should not end until after SSI benefits are fully phased out. If the DWTC begins to phase out before SSI benefits are fully phased out, the result will be a high cumulative marginal tax rate.[15]

4. A reasonable phase-out rate for the credit. During the phase-out, the credit is reduced for each additional dollar of income. A high phase-out rate will mean high marginal tax rates and potential work disincentives for workers with disabilities. In the phase-out range of the credit, the worker will already be experiencing a marginal tax rate that includes the 7.65 percent payroll tax for

15. Dropping the SSI $85 per month exclusion on earned income or increasing the SSI tax on labor earning would result in a lower SSI phase-out point. For instance, ending the $85 exclusion would move the SSI break-even point from $12,012 to $10,997.

Social Security and Medicare (FICA taxes), the 15 percent federal income tax, and any state and local taxes.

5. Minimize cost by having break-even points that target the DWTC to workers with only modest incomes. Balancing these goals may require extending the phase-out range beyond the break-even points for the existing EITC. When setting the credit's parameters, break-even points should be chosen that will ensure that the DWTC remains targeted to workers with modest incomes as a way to minimize costs. One could simply adopt the current EITC break-even points, but this would require either a substantial increase in the phase-out rate, a shortening of the plateau range, or a reduction in the phase-in rate.

An Illustrative DWTC Proposal

Based on these goals, a set of parameters was chosen for the Panel's illustrative DWTC for disabled workers with no qualifying children, one child, and two or more children (see table 3-2).

Figure 3-1 graphically illustrates how the DWTC and EITC phase in and phase out as earnings levels rise. The illustrative proposal is one way to achieve the five goals:

—At all earnings levels, the DWTC is larger than the EITC, thereby achieving a higher wage subsidy for disabled workers than for other workers of similar family size (goal 1).

—In each case, the phase-in rate is more generous than the EITC, thereby creating additional work incentives for workers with very low earnings (goal 2).

—The plateau range—from $10,000 to $13,000—applies to workers of all family sizes and is coordinated with the work incentive features of DI and SSI (goal 3).

—The phase-out rate of 25 percent for all disabled workers is set to minimize work disincentives in the phase-out range and yet avoid paying the DWTC to workers with more than modest incomes as a way to minimize costs (goals 4 and 5).

Comparing the Maximum DWTC with the EITC

In this proposal, the maximum credit varies by family size, with the greatest increase over the existing EITC going to low-income disabled workers without qualifying children because they are eligible for only a small credit from the EITC.

Table 3-2. Illustrative DWTC and 1996 EITC Parameters

Program	Phase-in rate (percent)	Beginning income for plateau range (dollars)	Ending income for plateau range (dollars)	Maximum credit amount (dollars)	Phase-out rate (percent)	Break-even point (dollars)
Worker with no children						
DWTC	25.00	10,000	13,000	2,500	25.00	23,000
EITC	7.65	4,000	5,000	306	7.65	9,000
Worker with one child						
DWTC	38.00	10,000	13,000	3,800	25.00	28,200
EITC	34.00	6,160	11,290	2,094	15.98	24,395
Worker with two or more children						
DWTC	45.00	10,000	13,000	4,500	25.00	31,000
EITC	40.00	8,900	11,620	3,560	21.06	28,524

Source: U.S. House of Representatives (1994).
Note: DWTC = disabled worker tax credit; EITC = earned income tax credit.

—For disabled workers without qualifying children, the maximum DWTC is $2,500, nearly $2,200 more than the maximum EITC for childless workers.

—For workers with one child, the maximum DWTC is $3,800, about $1,900 more than the maximum EITC.

—For workers with two or more children, the maximum DWTC of $4,500 is $940 more than the maximum EITC.

Estimated Cost and Benefits

The estimated costs and benefits of the illustrative DWTC proposal are for 1996 and, unless otherwise noted, represent the increased tax credits and cost of the DWTC over and above any EITC that workers might receive.[16] The estimates assume no changes in behavior as a result of the new DWTC,

16. The estimates are based on the 1996 EITC rules established by the Omnibus Budget Reconciliation Act of 1993. Data from the 1990 *Current Population Survey* were used to estimate the size of the eligible population with disabilities and the impact of different credit options upon incomes. For the definition of the eligible population with disabilities, see box in appendix. While this definition is not identical to the proposal discussed here, it is sufficiently similar to it to estimate the impact of the Panel's proposal.

To estimate the cost and impact of the DWTC for 1996, income and earnings from the 1990 *Current Population Survey* are adjusted by the increases in the consumer price index through 1993 and by 3 percent thereafter. The estimates assume no demographic changes, such as changes in population size, health and disability status, family size, and so on. In addition, they assume no changes in behavior as a result of the new DWTC, although the DWTC is expected to influence the work effort of people with disabilities. For a fuller discussion of the methodology used in the paper, see the appendix.

Figure 3-1. Comparisons of Illustrative DWTC and 1996 EITC

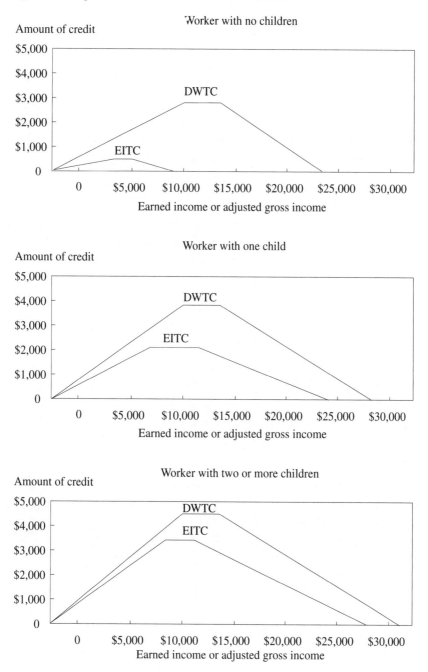

Note: DWTC = disabled worker tax credit; EITC = earned income tax credit.

although the DWTC likely will influence the work effort of people with disabilities (see tables 3-3 and 3-4).

—About 3.1 million low-income working people with disabilities who live in low-income families would receive the DWTC, at an additional cost of about $3 billion, in 1996. The additional wage subsidy from the DWTC would average about $1,000 a year over any subsidy the individual might receive from the EITC.

—Working individuals without children are the most likely to gain from the DWTC. They account for about 2.1 million of those who would receive the DWTC and about $2.3 billion of the DWTC paid. Their additional wage subsidy from the DWTC would average about $1,100. Individuals without qualifying children are targeted because they receive very little from the current EITC. The EITC for workers without qualifying children is a maximum of just $306 and is payable only to those aged twenty-five to sixty-four.

—The DWTC would also benefit about 1 million low-income working persons who have children. Their additional wage subsidy based on the DWTC would average about $750 a year.

—Most of those who would benefit from the DWTC are not receiving Social Security, SSI, or other payments based on their disability, such as workers' compensation; federal, state, or local government employee disability; or company or union disability. About three in four are not receiving any disability-based income. As such, the DWTC holds potential for encouraging and assisting low-income workers with disabilities to remain at work and not turn to disability income support.

—Young workers account for the majority of those who would receive the DWTC. About two in three of those who would receive added DWTC subsidies are under the age of forty-five. To the extent that the DWTC encourages and enables them to remain in the work force and to add to their human capital through on-the-job experience, it holds potential for enhancing their independence and self-sufficiency over the long run.

—The youngest workers—those ages eighteen to twenty-four—account for about one in six of those who would gain an added wage subsidy from the DWTC. Workers in this age group are not eligible for the current EITC unless they have children.[17]

---

17. The current modest EITC for childless workers is not available to those under the age of twenty-five on the theory that low-earning individuals in this age group include college students or others who are not genuinely at risk of long-term economic disadvantage. The DWTC targets only those in this age group who have significant disabilities and, therefore, are at considerable risk of long-term economic disadvantage.

Table 3-3. Distribution of DWTC Recipients and Marginal DWTC Benefits, 1996

Population characteristics	Recipients (in thousands)	Added DWTC benefits (in millions of dollars)
Disabled workers: Family status		
No children	2,133	2,321
One child	474	418
Two or more children	509	315
Percentage distribution: Age		
18 to 24	17	19
25 to 34	27	26
35 to 44	22	22
45 to 54	16	16
55 to 64	19	17
Percentage receiving benefits[a]		
SSI	18	15
DI	10	8
Veterans' disability	2	2
Other disability income[b]	9	10
None	74	78
Total	3,088	3,053

Source: Tabulations are based on the 1990 *Current Population Survey.*

Note: DWTC = disabled worker tax credit; SSI = Supplemental Security Income; DI = Social Security disability insurance.

a. Percentages do not add to 100 because some individuals receive benefits from more than one program.

b. Other disability income includes workers' compensation, company or union disability, federal government disability, U.S. Military Retirement Disability, U.S. Railroad Retirement Disability, state or local government employee disability, and accident or disability insurance.

—The benefits of the DWTC are targeted to workers living in low-income families. The target efficiency of the DWTC is shown by comparing the recipients' family income before the DWTC with the official poverty line. Nearly one in four workers with disabilities who would receive the DWTC have family incomes below the poverty line for a family of their size. Nearly six in ten have family incomes below twice the poverty line.

The DWTC is more precisely targeted on low-income persons when only the income of the tax filing unit is considered, instead of the total income of the family where the worker resides.[18] Some workers with disabilities, particularly young workers without children, live in families with additional earners, even though these earners are not included as part of their tax filing unit. For example, young single people with disabilities may be living with their parents but qualify as an individual tax filing unit. Using tax unit income as the

18. In these simulations, family income includes the incomes of all related people living in the household. Tax filing unit income would determine eligibility and amount of the DWTC. In these data, a tax filing unit consists of married couples or single individuals plus their minor children. An unmarried adult who lives with adult relatives would be considered a single individual as a tax filing unit.

Table 3-4. Distribution of DWTC Recipients and Payments by Ratio of Income to Poverty Threshold, 1996

Ratio of income to poverty[a]	DWTC recipients		DWTC payments	
	Family unit	Tax unit	Family unit	Tax unit
Less than 1.0	24	34	14	18
1.00 to 1.49	17	19	20	26
1.50 to 1.99	17	20	22	27
2.00 to 2.99	23	21	24	23
3.00 or more	18	6	21	6

Source: Tabulations are based on the 1990 *Current Population Survey*.

Note: DWTC = disabled worker tax credit.

a. This is known as the income-to-needs ratio. The second and fourth columns base the income-to-needs ratio on the total income of the family in which the disabled worker resides. The income-to-needs ratio in these columns is the ratio of the family's income divided by the family's size-adjusted poverty line. The third and fifth columns base the income-to-needs ratio on the income of the tax filing unit, not the total income of the family unit in which the worker resides.

measure of economic status, about one in three workers who would receive the DWTC have incomes below the poverty line. Nearly three in four have tax unit incomes below twice the poverty line.

Conclusion

The staggering growth in the relative disability beneficiary population in the United States between 1990 and 1994 far exceeds that of the Netherlands, Germany, or Sweden over the same period. The disproportionate growth in the younger benefit population is rapidly changing the disability benefit system from one that was primarily meant to ease the transition into retirement for older workers to a program providing benefits from cradle to grave. The growth in the younger disability benefit population is unprecedented in the history of the U.S. system and is counter to the goal of integrating people with disabilities of working age into mainstream employment.

Increasingly, SSI and DI are being used as alternatives to a more general income maintenance program. This is neither good social policy nor good for the children and young adults who are coming onto these programs. SSI childhood beneficiaries are rapidly approaching the 1 million mark. Over the next decade, the vast majority of these children who survive will come onto the SSI disability rolls unless concerted efforts are made to provide them with work-based alternatives. Because many of these young potential workers, even on a level playing field, will earn low wages or work less than full time, targeted work-based subsidies will be necessary to ensure them a minimum level of economic well-being.

A disabled worker tax credit developed along the lines proposed by the Academy's Disability Policy Panel targets subsidies on people with disabilities who work but nevertheless have low family income. This credit would not be costless. The plan illustrated in the Panel report has a price tag of approximately $3 billion per year over and above current EITC expenditures.[19] Yet when compared with the $51 billion in DI payments or the $21 billion in SSI disability payments made in 1994, it is not an overwhelmingly large amount. More important, money is paid based on work. A DWTC would be a major step toward shifting disability policy toward the goal of integrating people with disabilities more fully into the work force.

Technical Appendix

This appendix describes the simulations for the earned income tax credit (EITC) and the disabled worker tax credit (DWTC) used in the paper by Richard V. Burkhauser, Andrew J. Glenn, and David C. Wittenburg. Because the DWTC builds on the current EITC program and the cost and distribution of DWTC benefits are critically related to the EITC, both programs are simulated.

EITC Simulations

Because the EITC is an income tax-based program, the retrospective income data from the March 1990 *Current Population Survey* (CPS) was used for the simulations. In all simulations, a structure was set up for the EITC as specified by the Internal Revenue Service for 1996. These guidelines specified two sets of criteria: family type and income. While the unit of analysis for EITC eligibility is the family, the federal income tax filing unit is the unit for the income criteria. In most cases, these will not be the same, as many families file more than one tax return.

Family Eligibility

Family eligibility depends upon the presence of a qualifying child. That child must be under age nineteen and a direct descendent (for example, son, grandchild, stepdaughter) of someone in the family.

This age restriction is increased to age twenty-four if the child is a full-time student, and it is eliminated altogether if the child is totally or permanently

19. Because this simulation uses a broad description of disability, the actual population and costs are likely to be much smaller. In addition, to the degree that the DWTC reduces the flow onto the SSI and DI rolls or induces current recipients to leave, the costs of these programs will fall.

disabled. The child must also live in the main home of the household for more than six months of the year.

With the data available in the CPS, both the age and relationship criteria can be applied in a straightforward manner. The only exception is the disabled child, who has no age restriction. The CPS survey only asks respondents whether they were unable to work at any time during the previous year because of health problems and does not ask about disabilities directly. Thus, no attempt was made to identify permanently disabled children.

Once the age and relationship test are met, the family is assumed to be eligible for the program in the simulation. The next step is to apply the income tests to the appropriate tax filing unit within the family.

Only one tax filing unit within a family may claim the credit. That is, only one credit is available per family. All domestic tax filers who meet the income and family criteria are eligible for the credit except couples who are married and filed separately. In the simulations, the assumption was that all eligible married couples filed jointly.

Multiple-generation families will generally have more than one tax filing unit who can claim the qualifying child. In these situations, the IRS has two rules to determine who gets the credit. The first rule is that tax filers who are qualifying children cannot themselves be eligible for the EITC. The second rule applies when more than one tax filing unit can claim the qualifying child. In this case, the tax filing unit with the higher adjusted gross income will be the one to claim the credit. If either tax filing unit's adjusted gross income falls outside the range of the credit, then no credit will be paid out.

Income Criteria

Once the appropriate tax filing unit is determined, the income criteria are applied. In general, even though the CPS has detailed income data, any attempt to carry out IRS rules with respect to income will be much less precise than what can be attempted with respect to the family characteristic rules. Hence, any attempt to simulate the completion of a tax return will be crude. However, this problem should be mitigated by the sample population. Low-income families generally have few (and uncomplicated) income sources.

The two income measures used to calculate the EITC credit are labor incomes and adjusted gross income. All income figures are adjusted for inflation using the consumer price index (CPI–U). For the years 1994–96, the 1994 inflation rate of 2.9 percent was assumed. The simulations included as labor income: wages, salaries, tips, net earnings from self-employment, and union strike benefits. Adjusted gross income starts with labor income as the base and then both adds in other sources of income and subtracts out various credits. The following sources of income were added into the simulated measure of adjusted gross income: interest income, dividends, alimony, rental income, royalties, and unemployment compensation. Only one credit adjustment was included in the measure of adjusted gross income—the one-half of the self-employment tax that can be subtracted out.

For married couples, the labor income and adjusted gross incomes of the family head and spouse are added together to get the labor income and the adjusted gross income measures that apply to the appropriate tax filing unit. In the case of a single parent who receives the EITC, the individual's labor income and adjusted gross income are the appropriate measures.

For families that have both labor income and adjusted gross income that fall within the range of the EITC, the next step is to determine which of the two measures should be used to calculate the size of the credit. Table 3-2 lists the EITC parameters for calendar year 1996. The maximum cutoff is $28,524 in 1996 for families with more than one child. Therefore, all families with labor and adjusted gross incomes with positive labor income below these amounts are eligible to receive the credit. As long as adjusted gross income does not exceed the beginning income of the phase-out range, the labor income measure is appropriate. For adjusted gross income above this level, the appropriate measure of income is the higher of adjusted gross income or labor income. The phase-in and phase-out rates varied depending upon family composition for 1996.

DWTC Simulations

To qualify for the DWTC, an individual has to first meet one of the specified definitions of disability (see box). Individuals who meet any one of these criteria are considered disabled. All families with a disabled individual over the age of eighteen and under age sixty-five were included as part of the eligible population.

The DWTC simulation is run after identifying families with disabled individuals. The parameters for the DWTC are listed in table 3-2. Similar to the EITC, the DWTC has an income requirement based on a maximum level of family adjusted gross income. However, unlike the EITC, the DWTC contains eligibility requirements that target individual income, not family income. Therefore, the level of the benefit in the phase-in and plateau region are based on the labor income of the person with a disability, not family income. As with the EITC, benefits are phased out by the larger of either family adjusted gross income or the individual's labor income in the phase-out region. The simulated

Definition of Disability

A person of working age—that is, from eighteen to sixty-four—is defined as disabled if he or she:

—Answers "yes" to the question "Do you have a health problem or disability that prevents you from working or limits the kind or amount of work you can do?"; or

—Cites the main reason for not working the previous year as "ill or disabled"; or

—Reports that the current reason for not looking for work as "ill or disabled"; or

—Lists "own illness" as the reason for working fewer than thirty-five hours per week last year; or

—Receives any of the following: Social Security disability insurance, Supplemental Security Income, Railroad Retirement Disability, company or union disability, accident or disability insurance, or state or local disability.

DWTC is then compared with the family's simulated EITC. Families are assumed to take the higher of the simulated DWTC or EITC. For all families with a larger DWTC, the marginal increase in benefits are calculated as the difference between the DWTC and the EITC. The results are listed in table 3-3.

Comment by Michael J. Graetz

The disabled worker tax credit (DWTC) proposal is a careful effort to create a tax-based wage subsidy similar to the earned income tax credit (EITC), while avoiding some of the weaknesses of the EITC.[20] One of the great strengths of the DWTC is its effort to match the plateau level of this new credit to the Supplemental Security Income (SSI) and the Social Security disability insurance (DI) levels. In addition, it keeps the marginal rate resulting from the credit phase-out down to a reasonable level—25 percent.

20. Yin and others (1994); and Alstott (1995).

The result is still a 55 percent marginal tax rate on wages, so the new tax credit is not without problems. However, problems would arise with any means-tested proposal, and the DWTC proposal endeavors to avoid excessive marginal rates. Also to be alleviated are the high burdens of entering the work force that stems from the potential loss of Medicaid insurance.

Other observations can be offered. First, moving the implementation of eligibility for this new tax credit away from the Internal Revenue Service (IRS) to other agencies is right, although problems may result from the agencies' differing incentives and responsibilities. How disputes between the taxing authorities and those other agencies will be resolved remains unclear.

The broad definition of disability seems likely to cause some serious disputes about who is eligible.

With the EITC, a determination must be made of the family's income and whether the worker has qualifying children or not. With the disability credit, someone will have to figure out whether the claimant meets the disability requirement. That is going to be a much more difficult determination. In the 1960s, Congress was stopped on several occasions from enacting an additional personal exemption for the disabled comparable to the additional exemption that applied to the blind. Congress simply did not think the IRS could administer a disability standard.

Second, because proponents of the DWTC have assumed no changes in behavior, the $3 billion cost estimate is probably on the low end. If the DWTC does not induce anyone to enter the work force, then why should the government spend so much money for it? The $3 billion should be regarded as the lowest estimate of cost, even though some offsetting factors exist that cut in the other direction.

Third, targeting this credit to low-income people involves a well-known trade-off between targeting a significant amount of dollars to low-income people and providing a tax benefit more generally to people with disabilities. All disabled persons have additional expenses of working because of their disabilities, without regard to their income. But extending the credit (or allowing a deduction) to all disabled persons would increase its costs or require a narrowing of the definition of disabled persons who would qualify. Targeting to low-income disabled workers seems a reasonable judgment.

Some caution should be taken in building on the EITC. These cautions relate to five points: the complexity of the EITC, issues of eligibility and compliance, the delivery of the credit, work incentives, and marriage penalties.

First, the EITC is remarkably complicated for what is supposed to be a simple provision to help low-income workers. It requires a two-page tax form—a separate form—that is accompanied by a thirty-two page booklet that describes how to fill it out.

The Commission on Tax Reform and Economic Growth, headed by former U.S. representative and secretary of housing and urban development Jack Kemp, took as its example of staggering income tax complexity the definition of a qualifying child under the EITC as set forth in the *Internal Revenue Code*. The tax law says: "The term qualifying child means with respect to any taxpayer for any taxable year an individual who bears a relationship to the taxpayer described in Subparagraph (b), except as provided in Subparagraph (b)(3) who has the same principal place of abode as the taxpayer for more than one half of the taxable year and who meets the age requirements of Subparagraph (c). . . ." It goes on like that.

That level of complexity reflects the problem of marrying a wage subsidy delivery program to the *Internal Revenue Code*. It is a genuine problem of differing cultures that is not easily solved.

The definition of earned income in the instruction form includes wages, salaries, and tips; union strike benefits; long-term disability benefits received before minimum retirement age; net earnings from self-employment; voluntary salary deferrals, for example, a 401(k) plan; pay earned in a combat zone, basic quarters, and subsistence allowances for the U.S. military; the value of meals and lodging provided by an employer for employees; and housing allowances or rentals of a parsonage.

The EITC instructions say earned income also includes tax-excludable, employer-provided dependent care benefits and anything else of value received from someone for services performed even if it is not taxable.

The definition of earned income under the EITC is much broader than the definition of earned income subject to income or payroll taxes. This new disabled worker tax credit builds on this EITC definition.

The tax law definition of adjusted gross income, which would be used to determine the phase-out levels under the DWTC, is far more complicated than this earned income definition. This definition of earned income is child's play compared with determining the adjusted gross income level. Moreover, in making the adjusted gross income level determination for the DWTC, the claimant would have to take into account family members' incomes as well as that of the individual claiming the credit.

Second, in the case of the EITC, more than 100 percent of potential benefits are being paid to about 75 percent of eligible beneficiaries. People are being paid credits who are not eligible and people who are eligible are not claiming credits. Errors are taking place in both directions—overinclusiveness and underinclusiveness. Compliance problems are significant.

For example, the IRS decided in 1992 to pay out EITCs to those people who had not claimed the credit but were eligible based on the IRS's review of their income tax forms. The IRS paid out EITCs to 600,000 people, then found that 270,000 of them were not eligible. This experiment cost the federal government $175 million. The IRS subsequently terminated the program, having discovered that its ability to pay out money was worse than its ability to collect money. But, given the complexity of the law, eligibility for the EITC is difficult to get right.

Many people who would be beneficiaries of the new DWTC are mentally impaired or young, low-skilled disabled people. They will have enormous difficulty in dealing with a complicated system, perhaps even more difficulty than the average low-income worker.

Reviewing the work of tax return preparers and their records, the General Accounting Office found that half of the preparers got the EITC wrong. This is not an encouraging compliance record. Tax return preparers also share in the credit dollars.

The EITC also has been the subject of considerable fraud, particularly electronic filing fraud. The IRS had some success in 1995 in reducing electronic filing fraud, but fraud remains one reason for the large EITC overpayments.

Third, one of the big problems with the EITC, which will also be a problem with the DWTC, is that the money is delivered in a lump sum when the claimant files his or her tax return, instead of being delivered periodically as the worker earns the wages.

An advance-payment option exists under the EITC, and the IRS and many social service agencies have tried to get employers and employees to both understand and use it. But only one-half of 1 percent of eligible people use the advance-payment option. It is not working. Analysts who have looked at this issue believe the advance-payment option cannot work, in part, because of the need to recapture these benefits if the IRS pays them to ineligible people. That is not an easy or straightforward task.

The compromise proposal would make the advance payment option available for only 60 percent of the disabled tax credit benefits, which decreases the current value of the DWTC. Remaining unresolved is the important recapture problem, because eligibility depends on both income levels and meeting some definition of disability.

Fourth, the proposed DWTC has some adverse work-incentive effects. Work incentives are positive for people with very low incomes. This is one of the major purposes of the DWTC. But the work incentives become negative as the DWTC phases out. This has been acknowledged but remains a problem.

Finally, the EITC has serious marriage penalties. People who marry often pay much greater taxes than if they had remained single. In some odd cases, the marriage penalties are as high as 25 or 30 percent of income for some people. This situation is not widely recognized within Congress.

A couple of years ago, picking the EITC as a basis for designing a new benefit for disabled workers would have been building on a universally popular program. However, the recent efforts of the 104th Congress to cut back on the existing EITC are troubling. Further erosion of its political support will occur once people discover the marriage penalties, which are going to be expensive to fix. The EITC is now a much more shaky foundation for building a politically popular subsidy for working disabled people.

All of this is by way of caution. The EITC nevertheless remains a good place to start.

Two tax alternatives to the DWTC are available. First, a certain amount of wages of disabled workers could be exempt from Social Security taxes. This has the great advantages of being relatively simple and delivering the benefits in each paycheck that the worker gets.

At current minimum wages, the employees' share of Social Security is about $600 a year, so an exemption just from the employees' share would deliver substantial benefits. The DWTC proposal is somewhat more generous than that, and it reaches higher in the income scale than minimum-wage workers. The DWTC ranges from about $600 to about $2,500, with an average benefit of about $1,000 in the proposal.

A Social Security tax exemption could go higher than the level of the minimum wage, and the employers' share could also be eliminated. In the short term, this might create an incentive for employers to hire disabled workers. Other than its cost, no reason exists to limit an exemption to the level of the minimum wage.

The difficulty with the exemption alternative is that limiting an exemption to low-income people is not easy, and, without a limit, it will be considerably more expensive. When asked how many people would meet the definition of disability if no income limits exist, Richard V. Burkhauser said about five times as great as the number of people who are in the income range that he discusses. In rough terms, the cost of the disabled workers subsidy would increase by a bit less than five times the cost of the DWTC because of phase-outs and so forth. This alternative would therefore be considerably more expensive unless the definition of eligible workers is curtailed. This is the trade-off.

In terms of fairness, this kind of exemption is a good idea without regard to income level. An exemption of this sort takes into account the additional expenses that all working disabled people have. On this ground, it can be defended all the way up the Social Security wage scale.

The question of how to pay for the exemption is going to be a problem. Lawmakers could increase the Social Security earnings ceiling or increase the tax rate for wages above a certain amount and pay for this disabled workers exemption, but politically those are extremely difficult things to do.

Some people argue that one disadvantage of this alternative is that an exemption in Social Security would be created, thus opening the door for other exemptions. A Social Security tax exemption for disabled workers as the start of exemptions from Social Security taxes for all workers at the bottom end of the wage scale is not undesirable, as long as such exemptions do not eliminate or decrease benefits for low-income workers.

A second alternative would be to give a tax credit to employers who hire disabled workers. Such an employer tax credit could be modeled after the targeted jobs tax credit rather than the EITC. The advantage is that this alternative puts all of the complexity at the employer level. The largest disadvantage is that the employers might keep the money instead of passing it on to disabled workers as additional compensation.

Comment by William G. Johnson

Both the disabled worker tax credit (DWTC) and the return-to-work (RTW) ticket proposals address persons with impairments that limit their ability to work but do not prevent them from working. Whether they are employed depends upon economic and market influences, as well as the nature of their impairments. Individuals with impairments that limit their capacity to do the jobs for which they are qualified by education and experience are unlikely to find employment. Individuals with the same types of impairments but different qualifications will be more successful. The ability to work is not, therefore, a guarantee of employment. Employment is a bargain between two actors, each influenced by different incentives and by markets that neither control. The fact that the nature and severity of permanent partial impairments influence but do not completely determine a persons' chances for employment makes determining the probable effects of an impairment on employability extremely difficult.[21]

21. Workers' compensation plans and some veterans disability plans pay disability benefits for permanent partial impairment but calculate benefits on the severity of impairment without regard to the employment and post-injury earnings of the beneficiary.

The uncertainty surrounding the effects of partial impairments on an individual's capacity for work is one reason that Social Security disability insurance (DI) and Supplemental Security Income (SSI) are restricted to permanent total disability. The uncertainty is so great, however, that the application of the most strict definition of disability does not eliminate the possibility that some beneficiaries could work. The DWTC proposes to tap this potential by providing economic incentives. The RTW ticket proposal is based on the notion that innovative approaches to vocational rehabilitation will increase employment.

The target population for either proposal is small relative to the total number of DI or SSI beneficiaries. The only DI or SSI beneficiaries who are employable are those persons for whom the determination of permanent and total disability is incorrect. Persons with conditions that require institutional care are not candidates for reemployment nor are long-term beneficiaries whose lifestyle has adapted to disabled status. The potential increases in employment among DI or SSI beneficiaries with marginal skills and work experience must also be limited, given the existence of unemployment among persons without mental or physical limitations.

Another limitation is the effect of the process by which eligibility for disability benefits is established. Many DI or SSI beneficiaries become eligible for benefits through a lengthy process that can involve multiple applications over time, extensive clinical evaluations, and sometimes several appeals. The process requires that applicants demonstrate, document, and sometimes hire lawyers to argue that they are unable to work at any job available in the economy. The process does not encourage successful applicants to return to the labor force and risk subsequent unemployment because their health deteriorates or because of shifts in the demand for labor.

The idea that vocational rehabilitation services can significantly increase the employment of DI beneficiaries is (like a second marriage, according to Samuel Johnson) a "triumph of hope over experience." Many years of results from DI rehabilitation programs suggest that Monroe Berkowitz's characterization of current efforts as marginally effective is extremely charitable.

The low rates of success are not surprising given the eligibility criteria for these programs. Nor are the potential benefits likely to exceed the costs of the proposed services. A cost-effectiveness analysis of the rehabilitation interventions relative to alternatives that include not attempting to rehabilitate beneficiaries would improve the proposal. The RTW proposal is based on an implausible model of market behavior and, as such, should not be implemented.

The DWTC can be implemented, but its potential for success is constrained by the disincentives associated with the health care insurance provided by DI or SSI. The DWTC proposal is well written and well grounded in economics.

Persons with permanent partial impairments are the target group. Permanent partial disability is much more prevalent than the totally disabling conditions for which DI and SSI are designed, but it is a risk for which social insurance coverage is almost completely limited to veterans and persons who are covered by workers' compensation.

One benefit of the DWTC proposal is that it recognizes the importance of the problems of permanent partial disability and offers a partial solution to them. However, the contention that the DWTC will deter applications for DI or SSI begs disagreement, based on the incentives associated with the health insurance coverage provided by DI or SSI. Disability benefit payments are, for most workers, lower than their wages if they are able to work, suggesting that persons able to work will reject the benefit alternative unless they place a very high value on leisure time or on the health insurance coverage provided by the disability programs. The value of the health insurance provided by DI or SSI is greater than the value (net cost to the insured) of the health insurance coverage available to persons with impairments who work.

Most permanent impairments are associated with chronic conditions, which often worsen over time, suggesting the workers in the DWTC target groups consume above-average amounts of health care and experience above-average increases in consumption of health care as they age. The target group includes a relatively large number of part-time workers and of persons with spells of work disability, characteristics that reduce their opportunities to obtain work-related health insurance at affordable premiums.

Health insurance or managed care coverage in the private sector often limits coverage for persons with chronic conditions. The restrictions include exclusions of persons with preexisting conditions; the exclusion of certain types of chronic conditions; the practice, which is increasing, of restricting employment-related health insurance to full-time, year-round workers; and the practice of charging very high premiums or limiting coverage for high-risk individuals.[22]

The DWTC target group consists of low-income workers with chronic conditions, whose employment has been interrupted and who are unlikely to afford high-risk insurance premiums. These are the types of persons for whom the difference between the value of DI– or SSI–related health insurance and the health insurance they can obtain if they work is relatively high. The boundary example is the situation where a person with an above-average demand for health care is excluded from employment-related health insurance. A nice

---

22. Dallas Salisbury reported that the number of covered lives in employment-related health insurance plans fell by 2.8 million in 1995 and that it continues to decline.

empirical estimate of the potential effect of the DWTC would be to calculate the expected benefits of DI or SSI health insurance coverage; add the health benefit to the disability benefits and compare the sum with the comparable amounts plus the DWTC for impaired persons who are employed.

The RTW proposal stems from the hope that a new approach to the delivery of rehabilitation services to DI or SSI clients will be more successful than the provision of similar services to similar clients in the past. The proposed difference rests on introducing consumer choice, through a voucher system and provider incentives in the form of payments restricted to successful outcomes. Providers must, therefore, accept the costs of failures. The rationale is a variant on the idea of capitated care, in which a health care provider agrees to provide all necessary care for patients who pay them a fixed fee in advance. The important differences between the RTW proposal and the capitation concept are that the RTW has the payer setting the payment amounts and the providers are paid only for successful outcomes.

The first thing to remember is that the hoped-for effects on employment are, at best, modest. As Monroe Berkowitz notes, the demonstration project (Project Network) has a success rate of 1.2 percent and private providers succeed in 2 to 3 percent of the cases. In a cost-effectiveness analysis, the marginal benefit of the proposed program is the difference between its employment results and the results of the previous or existing programs. The benefit, therefore, is smaller than the 1.2 to 3 percent success rates. The potential benefits are also diminished because not all of those who return to work will maintain their employment. The recent, first study of the employment experiences of workers with permanent partial impairments evaluated nearly twelve thousand Ontario workers. It estimates that more than 40 percent of those who returned to work left the labor force because of the longer term effects of their conditions.[23] An additional 21 percent remained in the labor force but suffered subsequent episodes of work disability related to their impairments. The subjects of the study were experienced workers who were much less severely impaired than the average SSI or DI recipient.

Ignoring the upward bias in potentials for employment, the application of the Ontario results to the rehabilitation results from the United States suggests that only approximately 39 percent of the rehabilitation clients who returned to work will be defined as successful outcomes by evaluations that do not end with a return to work. The successes for which a rehabilitation provider can expect to be paid are, therefore, between 0.5 percent and 1.2 percent of the

23. Butler, Johnson, and Baldwin (1995).

cases that participate in the proposed rehabilitation activities. Thus, the costs of services to participants in RTW must be compared with the benefits of returning to work less than one client in a hundred who receive services.

The most serious obstacle to the success of the RTW is the structure of the payments systems, namely the retrospective payment to rehabilitation providers of amounts calculated from savings in disability benefits, measured in terms of potential benefits to persons who participate in the RTW program and the reductions in their expected durations on SSDI.

The relatively high prevalence of instability of employment after a return to work suggests that the outcomes of RTW services and the associate payments are difficult to predict. Consider, for example, a person who returns to work after receiving rehabilitation services and then experiences several episodes of employment interrupted by periods of work disability. After three or four years of this pattern, the person reapplies for DI and is accepted as a beneficiary. The formula for the expected payments that a provider of rehabilitation services will receive for providing services to this patient includes terms for the probability that this pattern will occur among all patients accepted; the predicted durations of the episodes of employment and work disability; the probability that the episodes of work disability are attributable to the effects that were treated (a failure) versus some new condition (not a failure); if not a failure, the granting of a new voucher to the person with impairments to obtain new rehabilitation services; and if services are received, the payment to designated persons for a successful return to work and the determination of the present value of the expected payments for a successful outcome. If this seems too simple to require attention, add the fact that the milestone approach requires a calculation of a payment at different times when expectations are conditional on the result at the previous milestone.

The target group is composed of persons with permanent partial impairments, conditions whose effect on employability is so difficult to determine that disability insurance programs either exclude them from coverage or pay a benefit based on clinical criteria instead of measures of earnings loss or employability.

The administrative costs of the RTW plan would appear to be high. Because the economic incentives of rehabilitation providers and federal administrators (the payers) are opposed, the determinations of the reasons for the outcomes require separate evaluations of the information regarding a patient and some administrative mechanism for resolving disputes that could also include the patient. The proposal would be greatly enhanced if it included an estimate of the administrative costs of the program with some examples of the problems to be encountered in dealing with first returns to work and subsequent periods of work disability.

Both the DWTC and the RTW ticket proposals are directed toward persons with permanent partial impairments, which is the largest subset of people with disabilities and the group that has the least access to social insurance and training programs for people with disabilities. The importance of the group and its problems are beginning to be revealed in the nature of the litigation filed under the Americans with Disabilities Act (ADA). The most prevalent cases involve work-related injuries, often low-back conditions, that affect experienced workers in middle age. This is not the group envisioned by the creators of the ADA. Both proposals are to be applauded for alerting policymakers to the existence and importance of disabilities that limit the ability to work but that do not prevent working.

The DWTC, carefully designed by well-qualified experts, is crafted to avoid the notch problem that has so bedeviled the welfare system. It is a reasonable type of economic incentive to subsidize persons who can and do work instead of seeking the alternative of social insurance benefits for disability. Its objectives, however, will not be realized unless it is altered to recognize the work disincentives created by the large and increasing gap between the health insurance coverages provided by SSI or DI and the employment-related insurance coverage available to persons with impairments who work for wages.

Monroe Berkowitz made the RTW proposal difficult to criticize by promising nothing. Unfortunately, the proposal leads to less than nothing because its potential benefits are small, its administrative structure promises to be costly, and, most important, the proposed payment system is so complicated to administer and the incentives so uncertain for the providers, that it is unworkable.

A commentator from the floor, Gerben deJong of the National Rehabilitation Hospital and member of the Disability Policy Panel, disagreed: "In the brain injury rehabilitation area . . . providers have moved into that kind of a market, have gained the experience, have developed the data . . . have determined what outcomes are going to be, and have developed prediction models . . . to predict outcomes and . . . costs."

A provider based in California, referred to by deJong, provides a capitated service that does require some assumption of risk. Payment, however, is not conditional on outcomes, and the payment system is not retrospective. Capitated payment for care is substantially different from the system described in the RTW proposal.

The proposals are honest attempts to deal with old problems that have not been solved to anyone's satisfaction. A number of problems exist with both, but the objectives of both are laudable. Supporting the possible imperfect improvements is preferable to simply criticizing the improvements for their failure to be perfect.

Comment by Tony Young

The American Rehabilitation Association, for whom I work, represents private providers of vocational rehabilitation services, along with medical rehabilitation services and residential services. The association suggested the risk-reward payment system in testimony before the House Subcommittee on Social Security in June 1991. At that time, the purpose was to create a private market for return-to-work and go-to-work services that was funded through outcomes instead of fees for service. The association's proposal also featured follow-up that kept people in jobs, not just place people in jobs. And, most important, it emphasized consumer choice among service providers.

Following the congressional hearings, members began making their views known—somewhat loudly in some cases. They felt that a pure risk-reward model was not feasible. Unless they had a certain size or a certain economy of scale, they could not afford to put the money up front into rehabilitating a person with the risk that they would not get it back. Even if they did get it back, resources would be drained out of the organization for any other purpose.

Members pointed out that the proposal would encourage the development of a new industry of large private providers. That is not what was intended. The association concluded that consumer choice, limited to a few large private providers, is no better than choice limited to a few large public providers, which is essentially the system in existence. Furthermore, participation should not be limited to only those beneficiaries who would require small up-front costs. All people who wanted to go back to work should be able to participate.

Small providers may enter the market as consortia providers or through some new funding mechanisms yet to be developed. But if those small providers are excluded initially, the result would be limited choice, a slowing of the return to work of individuals with disabilities, and a curb on the trust fund savings that would otherwise occur.

Monroe Berkowitz errs in stating that the return-to-work ticket proposal promises gain with no risk of harm. A monumental problem has arisen in the growth of the Social Security disability insurance (DI) and Supplemental Security Income (SSI) rolls. A choice must be made between helping people get off the two programs by going to work or having the programs shut down by external budgetary pressures.

Everything that can be done must be done to make the return-to-work proposal work. The purpose of milestone payments is to marginally assist providers. In one such plan, providers would be paid for milestones that are achieved at four points. A milestone would be achieved when the vocational assessment was done and the plan was developed to contract between the provider and the individual. A milestone payment is wanted there to assure a good vocational assessment and a solid plan for the individual. The second milestone would be a payment when the individual is at work for sixty days. It is not a full payment and does not cover the costs incurred up to that point. It is a financing mechanism that enables more providers to get into the game. The third milestone would be at the one-year point after the person was at work and benefits started to accrue to the trust fund. The last milestones would be yearly after that for three, four, five, or ten years. The provider reaps the benefits of the savings to the trust fund.

Some additional comments are now offered. The return-to-work estimates— 1.2 percent for Project Network and 2 to 3 percent for private providers—were disappointing. And they lead to very disappointing savings estimates. The situation must be bettered. The program cannot be kept the way it is unless something is done to improve the rate of return to work.

The providers should be certified but only in a minimal way. Providers need to have the financial ability to maintain the services over the course of the individual's contract. And some protections against abuses of all kinds are needed. But a whole new accreditation process for these providers is not desirable. It will drive up the costs. Besides, if the provider does not put the person to work, there is no savings to the trust fund and no payment to the providers.

A number of outstanding issues have to be settled. The administrative structure of the program has to be determined. Strong information systems need to be set up so that the consumers, the DI beneficiaries who are going to choose these providers, know which providers are providing what kinds of outcomes so they can choose their best option. Some sort of mechanism against providers moving around needs to be devised so that beneficiaries do not move from place to place. Some measure of consumer protection is necessary so that consumers do not get abused, as well.

If these outstanding issues are resolved, choice among the wide variety of providers would be ensured. Such a system could achieve the goals of returning people to work.

For disabled workers trying to work, the disabled worker tax credit could be the second most important feature of the whole program, right after extending medical coverage. As Lex Frieden says, an attempt has been made in the last thirty years to put this patchwork quilt in place. Then people are expected to leap from patch to patch to patch, sometimes over huge holes in the garment. That has not worked. It will not work in the future.

The disabled worker tax credit substantially eliminates what advocates call the earnings cliff; that is, the point at which benefits are lost, but income drops precipitously for a long period of time before earnings catch up with what had been received in benefits. It is the second barrier to people not going back to work.

The wage subsidy is much more efficient and cost-effective than a sliding scale benefit reduction and would be much more successful for individuals with disabilities. It makes the best use of eligibility determinations that are already made, does not create new administrative structures, and is targeted to the most significantly disabled. The component to assist the maintenance for work for as long as possible will ultimately save a great deal of money. In addition, it has a well-constructed phase-in and phase-out, is an excellent use of tax policy, and will enable many disabled workers to accept and retain work.

References

Aarts, Leo, Richard V. Burkhauser, and Philip de Jong. 1996. *Curing the Dutch Disease: An International Perspective on Dutch Policy Reform.* Aldershot, Great Britain: Avebury.

Alstott, Anne L. 1995. "The Earned Income Tax Credit and the Limitations of Tax-Based Welfare Reform." *Harvard Law Review* 108: 533.

Berkowitz, Edward D., and Richard V. Burkhauser. 1996. "A United States Perspective on Disability Programs." In *Curing the Dutch Disease: An International Perspective on Disability Policy Reform,* edited by Leo J. M. Aarts, Richard V. Burkhauser, and Philip P. de Jong. Aldershot, Great Britain: Avebury.

Bound, John, Sherrie Kossoudji, and Gema Ricart-Moes. Forthcoming. "The End of General Assistance and SSI Disability Growth in Michigan." In *Growth in Income Entitlement Benefits for Disability: Explanations and Policy Implications,* edited by Kalman Rupp and David Stapleton. Kalamazoo, Mich.: E. W. Upjohn Institute for Employment Research.

Burkhauser, Richard V., J. S. Butler, and Yang Woo Kim. 1995. "The Importance of Employer Accommodation on the Job Duration of Workers with Disabilities: A Hazard Model Approach." *Labour Economics* 3: 1–22.

Burkhauser, Richard V., and Mary C. Daly. 1995. "Childhood Disability and Family Economic Well-Being: A Dynamic Analysis." Paper prepared for the Seventeenth Annual APPAM Research Conference, Washington, D.C., November 2.

―――. 1996a. "Employment and Economic Well-Being Following the Onset of a Disability: The Role for Public Policy." In *Disability, Work, and Cash Benefits,* edited by Jerry Mashaw and others, 59–102. Kalamazoo, Mich.: W. E. Upjohn Institute for Employment Research.

―――. 1996b. "The Potential Impact on the Employment of People with Disabilities." In *Implementing the Americans with Disabilities Act,* edited by Jane West, 153–92. Cambridge, Mass.: Blackwell Publications.

Burkhauser, Richard V., and Robert H. Haveman. 1982. *Disability and Work: The Economics of American Policy.* Johns Hopkins University Press.

Butler, Richard J., W. G. Johnson, M. L. Baldwin. 1995. "Managing Work Disability: Why First Return to Work is Not a Measure of Success." *Industrial & Labor Relations Review* 48 (April): 452–69.

Goldman, Howard. Forthcoming. "Policy Implications of the Growth in Beneficiaries with Mental Illness." In *Growth in Income Entitlement Benefits for Disability: Explanations and Policy Implications,* edited by Kalman Rupp and David Stapleton. Kalamazoo, Mich.: E. W. Upjohn Institute for Employment Research.

Hoynes, Hillary W., and Robert Moffitt. 1996. "The Effectiveness of Financial Work Incentives in DI and SSI: Lessons from Other Transfer Programs." In *Disability, Work, and Cash Benefits,* edited by Jerry Mashaw and others, 189–222. Kalamazoo, Mich.: E. W. Upjohn Institute for Employment Research.

Mashaw, Jerry L., and Virginia P. Reno, eds. 1996. *Balancing Security and Opportunity: The Challenge of Disability Income Policy.* Final Report of the Disability Policy Panel. Washington, D.C.: National Academy of Social Insurance.

Stapleton, David, and others. Forthcoming. "Econometric Analyses of DI and SSI Application and Award Growth." In *Growth in Income Entitlement Benefits for Disability: Explanations and Policy Implications,* edited by Kalman Rupp and David Stapleton. Kalamazoo, Mich.: E. W. Upjohn Institute for Employment Research.

U.S. Department of Health and Human Services. Office of Inspector General. 1994. *Concerns about the Participation of Children with Disabilities in the Supplemental Security Income Program.* Government Printing Office. October.

U.S. General Accounting Office. 1994. *Social Security: Rapid Rise in Children on SSI Disability Rolls following New Regulations.* Report to the Honorable Gerald O. Kleezkay, House of Representatives. Government Printing Office.

―――. 1995. *Supplemental Security Income: Growth and Changes in Recipient Population Call for Reexamining Program.* Report to Chairman, Committee on Finance, U.S. Senate, and Chairman, Committee on Ways and Means, House of Representatives. Government Printing Office. July.

U.S. House of Representatives. Committee on Ways and Means. 1994. *Overview of Entitlement Programs.* 103 Cong. 2 sess. Government Printing Office. July 15.

U.S. Internal Revenue Service. 1994. *Your Federal Income Tax for Individuals.* Publication 17. Government Printing Office.

Weaver, Carolyn. Forthcoming. "Policy Changes to Improve Labor Market Outcomes." In *Growth in Income Entitlement Benefits for Disability: Explanations and Policy Implications,* edited by Kalman Rupp and David Stapleton. Kalamazoo, Mich.: E. W. Upjohn Institute for Employment Research.

Yin, George K., and others. 1994. "Improving the Delivery of Benefits to the Working Poor: Proposals to Reform the Earned Income Tax Credit." *American Journal of Tax Policy* 11: 225.

4

Challenges in Medicare and Medicaid for Persons with Disabilities

THE CONTRIBUTORS TO THIS CHAPTER focus on issues surrounding Medicare and Medicaid as they relate to persons with disabilities.

Confronting the Ambivalence of Disability Policy: Has Push Come to Shove?
Bruce C. Vladeck, Ellen O'Brien, Thomas Hoyer, and Steven Clauser

PERSONS WITH DISABILITIES ARE, above all, individuals. They are recognized as individuals by the Americans with Disabilities Act (ADA), and, as individuals, they pursue and enjoy the rights of citizens in U.S. society. The ADA is a recent statute, though, and does not explicitly alter the various federal programs that provide pieces of the disability puzzle. These programs—including Social Security disability insurance (DI), Supplemental Security Income (SSI), Medicare, Medicaid, and Vocational Rehabilitation—long predate the ADA. They, in turn, reflect a variety of conflicting views about disability, and their influence significantly affects how persons with disabilities fare in society.

For the Health Care Financing Administration (HCFA), the needs of our large and growing number of disabled beneficiaries are a central concern. But our current thinking about disability policy, and the relationship of Medicare and Medicaid to it, is very much in a state of evolutionary flux. What follows, therefore, are observations, not conclusions. This paper is less a policy statement than an extended meditation on the issues posed by the changing populations and changing social beliefs. As such, it provides an up-to-the-minute reflection of a process still under way.

Disability in a Medical Context

The traditional priorities of public, as well as private, health insurance are evident in the way the programs have been designed—with emphasis on the provision of acute inpatient hospital services and immediate posthospital care.[1] Therefore, not surprisingly, much of the debate around health policy concerns how best to manage resources in acute care settings. (For example, Will prospective payment slow the growth of hospital costs? Will bundling of payment for acute and postacute services encourage a more rational use of resources?) That is, the debate tends to be about the payments we make rather than those we do not make. By comparison, discussion of the relative priority among preventive, chronic, and acute care is far more limited.[2] Those issues are put off the same way saving for retirement years is avoided: forgetting that a person lives a whole life, not just a young life. Society seems more interested in the questions that affect access to acute, or critical, care services—probably because most people think they are more likely to use them. For "realistic" entertainment, people watch "ER," not "ICF/MR."[3]

These priorities are also evident in what does not get done. Medicare and Medicaid lack many of the services that the disabled would use. They give short shrift to mental health services; institutional long-term care services for the elderly and nonelderly disabled still outweigh community-based services; and access to assistive technology is limited.[4] The result has been that individuals with disabilities, who are most likely on any given day to have a need for medical care, generally find that they do not get enough help (or at least not enough of the kind of help that they prefer) from Medicare and Medicaid.[5]

Though Medicare and Medicaid lack a number of services that disabled beneficiaries would use, limited resources in both programs reinforce the skepticism of policymakers that new services will substitute cost effectively for old ones instead of just adding expense, as has been the experience with

1. See Starr (1982) for the history of how the scales came to be tipped out of balance.
2. Or how to prioritize allocations among different populations—children, pregnant women, disabled adults, the elderly.
3. ICF/MR stands for intermediate care facility for the mentally retarded.
4. Assistive technology refers to items used by persons with disabilities to compensate for functional loss and to prevent the progression of illness.
5. A rosier scenario is sketched by Fox (1989). He argues that growing epidemiological pressure—the rapidly increasing prevalence of chronic disease and disability—explains the priority accorded to disability by health care providers, researchers, government agencies, and insurers. Fox outlines a "political history of accommodation" whereby chronic disease has become "the principal focus of public and insurer payment for personal health services since the 1960s." (p. 258) In this paper, it is suggested, contrary to Fox, that policy lags behind where the world is at.

virtually all benefit expansions. Policymakers are especially loath to abandon the security of well-established programmatic limits, even when those limits stimulate alternative utilization patterns that produce counterproductive results for disabled clients. As a result, for want of alternatives, many disabled clients of both Medicare and Medicaid are now making expensive and inefficient use of existing services—a situation that not only reduces the solvency of public programs but that, more important, may damage the clients themselves.

At HCFA our attention to the needs of the disabled has grown in recent years. In Medicaid, the desire has been to add flexibility to combat a putative "institutional bias," to stretch both state and federal dollars. But more fundamental questions have also begun to shape our conception of the issues. A fundamental shift in attitudes of the disabled toward themselves and in society's attitudes toward them have led to a reconceptualization of the problem of disability and of public solutions to address it. Here, as everywhere, the definition of the problem is the first critical challenge. What various groups (the public, the press, and policymakers) perceive as problems (solutions) relates to their conceptions of disability. These conceptions underlie the programmatic responses to disability that they advocate and also provide the perspective from which they evaluate success or failure. The challenge is to create a critical mass of seeing to set the stage for solving the problems.

The story to be told here is one of a basic tension between old paradigms and new realities in Medicare and Medicaid. The pressure to resolve the problems leads in turn to a reexamination of them and the context in which they exist. The right answer is not being found any more. Maybe the equation is no longer right or maybe the time has come to look at the disability paradigm that structures thinking about the problem and the solution.

The time to change a paradigm is when it no longer serves to answer the full range of questions or needs for which it is intended and when an engine powerful enough to produce better or broader solutions is at hand. The question for disability policy is whether that moment is soon to arrive.

Accounting for the Ambivalence of Disability Policy

Persons with disabilities have traditionally been viewed as among society's most vulnerable and neglected minorities. A long-standing belief has been that the disabled, more than impoverished children or the elderly, should benefit from various social welfare programs because they are, by definition, unable to participate in the work-based distributive system.[6] Disability thus carries a set

6. Stone (1984).

of claims on the social welfare system, and these claims have been more secure than the protections offered to other groups. For example, income and asset eligibility standards for SSI are set nationally and adjusted annually, so federally administered benefits for the disabled have largely kept pace with inflation. At same time, with income and asset eligibility levels left to state discretion, income payments to those receiving payments under the Aid to Families with Dependent Children program have eroded in real terms.[7] However, while society is willing to see the disabled population as unique in its claims to basic incomes support, society's ambivalence about the disabled is clearly reflected in the Medicare and Medicaid benefit structures that do not have embedded in them benefits that address the unique needs of this population.

A number of stories may be constructed to explain this ambivalence.[8] One possible story is that it is an artifact of priorities that were established decades ago. In the case of work disability, medical care has historically been a lower priority than the other elements of the governmental response: workers' compensation, income support, and vocational rehabilitation. Income support was the first priority as social programs evolved because the problem was seen primarily as one requiring an alternative source of income for those who could not support themselves or their families by working. Health care and health insurance were seen as a separate set of issues, disconnected to disability. In that context, the disjunction between the social view of income and the social view of health care is clearer. Health care benefits were not important in early responses of private disability insurance, and when Medicare was eventually extended to the disabled, the limitation of a two-year waiting period reflected this bias.

Even as disability income policy has increasingly focused on work incentive and self-support provisions, the de-emphasis on health insurance has persisted. Policymakers have been hesitant to enhance medical and social services for the disabled because the likelihood that they would use those services to achieve a level of rehabilitation that would allow them to return to work is thought to be slim, with recent estimates that fewer than 3 percent of all beneficiaries exit the DI program because of a return to self-supporting work.[9] Without rehabilitation

---

7. Coughlin, Ku, and Holahan (1994).

8. This paper will focus on the special challenges that disability creates for Medicare and Medicaid. More encompassing looks at the government's response to disability are available elsewhere. See Berkowitz (1987) and Stone (1984).

9. Congress ended funding for rehabilitation of SSI and DI beneficiaries in 1982. See Hennessey and Muller (1994).

to justify the expense, the cost-effectiveness of additional services is hard to see when the disability paradigm is mainly work- and income-based.

A second story has to do with ambivalence about the meaning of disability itself. Disability determination is not a primitive choice. The truly disabled—those who have a clear right to protections—cannot be easily identified in the modern social context in which disability is a matter of degree. Once reducible to a narrow set of conditions or symptoms, disability is subject to ever more expansive classifications and codifications. Disability consists of a hard physical core with an expanding penumbra of mental and psychosocial nuance not generally as visible (or acceptable) to society. As a result, gaps in services betray a deeply rooted ambivalence toward certain classes of the disabled. Most especially, a fundamental skepticism of those who are disabled because of a mental illness, alcoholism, or drug addiction seems ingrained in the culture. This ambivalence has manifested itself through periodic attempts to clamp down on growth in the SSI and DI populations. For example, during a particularly dark period in the mid–1980s, because of a public perception that disability rolls were swollen with thousands of undeserving individuals, massive reassessments were done and thousands of individuals were abruptly removed from the rolls, with the mentally ill disproportionately represented among those who lost their eligibility or were denied benefits upon application.[10]

Another such period seems right aroound the corner. The 1995 welfare reform debate included extensive discussion of disability benefits for children and for the drug addicted. In the aftermath of the 1990 *Sullivan* v. *Zebley* decision, in which the Supreme Court found the government's disability criteria biased against disabled children, public perception is growing that the Social Security Administration is awarding benefits to more and more children who are not truly disabled, even though a General Accounting Office report on the topic found limited empirical evidence to support such claims.[11]

People will continue to give diverse answers to the service question if they continue to have varying ideas about the nature of disability. Even the language in which policymakers characterize the effects of coverage betray a fundamental bias against the populations for whom aid is provided. The term "woodwork effect" seems to imply that more attractive bait will entice more pests "out of

10. A thorough examination of SSA actions during this period is contained in Goldman and Gattozzi (1988). The somewhat perverse result of the Social Security Administration's actions during this period, as Goldman and Gattozzi describe, was enhanced visibility of the long-term, disabling effects of mental illness together with a growing perception of mental illness as a medical problem.

11. U.S. General Accounting Office (1995a).

the woodwork" to enjoy them. The overall insurance term that describes the danger that someone, somewhere, might submit a claim is "moral hazard." Offer a benefit, and a moral hazard exists that some unworthy will advance to claim it. When the political culture accepts a disability paradigm grounded in a false conception of benefits users as unworthy or immoral, it is difficult to see how the problem can be impartially studied, let alone resolved.

Third, suggestions often have been made that the cost implications of disability-related services are so inherently unpredictable as to frighten policy-makers away from contemplating all but the narrowest of expansions. What looks like a half-empty glass when benefits are being designed may be a bottomless pit once the payments begin to flow. Those who have experienced the unpredictable costs that have given rise to concern about the woodwork effect believe that efforts to enhance services for the disabled run the risk of eroding informal support networks that currently fill in the gaps in needed services or of serving a wholly new population, namely those who otherwise would not use institutional long-term care services. Consequently, many attempts to expand coverage for the disabled have encountered resistance and have subsequently been abandoned.

For example, the Omnibus Budget Reconciliation Act of 1990 included a significant change in the coverage of personal care services as part of the Medicaid home health benefit. The original change was mainly intended to enable states to offer nonmedical or semimedical personal care without the need either to follow the federal regulations relating to the optional Medicaid benefit or to seek the flexibility of a home and community-based waiver. Congressional supporters saw it as a legislative concession to state flexibility. However, states soon realized that the new benefit would be subject to Medicaid's requirement that the personal care services be adequate in amount, duration, and scope to serve their purpose (that is, to meet the personal care needs of the whole Medicaid population in the state) and began to fear an explosion of cost. New eligibles would come forward for the more attractive benefits, and the cost of additional services to them would be quantitatively more important than any savings resulting from diminished use of other services. The states subsequently began to demand and did achieve repeal of a provision that many of them had originally favored.

The fourth story is political. According to this version of events, the ambivalence reflects a basic contradiction between the presumption of absolute need that underlies the income preference and the mainstreaming arguments that are made by advocates of services to enable expanded independence for the disabled. This fundamental tension arises because the force behind the claim to social welfare benefits comes out of the conviction that this population compels special consideration because of its presumptive absolute needs. That is, society presumes that the disabled are so helpless as to require the assurance of income. That presumption nails shut the door to the community and the services and devices available there. If a person is disabled enough to get SSI or DI, then he or she is too disabled to use these community services for a productive purpose, so paying for them is a social luxury for which no offsetting contribution through productive work exists. The Catch–22 here is that any demonstration of independence attenuates the support for disability payments.

A fifth story locates the source of ambivalence in the structure of the medical profession. Because physicians have traditionally accorded lower priority to chronic disease, disability, and function, those priorities, not surprisingly, are reflected in Medicare and Medicaid. As physicians who are concerned with disability—those in the field of medical rehabilitation, for example—seek to enhance their status, they have begun to reconceptualize their role within a reformed service delivery system for the disabled.[12] Within the reformed system, chronic disease, disability, and function would receive higher priority, and the physicians who specialize in the treatment of individuals with disabilities would see their status within the hierarchy of the medical profession elevated.

To some extent, this medical bias gets back to the original social predilection to look at medicine as an acute intervention that takes a fully functioning person with a short-term, acute problem and repairs that person so he or she can resume functioning. Insurance payments for health care have always tended to be keyed to rehabilitative potential with the assumption that treatment should be withdrawn when progress toward full recovery stops. In terms of medicine and medical insurance, this has played into the notion that the people who do not return to the regular world of the healthy lose their claim on the services that these people can get and join the ranks of people who merit subsistence support instead of treatment.

The sixth story is a synthesis of the others. It consists of a recognition that disability is a socially and economically crosscutting phenomenon that is not susceptible to an analysis limited to income strategy or medical care but must be viewed as a whole. As a result, Medicare and Medicaid lack the scope and resources to accommodate the needs of the disabled, and their medical and rehabilitative missions touch only a part of the problem to be resolved. The solutions that are required must be broad-based. Unfortunately, legislative solutions that put together the various pieces of the disability puzzle—housing, income support, personal assistance, educational and vocational services, and

12. ACRM (1993).

rehabilitation—are close to impossible in a Congress that divides jurisdiction for these items into a variety of committees in both the House and the Senate and funds the needs through numerous unconnected appropriations, and an executive branch that then addresses these needs with several cabinet departments whose constituencies are different and whose accounts are separately addressed at the Office of Management and Budget. The legislative and bureaucratic structures we have created do not provide us with the tools to do the job right, even if we could conceive of a solution to implement.

People telling these six stories make plausible cases, as could a number of other storytellers with different tales. They are all attempts to explain the failure of the old paradigm in terms of the old paradigm. The old paradigm, however, is increasingly incapable of providing a context in which the current issues and needs can be properly viewed, let alone providing a structure of organized thought to assist us in responding to them.

Long-Term Care: Resolving a Distributive Dilemma

The government's response to the long-term care needs of the disabled can be understood in terms of the basic distributive dilemma: It is a response to the question of what share of the government's scarce resources will go to caring for the disabled. The initial response was to rely on a limited, "bright line" conception of treatment.[13] Physical walls are the brightest of lines, and for the disabled, the walls of the institutions that had been designed to provide an asylum for this population also limited the range of responsibility of the state. State-run institutions for mental diseases (IMDs), intermediate care facilities for the mentally retarded and persons with related conditions (ICFs/MR), and nursing facilities—differently named over the history of the benefits—were the whole range of options for the disabled population. The conception of treatment as institution-based gave rise to the structure of the eligibility process and locked in the institution as the source of care.[14]

This system has come under increasing attack because the people who present themselves for services have stopped fitting the mold into which the programs have been putting them. Their united resistance has at last challenged the conventional way in which public health insurance has been structured. A

13. "Bright line" is a legal term referring to sharp, yet arbitrary, distinctions that are necessary and difficult to determine but must be clearly and quickly made.

14. The discussion here is largely confined to examples relating to persons with mental impairments, such as mental retardation, developmental disabilities, and mental illness. A more complete story would include the VA hospitals, tuberculosis hospitals, and polio places where the physically disabled were stored during this period.

profound cultural shift is occurring, symbolized both by the ADA and, more important, a change in the attitudes of the disabled toward themselves. The ADA was devised in response to what members of both the Senate and the House identified as a "compelling need to provide a clear and comprehensive national mandate for the elimination of discrimination against individuals with disabilities and for the integration of persons with disabilities into the economic and social mainstream of American life."[15] Such a broad mandate would seem to suggest some obligations on the part of the health care system—and especially the publicly financed insurance systems through which so many of the disabled receive access to care. If we are truly to have persons with disabilities "among" us, then the services they receive should be part and parcel of the insurance programs, housing programs, jobs programs, and all the other mechanisms through which the needs of citizens are currently addressed.

For a number of years, the disability community has pushed for the right of persons with disabilities to live independently. This has fueled enthusiasm for consumer-directed care models and insistence upon access to services that are necessary to make an independent living model work. In some places in the health care system, the shift in thinking and in practice is evident. Progress along a variety of fronts has already been made. The population living in large state ICFs/MR has declined markedly since the mid–1960s. While many individuals with mental retardation and developmental disabilities continue to live in residential facilities, not in a family home or their own home, the residential facilities in which they live are now much smaller. The shift has been fueled by changing expectations about what kind of care persons with mental and physical disabilities should receive.

Persons with mental retardation and developmental disabilities and their advocates were particularly successful in using the judicial system, initially as a means to improve the quality of care in state institutions. The recognition of the right to habilitation (or active treatment) resulted from more than ten years of federal and state court involvement in state institutional care systems. Judgments in federal courts frequently declared that habilitation programs should be delivered in settings appropriate to the habilitative goal—generally the least restrictive alternative. While recourse to the courts did not guarantee a right to habilitation in the least restrictive setting, it certainly fueled increasing expectations for community-based placements for persons with mental retardation.[16]

15. Americans with Disabilities Act of 1990 (P.L. 101-336); U.S. Senate (1989); and U.S. House of Representatives (1990).
16. Lakin, Hill, and Bruininks (1995).

Bearing these successes in mind, lawsuits recently filed by persons with physical disabilities have argued that the failure to provide appropriate community-based services (as a substitute for institutional care) is a violation of their rights under the ADA. At least one court has found, however, that states have a right to choose how they will provide for the disabled (in nursing homes or in community attendant programs) so long as services provided to the non-disabled are available on an equal basis to the disabled.[17] The boundaries, for now, retain their legitimacy in the eyes of the courts; the ADA does not guarantee the kinds of changes in services that the disabled would like to see.

While public discussion of the merits of community-based care has not run its course, the consensus seems to be that independent living should be the goal for all but the most severely disabled. For the severely disabled, the adequacy of protections outside of institutions is still being debated. But progress toward that objective has been more limited for the working-age disabled population, those with physical limitations or suffering from chronic mental illness, alcoholism, or substance abuse.

Home and community-based waivers in the Medicaid program—originally provided for legislatively in 1981—represent both a response to the decreasing legitimacy of the institutional approach to care and an instructive phenomenon because they represent an attempt to deal creatively with many of the effects discussed earlier. The initial waiver program, designed to placate concerned policymakers and Congressional Budget Office actuaries, kept to the bright line institutional test that was used for traditional eligibility and even—with notable disingenuousness—to the traditional eligibility tests. This so-called 1915(c) waiver authority originally permitted states to substitute home and community-based services for nursing home care in limited circumstances. First, the waivers had to be cost-effective; the state was required to demonstrate that all the waiver services in the home and community would not cost more than caring for the waiver population in nursing facilities under the state's Medicaid program. Second, the waivers could apply only to specific individuals for whom the state had made a determination that, but for the waiver, they would occupy existing nursing home beds.

The law contemplated that the vast preponderance of waiver clients were to have been discharged or diverted from skilled nursing facilities (SNF) or intermediate care facilities. To get an eligible person into the waiver, the state needed to make the necessary certification that, but for the waiver services, that individual would be an inpatient of an SNF or ICF. Yet the test for eligibility for SNF care was that the services "as a practical matter can only be provided

17. U.S. Court of Appeals for the Third Circuit (1995).

in a skilled nursing facility [currently, nursing facility] on an inpatient basis" (Section 1905(f)) and for ICFs, that the individuals require services that "can be made available to them only through institutional facilities" (Section 1919(a)(1)(C), formerly 1905(c)). Thus, the key to getting a client into a waiver was to certify that only an institutional setting would suffice for the care and services. This is the point at which the fundamental contradictions of the "medical model"—at least in Medicaid—were exposed in the federal statute.

HCFA initially administered the program as formally described by the law. To ensure that waiver services displaced institutional care, the waivers were initially premised on a "cold bed" theory. Proof was required that an institution had the capacity to serve the individuals who would be receiving waiver services. Furthermore, states were asked to take out of service the beds that would have been occupied by waiver clients. They could do this by canceling certificates of need or decertifying facilities or beds. Undoing the existing paradigm required establishing this kind of equivalence. Early on, as well, HCFA attempted to enforce the cost-effectiveness test. In the face of criticism from Congress and others, HCFA subsequently abandoned strict application of the cold bed test. Changes to the waiver provisions have progressively decoupled them from both the rigid interpretation of institutional substitution and cost-effectiveness. Now that the cold bed and cost-effectiveness fictions of the waiver program have been exploded, the boundary between the disabled and other Medicaid beneficiaries—never more than a putative one under state administration—has disappeared.

In Medicaid, the distributive dilemma has been brought to a new boil by the increasing consensus around expanded state flexibility and the support for elimination of waivers as a category of services outside the usual range of Medicaid rules. Under current law, waivers are considered to be outside the state's general Medicaid program and are therefore free of the basic Medicaid requirements relating to access and freedom of choice. A state can pick the population it wants to place in a waiver and the range of services it wants to provide. These limits mean states can design waivers to meet both their fiscal constraints and their own conception of which categories of clients deserve waiver services. These limits provide the states with flexibility in choice of populations and services. However, states are limited under waivers to the populations and services approved under a relatively complex process for granting and renewing the waivers. They do not like that process.

Under Medicaid's current structure, states thus have an option to accept the burdensome waiver apparatus (which protects them from much financial exposure) or militate for the services to be built into the mainstream Medicaid program (which requires general access for all similarly situated Medicaid patients). A good bit of the current Medicaid debate among well-informed state officials is concerned with this distributive dilemma. Once the disabled are in the Medicaid mainstream and the kinds of home and community-based care they need are also generally covered, how can states limit their exposure to explosive increases in costs? States dream of block grants as a way of solving the problem, but from a policy perspective such grants would only dump the problem more fully in the states' lap and diminish the extent to which states could hide behind federal requirements to avoid facing them.

The same distributive problem, to a lesser extent, affects Medicare because the disabled in the community are raising the same issues about the limits that the service paradigm places on their ability to have the items and services they need for independence. Now the question is, what kinds and volume of services should the disabled residing in the community receive? One solution to the distributive dilemma is to subdivide the disabled or their needs into subclasses whose needs are discrete and deal with them piecemeal. The problem with this type of approach is that the rules of thumb needed to make these distinctions must create bright lines for purposes of administration and be politically acceptable. Unfortunately, ways to measure the degree of need for the purposes of payment are mostly primitive or nonexistent. Where they exist, they can be gamed mercilessly. For example, in the domain of personal assistance services, the mechanisms for making such determinations (inventories of limitation in activities of daily living (ADLs) or instrumental activities of daily living (IADLs)) are still in the early stages of development.[18] Moreover, no determination has been made of what personal assistance services should be. States adopt a variety of definitions. The boundaries are in flux.

A similar set of issues is confronted in the area of assistive technology, which includes assistive communicative aides, wheelchairs, prosthetic and orthotic devices, computer-assisted environmental control units, and other items used by persons with disabilities to compensate for functional loss and to prevent the progression of illness. While "assistive technology" is a term that has no specific meaning in the context of either Medicare or Medicaid laws, people with disabilities and advocacy groups have focused attention on this area because—as with personal assistance services—adequate access to assistive technology is key to independent living. However, access to assistive technology devices has been limited by the reluctance of third-party payers to reimburse for them.

Medicare is fairly typical. While some assistive devices (canes, crutches, walkers) primarily serve a medical purpose, other devices largely serve to

18. Jackson and others (1992).

augment a user's functional abilities and cannot be considered medical equipment for the purposes of payment under Medicare's durable medical equipment (DME) coverage definition (Section 1816(m)). For example, specially adapted computer keyboards or screens may allow workers with functional limitations to perform job-related tasks. Items that contribute to convenience and quality of life, but not necessarily medical treatment, have always been excluded from most insurance plans and are listed in the Medicare statute's exclusion of personal comfort items (Section 1862(a)(6)).

The perceived defects of the processes by which DME is authorized and paid for are exacerbated when the question turns to the needs of those with chronic impairments that limit function. Traditionally, HCFA has drawn a line requiring that DME serve a medical purpose (necessary to treat a beneficiary's illness or injury) and that its cost is reasonable given the expected benefit. Even within this traditional framework, a number of ambiguities exist. Concerns have been raised that the government is making unnecessary payments for equipment that is not medically necessary or that is more sophisticated than is needed. There is already a sense that HCFA's coverage criteria are vague and subjective and an expressed desire on the part of carriers and other experts that more specific coverage criteria be developed.[19] Furthermore, as concerns about weeding out fraud and abuse in the system increase, DME has been a prime target.

Assistive technology addresses a range of needs that go well beyond the scope of Medicare's currently stated purposes and benefits. Such technology may serve at least three distinct purposes. It can be used to improve function, for health and homeostasis (to prevent the progress of disease or illness) and for vocational purposes. Making determinations of medical necessity are difficult enough, but the effects of chronic illness and the relation of equipment and functional improvement are even more elusive. The impact of assistive technology on function, health, and disease prevention are embedded and idiosyncratic, personal and subjective. Professional consensus around appropriate use of assistive technology is still lacking. Moreover, primary care physicians are often ill-equipped to deal with these determinations. Measuring the outcomes—the benefits to health and function—is difficult, and the personal assessment of the user of the technology must generally be relied upon. The law includes coverage of a range of devices much narrower than even a conservative disability advocate would favor.

HCFA's ability to respond is severely limited by the statutes under which it operates. Still, HCFA has increasingly sought to identify areas in which a growing recognition can be incorporated that many determinations require a

19. See U.S. General Accounting Office (1992).

consideration of the whole patient. Treatment is no longer limited to that arising from a medical diagnosis. The range of outcomes extends beyond those associated with acute care to include function. Most current efforts are confined to conditions of participation, the federal standards that describe the types of behavior expected of facilities that sign agreements to provide care to Medicare and Medicaid patients. In ICF/MR policy, more weight is given to functional status than to raw IQ (intelligence quotient), and functional independence can be looked to as an indicator of health. Function is recognized as an outcome of care in quality assurance activities and is used to adjust payments to providers in various settings. These changes are, where possible, blurring the boundary between disabled and nondisabled, and between acute and long-term care. However much sensitivity is achieved within the bounds of the programs, the fundamental paradigm issue that has established those bounds must still be dealt with.

Legislative and executive branch custodians of Medicaid and Medicare have attempted to resolve the issues of the disability paradigm and of distribution of resources within the context of the current structure. Disability policy has operated first to resolve the thorny distributional questions by limiting the concept of treatment. As these institutional boundaries have been called into question—and the distributive dilemma is more forcefully presented—policy has faltered. Changes in the world (shifting attitudes toward the disabled and changes in the way persons with disabilities perceive themselves) have given rise to new distributive questions. The next section examines how the existing paradigm in mental health care has been reinforced (actually, made) by Medicaid policy and may be coming undone.[20]

The "Medicaidization" of Mental Health

Mental illness is an important cause of disability. In the SSI and DI populations, the number of individuals with a primary diagnosis of a mental illness has grown steadily over the past decade. Despite the large number of persons with mental illness in the traditional Medicaid and Medicare populations, the criticism is commonly made that Medicare and Medicaid give short shrift to behavioral health care services. State mental hospitals were the mainstay of mental health care in the years before the enactment of the Medicare and

20. This paradigm problem is not confined to the disabled and mentally ill; it is a problem for every group of patients whose needs have changed as a result of refinements in diagnosis or treatment that have come after the basic structure of programs have been established. For example, home IV therapy, many outpatient drugs, and items of equipment do not fit the Medicare coverage mold because early on these examples were not in the continuum of care considered by the drafters.

Medicaid programs, and both programs had features designed to avoid payments for services in those settings. The theory was that states needed to maintain their effort so that new program funds could go to new beneficiaries for new services. However, a gradual shift in the location of mental health care and, as a result, in the responsibility for mental heath care from the states to the federal government began in the 1960s and 1970s with deinstitutionalization. Consequently, federal programs have become increasingly important for chronically mentally ill populations first by default, as deinstitutionalization proceeded, and then with the expansion of entitlements to include SSI and Medicaid benefits.[21] This "Medicaidization" of mental health, and the perception of a need to level the playing field by expanding mental health services, is forcing consideration of how policy should respond to serious mental illness.

The term "institution for mental diseases" and its complex history are a reminder of how both Medicaid and Medicare initially avoided most of the care of the mentally ill and how, in the shadow of outdated benefits policies, they continue to pursue policies that drive the mentally ill into Medicaid, mainly into institutions. The IMD exclusion was originally included in Medicaid (as it had been in the predecessor Kerr-Mills legislation) as a means of ensuring that states did not use newly available Medicaid matching funds to refinance their state mental hospitals. Originally, the law simply said that no Medicaid benefits would be available to an individual who was a resident in an IMD. In a single sentence in section 1905(a) of the Social Security Act, Congress stipulated that the institutions that treat persons with mental illness would remain discrete (as they had been for more than one hundred years) and that their inpatients would remain outside the reach of most Medicaid benefit.

The IMD exclusion was premised on the belief that mental health was separate from physical health and that treatment for mental health could be compartmentalized. That is, the focus has been on the treatment of mental illness and not on the treatment of a person who has physical health and mental health needs. The attempt to separate the two is no longer valid, yet in various ways, Medicaid policy continues to reinforce the mistaken presumption that mental health care is not mainstream health care.

Consider the intent of one piece of the Omnibus Budget Reconciliation Act of 1987 nursing home reforms: Pre-Admission Screening and Annual Resident Review (PASARR). The gradual release of people from state hospitals resulted in a concomitant increase in the admission of persons with mental illness to nursing homes, a practice that was widely condemned as gaming the IMD exclusion to get federal matching funds and a means of reducing populations in

---

21. Tannenbaum (1986).

overcrowded state ICFs/MR. At the time the provision was enacted, HCFA had forced a number of states to establish concrete plans to move inappropriately placed persons with mental retardation from nursing facilities to ICFs/MR. In response to the growing perception that "substantial numbers of mentally retarded and mentally ill residents (were) inappropriately placed at Medicaid expense" in nursing facilities, a two-stage approach—that is, PASARR—was adopted to curb the inappropriate use.[22]

PASARR was an attempt to make the IMD policy a reality, to separate physical from mental illness and to compartmentalize their treatment, by identifying and relocating those nursing home residents who were inappropriately placed. PASARR's premise was that the mentally ill ought to get the active treatment they needed and that the treatment was to be found somewhere other than the nursing home. What the implementation of PASARR has revealed, however, is that the boundary lacks legitimacy. The lesson from PASARR is that much mental health care is mainstream health care.

The simple mechanics of PASARR were as follows. Every potential Medicaid nursing facility patient with a mental disorder listed in DSM-III (*Diagnostic and Statistical Manual of the American Psychiatric Association,* third edition) would be required to be screened by the state mental health organization, which would determine whether the patient needed active treatment and needed nursing facility services. If a patient needed both (a situation that was expected to be infrequent), the state was required to provide the active treatment services in the nursing facility. The anticipated result was that persons with mental disorders who needed active treatment would be identified and diverted to appropriate facilities, likely IMDs where Medicaid payment was excluded. A similar screening and determinations process was set up for persons with mental retardation.

States made significant expenditures to implement PASARR but found that most of the persons with mental disorders did require nursing facility care. The law was thus amended to limit PASARR to persons with serious mental illness. Most significant, in 1990, language was added to the Medicaid statute requiring that mental health services be part and parcel of nursing home services (Section 1919 B(4)(a)(vii)). The Medicaid experience with PASARR shows a positive evolution toward congressional acceptance of the position that mental health care is mainstream health care and that the mentally ill ought to be integrated. However, the breakthrough was limited. Congress also commissioned a study of the IMD exclusion to determine whether it was still appropri-

---

22. Omnibus Budget Reconciliation Act of 1987 (P.L. 100-203); and U.S. House of Representatives (1989, p. 459).

ate.[23] The report did not lead to repeal of the provision, in part because it demonstrated that the pressure of the IMD exclusion had led to widespread innovation in areas of ambulatory mental health care and care in small facilities (the law was changed in 1988 to restrict the IMD designation to facilities with more than sixteen beds).

The impact of the continuing Medicaid exclusion for services delivered to certain patients in IMDs is to reinforce the separation of mental and physical health. Some advocates have argued, to the contrary, that the IMD exclusion may be working, paradoxically, to enhance the integration of the mentally ill and the mainstreaming of mental health. According to this logic, the states respond to financial incentives to shift more of their costs into federal programs. Confronting in the IMD exclusion a sizable barrier in their attempts to shift costs of care into federal programs, states have responded by changing the basic structure of their mental health delivery systems. Large state facilities have been closed or downsized, and many smaller, mostly private, facilities have been opened. Evident are dramatic declines in the total days of care in state hospitals and corresponding increases in outpatient admissions and partial care services. Once the primary source of inpatient care, state and county mental hospitals are now far less important than general hospital inpatient psychiatric units.[24]

Certainly it is possible to question whether states' urgency to circumvent the IMD exclusion has fostered more inventive approaches or whether, viewed more critically, the redefinition of IMDs as facilities of sixteen or more beds (including nursing homes and units of general hospitals, whose primary purpose is to provide treatment for the mentally ill) ought to be viewed as evidence of states getting enough leverage to pay for the small personal care homes increasingly being used to house the mentally ill.[25] The response in this case would not be seen as particularly inventive; it is just more of the same in smaller containers.

The weaknesses of the prevailing paradigm in mental health care are thwarting the achievement of a consensus. Professional disagreements about the effectiveness of alternative treatments are in part responsible. Moreover, while Medicaid is paying for more mental health care, the IMD exclusion remains in place though its conceptual basis has come under increasing attack. Advocates think that it works—in a contradictory fashion. Although it is based on a

---

23. Health Care Financing Administration (1992).
24. Health Care Financing Administration (1992).
25. Section 1905(I) of the Medicaid statute was added by 411(k)(14) of the Medicare Catastrophic Coverage Act of 1988 (P.L. 100-360).

mistaken premise, the exclusion is believed to have the paradoxical effect of creating a basis for the expansion of more of the kinds of community-based services that they desire. In the case of mental health, a powerful enough engine may not yet be at hand to effectively challenge the prevailing paradigm and open up an avenue for better solutions.

Conclusion

So long as disability is viewed as being work- and income-based, resistance will exist to providing rehabilitative services and assistive technologies that exhibit little return on the investment. So long as persons with disabilities are viewed as dependents in need of subsistence support instead of treatment, opposition will arise to expanding community-based services. Yet persons with disabilities themselves, and all those who listen to them, are no longer prepared to simply accept the outcomes such advocacy produces. The once bright lines are no longer politically acceptable.

Many current policy initiatives are responses to the decreasing legitimacy of the outdated models of caring for the disabled. In some sense, they are attempts to do better within the constraints of a model whose usefulness has expired. Though constrained by the statutes under which it operates, HCFA's current policy efforts are directed toward trying to effect a fundamental shift in what is done for the disabled by giving greater priority to the needs and preference of persons with disabilities. These beneficiary-centered approaches are contrasted with outmoded institutionally based and professionally driven systems. Beneficiary-centered care involves a recognition of the needs of the whole person, with a view of care that extends beyond medical treatment to health, function, and homeostasis. This new paradigm is evident in changes in payment, quality assurance, and Medicare and Medicaid conditions of participation.

How will the distributive dilemma be resolved? What fraction of the scarce resources will go toward the care of the disabled? Even when considering a small piece of the whole, assistive technology, for example, the questions that need to be answered are difficult ones. Once the old paradigm is thoroughly undone—breakdown the boundaries between the disabled and the nondisabled, between acute and long-term care, and between physical and mental health care—what will the new paradigm look like? Though difficult, these challenges are impossible to avoid in light of how the world is changing. These are issues for the young disabled and the growing elderly population alike. The problem to be faced in the end is a universal one that cuts across the whole society's institutions and across a spectrum of ages.

Why Not the Best for the Chronically Ill?
Stanley B. Jones

WHEN EMPLOYEES OR BENEFICIARIES are offered a choice of multiple health plans—as in Medicare, some Medicaid programs, and many large employer groups—strong incentives are created for the competing plans to underinvest in and otherwise de-market care to chronically ill people. Because they cannot charge a fair premium for the chronically ill (they get the same premium regardless of whether the person is sick or well), health plans are driven to avoid these very employees and beneficiaries whose costs and care most need to be managed. One solution might be to allow plans to charge chronically ill people higher out-of-pocket premiums; that is, to make them pay for the costs of their condition. However, this would be unfair and unaffordable to the individuals (for example, in 1993, 10 percent of Medicare beneficiaries have average costs of more than $28,000 per year while 90 percent average slightly more than $1,300).[26] Another solution would be for Medicare, Medicaid, or the employer to adjust its share of the premiums paid to health plans to reflect how many sick versus well people the plan enrolls. Unfortunately, years will pass before premium adjustors are available adequate to adjust premiums well enough that health plans can invest in and market improved managed care to chronically ill persons. To achieve the best value for the chronically ill, large employer coalitions, Medicare, and Medicaid should consider radical new approaches, such as establishing separate prices for care to people with specific chronic conditions and purchasing such care both from health insurance plans and directly from provider systems.

Chronic conditions involve health care needs that seem particularly suited to the kind of improved coordination and capitated payment associated with managed care. Such conditions often require the patient to deal with numerous and varied providers of services over a protracted period of time. In addition, they frequently involve a progression (often downward) over time that requires adjustments in services—to both accommodate and retard further loss. And they affect patients differently, often requiring tailored services. In many cases, patients must comply with complex instructions to avoid acute episodes or more rapid deterioration. Health care providers need clinical time to work with such patients and flexibility to organize care to meet individual needs, beyond what is provided under the usual acute medical care fee schedule and coverage categories.

26. Henry J. Kaiser Foundation (1995, figure 8).

Moreover, the chronically ill incur high costs for employers and public programs. Health care costs for persons with moderate chronic disabilities, for example, may be as much as two to three times higher than those for persons without disabilities.[27] In addition, the morbidity associated with chronic conditions costs employers a great deal in absenteeism and lost productivity.

Given the opportunity managed care seems to offer for the chronically ill, existing payers—employers, Medicare, and Medicaid—by all rights might hope to see health plans competing to develop and market higher quality and more cost-effective plans for chronically ill employees. Purchasers might hope to see plans advertising aggressively to enroll chronically ill employees and beneficiaries, and they might well want to help channel these employees and beneficiaries to the plans that offer the best value. This hopeful scenario is not justified by the incentives in today's health plan market.

Adverse Risk Selection and Its Consequences

In the market of competing health plans, the threat of adverse risk selection encourages health plans to be at best ambivalent about investing in care for the chronically ill. On the one hand, such investments offer great potential for reductions in costs and improvements in value. On the other hand, if a plan becomes known among employees or beneficiaries as better than its competitors at caring for people with a particular chronic condition, it is likely to attract more such subscribers during open seasons, and its costs and premiums are likely to rise in comparison to its competitors'. In serving people with chronic conditions, being so efficient that the cost of care to a chronically ill enrollee is at or below the average for a plan's enrollees is hard to achieve. Ultimately, a plan cannot quote a competitive premium if it enrolls many more than its proportionate share of sicker employees or less than its share of healthier employees.

The importance of risk selection in determining premiums of competing health plans was first documented publicly in the Federal Employees Health Benefits Plan (FEHBP). In 1989, the actuarial values of nine FEHBPs studied varied by no more than 35 percent, but the premium of the highest-cost plan was 246 percent greater than the lowest-cost plan, primarily as a result of adverse selection. The high-option and standard-option Blue Cross and Blue Shield plans were virtually identical in benefit value, but the high-option premium was nearly twice the standard option's because of risk selection.[28]

27. Slesinger and Mechanic (1993).
28. U.S. House of Representatives (1989, pp. 184–88).

Wide variation in benefit value compared with premium among similar health plans is common where employees or beneficiaries are given the choice of multiple plans. Risk selection therefore can produce much larger variations in premiums than the 15 percent to 20 percent estimated savings achievable by the most tightly integrated health maintenance organizations (HMOs).

The implication of this phenomenon for health plans' competitive strategies is that health plans cannot rely on efficiency alone; they must compete based on risk selection. If plans were to advertise to enroll the chronically ill, or if Medicare, Medicaid, or employers were to channel beneficiaries or employees who are chronically ill into health plans that offer the best value (price and quality), or if large numbers of the chronically ill were to learn about these plans and seek them out, these plans' competitiveness would be damaged. Because of risk selection, health plans are not motivated to compete to market better value to the group purchasers' most costly and needy employees or beneficiaries, and the group purchasers would harm the best plans if they encouraged their most costly and needy employees to enroll in them.

De-Marketing to the Chronically Ill

How many health plan advertisements have been aimed at recruiting high-cost chronically ill people? With regard to the chronically ill, health plans have a strong incentive to de-market—or at least to stay in the pack of competing plans; that is, neither to stand out as a better value nor to appear scandalously behind.

Such a posture argues for investing less, at the margins, in improvements or plan features that increase value to the chronically ill and investing more, at the margins, in improvements or plan features (such as pediatrics) that can be marketed to subscribers who are healthier on average. It also argues for weighting the plans' marketing and de-marketing efforts in the same ways.

A primarily defensive posture requires steps such as the following:

—Investing in ways to contain costs of care to chronically ill people already enrolled as a way to keep down overall premiums while avoiding attracting more such enrollees.

—Investing in ways to meet the specific quality requirements of accrediting organizations and to gather the data they require on specific performance standards relating to chronically ill people, but avoiding going beyond these requirements.

—Taking care not to overinvest in costly services, new technologies, or benefits that are particularly desirable to a group of chronically ill employees and that are better than those of competing plans.

—Being careful not to outdo competitors in empaneling those types of providers of care (specialty clinics or physicians) widely known for their attractiveness to the chronically ill.

—Avoiding advertising care to chronically ill people unless extraordinary extenuating circumstances exist, such as the ability to keep an asthmatic child's health care costs low enough that they do not outweigh the advantage of enrolling an entire family.

A more aggressive posture regarding risk selection suggests further steps:

—Investing in research based on analysis of claims data and past enrollment and disenrollment patterns, as well as in focus groups and surveys, so as to determine which services, providers, plan features, and marketing and advertising approaches attract (or repel) low-cost subscribers.

—Avoiding specific health care providers favored by the chronically ill or, if it is necessary to contract with these providers for marketing purposes, using referral criteria that minimize their use.

—Discouraging the use of specific referral services favored by the chronically ill or their physicians by using unrefined review protocols that require special approvals or exceptions.

—Using primary care gatekeepers who are paid in ways that discourage referrals of chronically ill persons to specialists.

—Keeping the numbers and availability of specific types of health professionals, clinic facilities, and other resources that attract the chronically ill to a minimum, thus ensuring long waiting times.

—Identifying advertising images and slogans that give an impression the plan is designed for healthier employees instead of for the chronically ill.

—Paying physicians and hospitals in ways that pass on to them increasing amounts of risk (a practice seemingly welcomed by more and more providers across the country), as well as the problems of risk selection.

Depending on their organizational structures, health plans have different options and philosophies for underinvestment and de-marketing. For example, a group- or staff-model HMO has more power to control investment in various services through its budgeting process, while a loosely organized preferred provider organization (PPO) will rely on restrictive review protocols. Ironically, the integrated health plan, which has arguably the most potential to improve care to the chronically ill, also has the most options to avoid this population, because it controls the resources for care more directly. And as physicians and other providers assume more and more of the risk, they are likely to have to develop their own set of practices for de-marketing to the chronically ill, a frightening thought, given providers' better knowledge of which individuals in their practice are likely to be high-cost.

However it is done, staying in the pack and de-marketing produce at best weak competitive efforts to improve the quality and value of care to the chronically ill. These practices offer weak assurance of long-term improvements in care and can mean higher costs in the short run. As Medicare has documented, purchasers can end up facing higher costs for insurance and care as health plans compete to enroll the low-utilizing employees or beneficiaries and avoid those whose costs are higher.[29]

Chronically ill persons themselves face health plans that are encouraged to underinvest in their care, avoid marketing to them, construct obstacles to their complex referrals, and avoid the providers and services they have searched out as most helpful to them. If they choose to stay with these providers, the likely result is staying behind in higher-cost health plans while lower users opt into plans with better risk selection. In FEHBP, this can cost four times the out-of-pocket premium of other employees—thousands of dollars a year.[30]

If the computer industry were motivated to compete the way health plans compete, they would avoid investment in and marketing to the big users of computing for fear they could not get a fair price.

Premium Adjustors and De-Marketing

Frustrated policymakers and insurance consultants sometimes play down the importance of risk selection, saying that it is not a great problem in mature markets, where large managed care plans dominate the landscape, or that it is a transitional problem that will balance out over time in any system. The evidence, however, is more discouraging. For example, the variations in benefit value and premiums of Blue Cross's high and low options in the FEHBP in 1989 remain roughly the same today. The risk selection has not proved to be transitional. As for maturity, the FEHBP has existed for more than thirty-five years.

The greatest hope for correcting the risk selection problem that causes plans to de-market to chronically ill persons has been thought to be a premium adjustor; that is, a formula by which plans receive premium payments adjusted to take account of the extent of the favorable or adverse selection they experience. If a premium adjustor produced a fair premium for people who require a significant amount of health care, persons with chronic illnesses would become highly desirable subscribers to a health plan—and the providers they favor would likewise become highly desirable participating partners of the plan.

29. Brown and others (1992), cited in U.S. General Accounting Office (1994a).
30. U.S. House of Representatives (1994a).

Having a premium adjustor good enough to facilitate constructive plan competition to invest in and market to the chronically ill is a long way off. The ultimate test of an adjustor is whether it enables health plans to advertise to this population. Adjustors in use today do little to correct for risk selection in general. Those being researched hold promise for doing a good bit more, but none promises to meet this ultimate test of allowing advertising to the chronically ill.

As described in recent literature, to neutralize a health plan's incentives to risk select, a premium adjustor must explain predictable variations in costs of potential subscribers at least as well as the health plan can predict them and use de-marketing techniques to enroll more of the predictably low users and fewer of the predictably high.[31]

One important effort uses information available in employers' personnel files to divide employees into subgroups whose health care utilization varies, assign a relative future cost to employees based on the subgroup to which they belong, and then adjust the premium of each plan based on how many members of each subgroup it enrolls.[32] Other researchers have used multiple factors (for example, indicators of physiologic health, self-reported general health perceptions and chronic diseases, and prior use of medical services) to divide employees into many subgroups and assign relative premium cost to each employee.[33] Still others have defined subgroups based on diagnostic information.

Some research focuses on predicting future years' costs of the entire insurance group (for example, the employees of one employer enrolled in one of the health plans offered) and claims considerable success in predicting and potentially adjusting premiums to take account of risk selection.[34]

Approaches to predicting and correcting for risk selection are not nearly as successful at predicting the variations in costs at the individual subscriber level. Some agreement exists among researchers that being able to explain as much as 10 to 12 percent of the total variation in costs, or approximately two-thirds of the predictable variation at the level of individual subscribers, is unusual.[35]

31. Newhouse (1994, p. 142).

32. For example, "a recently hired, single, female clerk, 23 years old, would carry with her an annual contribution of $563; a single female professional, 60 years old with 10 years on the job would bring a contribution of $1,277; and a female clerk, married with children, 40 years old with 15 years on the job, would bring a contribution of $1,529 to whichever plan she chooses." Cited in Robinson and others (1991, pp. 107–16). See also Robinson (1993, pp. 65–75).

33. Newhouse and others (1989). See also Newhouse and others (1993, pp. 39–54).

34. For a recent review of this and related research, see Fowles, Weiner, and Knudson (1994).

35. Luft (1994). See also Physician Payment Review Commission (1994); and Newhouse and others (1989, p. 49).

Do health plans have the motivation, opportunity, and resources to predict future costs of individuals or small subgroups better than those who use risk adjustors? Can health plans identify and market (or de-market) to prospectively higher-cost and lower-cost individuals within the subgroups for which research can set premium adjustors?

Plans clearly have the motivation and the opportunity. Limitations in adjustors currently being used in research leave a wide margin for plans to profit by risk selection.[36] Moreover, most of these research adjustors have been developed based on historical data or in situations where the plans have not been strongly motivated to outmaneuver the adjustor. Plans have easily outflanked the Medicare adjustor, and their efforts likely will substantially reduce the predictive power of research adjustors. Group purchasers will find themselves in something of an arms race with health plans, when and if they attempt to use risk adjustors.

Unfortunately, plans are far more motivated than those who might use risk adjustors to buy from them. Few purchasers today have entered this arms race, because few are using risk adjustors as part of their efforts to manage competing health plans. The Pacific Business Group on Health, the California Managed Risk Medical Insurance Board, and the Minnesota Buyers Health Care Action Group have plans to use relatively sophisticated risk adjustors for the chronically ill. But most purchasers who do use adjustors have limited themselves to the most elementary, such as age, sex, and geographic location of the subscribers. Medicare is using by far the most sophisticated risk adjustor today, and it is flawed and easily outflanked by health plans. Why purchasers have been so slow to use adjustors is not clear; perhaps it is too complicated. But this reluctance does not augur well for the near-term development and use of practical adjustor systems.

When and if the race begins, health plans have formidable resources for attaining favorable risk selection beyond what the adjustor can correct for. Once plans are aware of premium adjustor subgroups and the premium each will carry, they can use the past claims and enrollment files as well as focus groups and survey techniques to characterize their own subscribers over the years within each subgroup or across subgroups so as to identify those to whom they want to market or de-market. The data and financial resources available to the health plans for such research are much greater than those available to the researchers.

Adjustors based on subgroups will also set up a pernicious incentive for plans to identify individual current enrollees whose costs are substantially

---

36. Newhouse and others (1989, p. 49).

higher than the premium paid for the subgroup and look for ways to limit their investment in care to the premium amount. This approach would be similar to the common hospital practice of encouraging staff to get patients out within the days covered by a diagnostic-related group (DRG) payment, as though the DRG amount were a target or limit for patient stays instead of an average for costs of all patients in the DRG.

A tough-minded assessment of the purchasers' chances of using risk adjustors to win this arms race comes from Joseph P. Newhouse, who argues that "risk adjustment technology has to take major leaps forward to render these incentives insubstantial" and that "the expectation for further research is for modest improvement."[37]

Because the potential of managed care is so high for the chronically ill, and because the costs and quality problems are so great, it makes sense for employers, Medicare, and Medicaid to look for new approaches to augment whatever premium adjustors they find practical.

Purchasing for People with Chronic Conditions

Unlike health plans, physicians and other providers of care have no ambivalence about marketing their services to patients with chronic conditions. Moreover, chronically ill persons on the whole are sophisticated consumers of such services and can be counted on to shop carefully for quality and price. If Medicare, Medicaid, and large private purchasers develop fair global prices or capitation rates to provider systems for specific chronic conditions, they facilitate the development of a market in which investing in and marketing to the chronically ill is desirable. Direct contracts between purchasers and providers for care to the chronically ill will force health plans to invest in and market to these subscribers if they are to hold on to them and to the large share of premium revenue they represent. If the system is structured well, chronically ill consumers will be educated to choose based on quality and value—and will use their relatively high level of sophistication about these matters to drive provider systems and health plans to serve them better.

The first key element of this approach is to guarantee that the price is right. Purchasers such as Medicare might use past claims data to set prices (as is done with DRGs), or they might ask plans and provider systems to bid on the provision of services for people with specific chronic conditions.

The second key element is to define specific chronic conditions as well as clinically and actuarially manageable service packages for which prices can be

---

37. Newhouse (1994, p. 141).

set. Ideally, a service package should encompass both comprehensive care and services for the specific condition. However, for some conditions, bidders might be able to set a price for specialty services only and work out agreements and separate prices with primary care providers for the remainder of the patient's care. The prices may be in the form of capitation or mixes of capitation and other forms of payment and risk bearing. Chronic conditions and the range of services and relationships of providers for them vary greatly. The packaging and pricing of services should be clinically driven, taking into account the nature and course of the condition being considered. This is another powerful reason to look to providers directly, not only to health plans, to shape the program and bid.

A third key element is choice. The consumer should be offered the choice of these different systems and allowed to discipline the market over time by choice. If the consumer wishes to stay in the traditional arrangement with traditional providers and plans, he or she should be allowed to do so.

Some employers as well as Medicare and Medicaid are already purchasing limited packages of health care from providers on a competitive basis. For example, large employers contract for transplants. Medicare contracts for coronary artery bypass grafts. Employers are purchasing disease management approaches to a variety of conditions, such as diabetes, pediatric asthma, coronary artery disease, pregnancy and childbirth, low-back pain, breast cancer, stroke, depression, knee care, attention deficit disorder, congestive heart failure, adult asthma, hysterectomy, Alzheimer's dementia, and hypertension.

HealthPartners of Minnesota is considering requesting proposals from provider groups (care systems) for capitated payment for comprehensive services to people with specific conditions (for example, insulin-dependent diabetes). This payment would augment an ambulatory care group (ACG)-based risk adjustor in 1997.[38]

Medicare, Medicaid, and large employers might take the following types of steps in pursuit of such arrangements:

—Request health plans and provider systems to propose global fees and capitation amounts for improved care to people with specific chronic conditions. The purchaser could use diagnostic groupings, such as ACGs, to determine a reasonable price, or it might supply the data to bidding plans and provider systems as a basis for their pricing.

---

38. The author interviewed George Halvorson, chief executive officer of Health Partners, and Stephen Wetzel, chief executive officer of the Minnesota Buyers Health Action Group, which is collaborating in this effort. For more on ACGs, see Starfield and others (1991).

—Request health plans and provider systems to bid on and arrange to offer all covered care to these persons or to demonstrate contractual or other agreements that permit all the covered care of the person to be clinically managed.

—Subtract the projected cost of these new condition-specific payments from the premium rates paid for other employees or beneficiaries.

—Contract with the provider systems and health plans offering the best value in the community or with the sole providers in rural communities.

—Allow chronically ill employees and beneficiaries to choose among health plans and provider systems. The choice might be made at the time of diagnosis as a point of service (POS) option or on a monthly basis as an enrollment shift. Medicare might offer the same choices to its beneficiaries who enroll in alternative health plans, as well as in the traditional Medicare program.

To encourage health plans and provider systems to bid on a global fee or capitation basis early in the program, purchasers might offer risk sharing arrangements to providers. For example, the employer might:

—Offer to share risks with plans and provider systems for all costs over a maximum for an individual case or for an individual over a year or longer period of time.[39]

—Pay provider systems and plans a blended rate or partial capitation; for example, capitation for half and payment based on current costs for half, with the blend including a higher percentage of current costs for higher-cost patients.[40]

—Allow health plans and provider systems to limit the number of patients they will take in their initial years.

To ensure quality, the purchaser's requests for proposals (RFPs) to health plans and provider systems might require management and clinical arrangements that clinicians and consumers consider critical to improved care for the person with the chronic condition. Accreditation by the National Committee on Quality Assurance (NCQA) might be used for this purpose, or Medicare might assemble experts and consumers to specify the best practices that high-value systems for patients with different chronic conditions should have and to develop performance measures for contracting with plans and provider systems. The RFPs might include:

—Possible organizational, risk sharing, and payment arrangements with providers.

39. Slesinger and Mechanic (1993).
40. Newhouse (1994, p. 142).

—Evidence of investment of capital in improvement of services, treatment protocols, and best practices.

—Collection and submission of performance data, including preventive services, especially measures of preventive services that forestall chronic illnesses for which a capitated rate is paid.

—Evidence that providers have needed expertise and that the ratio of types of providers to planned enrollment is adequate.

—Inclusion of providers with strong local reputations in care of the chronically ill in health plan panels or justification for not including them.

The employers, Medicare, and Medicaid would also undertake an extraordinary effort to inform the choices of the chronically ill among health plans and provider systems so plans and provider systems that invest in improved quality could be rewarded with larger market share. This effort might include:

—Developing plan performance data based on best practices for various chronic conditions.

—Informing employees with chronic conditions how to make an objective choice in their own interest and equipping them with materials such as premium-to-benefit value comparisons, quality surveys of health plans and provider systems, and surveys of consumer satisfaction.

Difficult Issues

A number of difficulties must be faced to facilitate competition among provider systems and health plans to manage care to the chronically ill. Three of these—and possible solutions—are listed below:

—Some chronic conditions affect too few people to support more than one (or even one) provider system in an area, especially if the employees of only one employer are involved. Even the enrollees of one health plan are often too few to contain the critical mass needed to facilitate organization of provider systems. The solution is for Medicare and multi-employer purchasers to take the lead. With Medicare's 37 million beneficiaries and a high incidence of chronic conditions in its population, Medicare in particular has enormous leverage in the market for services to chronically ill persons in most communities. Once a provider system is organized, smaller purchasers might buy from it. In rural areas or for rare conditions, sole provider arrangements might be negotiated.

—Many different chronic conditions exist, each requiring a different set of services. Even a large employer will find complex issuing RFPs to cover all these possibilities and reviewing competitive bids in each. The solution here is, again, relying on large group purchasers, such as Medicare and purchasing alliances, to take the lead. Large purchasers might work with agents such as the

NCQA or the Foundation for Accountability to solicit providers and consumer organizations to develop RFP criteria and provider system performance measures relating to chronic conditions. The effort can begin slowly by selecting the conditions that impact employees or beneficiaries the most or provide the best local market opportunities.

—Many patients have multiple chronic conditions. The solution here is for purchasers to solicit proposals from provider systems, such as geriatric centers for elderly patients, that can bridge multiple diagnoses. Although such systems may not be feasible for many complex diagnoses, clinicians should drive the systems' design wherever they can be developed.

Successful purchasing for people with specific chronic conditions will involve a steep learning curve. It will take considerable time and resources. And some chronic conditions may simply not be amenable to this approach. However, every condition for which this approach is perfected will yield that much more value for purchasers' health care dollars.

Managing Care for Persons with Disabilities: The Conflicts between Medicare and Medicaid
Patricia Riley

AN EMERGING DISABILITY POLICY concern in the rapid growth of managed care is whether and how persons with disabilities will fare, particularly as Medicaid programs move to enroll all eligibles into managed care. Bruce C. Vladeck notes that no clamor has been heard for case management services to better control utilization and costs of Medicare benefits for disabled beneficiaries and no rapid shift has occurred into managed care for that population. The same is not true of Medicaid. In Medicaid, states have begun to more aggressively enroll persons with disabilities in managed care; nineteen states include some enrollment of this population in their risk-based managed care programs and many states include persons with disabilities in their case-managed home and community-based 1915(c) waiver programs.[41] In the course of these efforts, states have learned of the critical interrelatedness of Medicare and Medicaid and the conflicts between the two programs that restrict state initiatives to manage care.

41. Under 1915(c) Medicaid waivers that were enacted in 1981, states with plans approved by the secretary of health and human services can provide Medicaid-financed social services in the community to people who, without those services, would require institutional care that would be covered by Medicaid. Services that can be financed under the waivers go beyond the medical services Medicaid traditionally paid for and include case management, homemaker or home health aid services, personal care, adult day care, and habilitation services.

Managed care holds the promise of improved coordination of care at predictable, predetermined costs as well as moving the Medicaid and Medicare programs from their bias in favor of institutional care toward community-based care. By capitating a managed care organization and holding it accountable for assuring the maximum independence of a person with disabilities, managed care can create incentives for those organizations to work with consumers to redesign benefits and provide an array of services outside of institutions. But advocates worry that managed care can also underserve persons with disabilities; it may sever existing relationships with specialists and other providers; and it may overemphasize a medical approach to their needs for ongoing supports. Consumers worry that a health maintenance organization (HMO) orientation may cause them to lose access to nonmedical care and consumer-directed personal care. If managed care is to meet its promise, these critically important issues of consumers must be addressed.

But compounding the complexity of how best to develop managed care for and with persons with disabilities is the conflict between Medicare and Medicaid. About 5.2 million people are dually eligible for both programs.[42] About 1.5 million of them are persons with disabilities under the age of sixty-five. In general, dual eligibles under age sixty-five are recipients of Social Security disability benefits, who become covered under the federal Medicare program after a twenty-four-month waiting period, but because they have limited income and assets they also qualify for the means-tested Medicaid program that is administered by the states.

From the perspective of the Health Care Financing Administration (HCFA), dually eligible beneficiaries represent only a fraction of total Medicare enrollment. But from a state's viewpoint, dual eligibles comprise virtually all their Medicaid elderly enrollment and one-third of all persons under sixty-five with disabilities who qualify for Medicaid. For those dually eligible, Medicare covers mainly acute and rehabilitative care. Medicaid pays mainly for long-term care and other services not covered by Medicare. Medicaid also pays for the copayments, deductibles, and premiums that beneficiaries are charged under Medicare. While the two programs have different orientations, considerable overlap and duplication exists between the two. A simple delineation of Medicare for acute care and Medicaid for long-term care is inaccurate. Both programs, for example, pay for home health and some nursing facility care, and

---

42. The process by which a beneficiary becomes eligible for both programs is a complex one. At least nine different ways are available to become dual eligible, and not all dual eligible clients qualify for the same services. For example, some qualify only for cost-sharing while others receive the complete array of Medicaid services.

Medicaid pays cost-sharing for all Medicare services for the dually eligible. More important, a clear line cannot be drawn that separates when acute care ends and long-term care begins. A chronically ill or disabled person goes in and out of both services, often over long periods of time. Beneficiaries, therefore, are caught between Medicare and Medicaid in a confused and fragmented nonsystem of care.

How Dual Eligibles Experience the System Today

States and consumers face numerous difficulties under the four possible combinations of fee-for-service and managed care arrangements for persons dually eligible for Medicare and Medicaid.

Fee-for-Service Under Both Medicare and Medicaid

Beneficiaries may receive services from both the Medicare and Medicaid programs on a fee-for-service basis. Coordination of care is compromised as different providers serve the beneficiary and cost-shifting between programs is likely to occur. Medicare beneficiaries have complete choice to seek and receive services, and Medicaid pays all cost-sharing but has no capacity to monitor or review the care for which it is partially paying.

Duplication between the programs is particularly evident in 1915(c) Medicaid waivers through which virtually all states provide long-term care to the elderly and to persons with physical disabilities, mental disabilities, or both. In these programs, case managers work with physicians, clients, and families to develop care plans to maximize independence and reduce institutionalization. But dual eligibles can receive care from many providers, and both the primary care doctor and specialists can order Medicaid services (for example, prescription medication), without regard to an existing care plan. Physicians may also order skilled home care directly from a home health agency. Administrators of Medicaid waiver programs express concern that Medicare tends to provide costly and sometimes unneeded skilled nursing care ordered by a physician directly through a home health agency with no gatekeeper to review cost and appropriateness of those Medicare services.

Medicare Fee-for-Service and Medicaid Managed Care

Some states have enrolled dual eligibles into their Medicaid risk-based managed care programs (Oregon, TennCARE, Minnesota). These programs do not cover long-term care. But dual eligibles receive most of their primary, acute, and rehabilitative care through Medicare.

States are interested in expanding their Medicaid managed care to cover long-term care. In its Arizona Long Term Care System, an HCFA demonstration that integrates acute and long-term care in a capitated Medicaid program, Arizona capitates long-term care for persons when they become nursing-home eligible. Florida has two HMO–based prepaid health plans that capitate all long-term care related services. But the conflicts between Medicare and Medicaid have stymied true coordination of care for the beneficiary, leading Minnesota to seek and receive federal waivers to experiment with coordination of both programs. Among the areas of conflict are:

—Beneficiaries may receive care from more than one physician and have more than one medical record.

—Medicaid plans have incentives to shift costs to Medicare and may hospitalize, where Medicare pays, instead of providing Medicaid home care services, for which they are at risk.

—The goal of reducing institutionalization is compromised if hospital stays and short-term nursing facility services are paid by Medicare on a fee-for-service basis.

—Liability for cost-sharing may be unclear to beneficiaries, plans, and providers. Some states wish to pay cost-sharing for Medicare-covered services only if they are provided through the Medicaid managed care plan in which the dual eligible is enrolled. Costs would rise and continuity of care would be compromised, they argue, if enrollees could go out of plan at will to receive care from a different Medicare provider and charge Medicaid directly for cost-sharing that is covered in the managed care rate of capitation. But the Medicare program must provide beneficiaries complete choice regarding whom delivers their care.

—Neither the federal government nor state governments have complete accountability for care that is fragmented, and holding a Medicaid plan accountable for care is difficult if enrollees can go out of the plan and receive Medicare services.

Medicare Managed Care and Medicaid Fee-for-Service

Medicare managed care plans are financed in two ways. Until 1982, they were financed under cost contracts. The Tax Equity and Fiscal Responsibility Act of 1982 (TEFRA) introduced the risk contracting program, whereby Medicare pays health plans a monthly capitated rate.[43] Today, about three in four

43. The capitated rate is based on estimated fee-for-service spending. The adjusted average per capita cost is a county-level estimate of the average cost incurred by Medicare for each beneficiary in the fee-for-service system. Medicare's capitation payment to a plan with a risk contract is 95 percent of the AAPCC for Medicare fee-for-service beneficiaries.

Medicare enrollees in HMOs are in plans with risk contracts, so-called TEFRA HMOs, while the rest are HMOs that are paid based on cost contracts.

Increasing enrollment by dual eligibles into these TEFRA HMOs for their Medicare-financed care presents several challenges. TEFRA plans will have incentives to shift costs to Medicaid and to place beneficiaries in long-term care arrangements that are financed by Medicaid. Many TEFRA plans recruit participants by covering prescription drugs, which currently are not covered by Medicare but are covered by Medicaid, and by eliminating or reducing copays and premiums that have been paid by Medicaid. Consequently, Medicaid's liability is reduced. Nonetheless, managing the oversight of cost-sharing is complicated because TEFRA plans may change incentives and states must watch who pays for what. TEFRA plans may also conduct marketing to avoid adverse selection, which could result in disproportionately costly dual eligible clients being left in Medicaid fee-for-service arrangements. As more TEFRA plans offer point of service options, which allow beneficiaries to use providers outside the plan's network, how will dual eligibles be assured that choice? Without resources to pay for out of plan services, will Medicaid be expected to pick up that cost? Finally, Medicare does not provide the capacity to ensure statewide managed care. Because TEFRA HMOs tend to be developed around areas of high adjusted average per capita cost (AAPCC) rates, dual eligibles are not provided full choice statewide.

Managed Care Under Both Medicare and Medicaid

A dually eligible beneficiary can be enrolled in managed care under both Medicare and Medicaid in two ways. One involves enrollment in two separate managed care plans. The other involves linking Medicaid services with a Medicare TEFRA HMO plan.

States may use their existing network of Medicaid plans or develop 1915(c) waivers to organize other providers with expertise in serving elders and persons with disabilities as their managed care plans (for example, Arizona, Minnesota, and I–CARE in Wisconsin). Those plans cannot qualify as TEFRA HMOs.[44] Therefore, dual eligibles could be enrolled in two different managed care organizations and have two different primary care providers and two

---

44. To qualify as a TEFRA HMO, a plan must be a federally qualified HMO or a competitive medical plan and must offer all Medicare-covered services under a capitation payment. Furthermore, health plans participating in Medicare must meet the 50/50 rule, which requires that at least half of the plans participants are private pay enrollees. Medicaid plans must meet a 75/25 rule, with at least 25 percent of participants being private pay enrollees. The 1915(c) waiver programs generally are for Medicaid recipients only.

different medical records. Each plan would have incentives to shift costs to the other, and no one has full responsibility for the total plan of care for a client. States have difficulty setting rates if TEFRA plans provide enrollment incentives, such as no cost-sharing and no cost for drugs, which were previously the liability of Medicaid. HCFA and states duplicate quality assurance and other accountability functions, and each pays duplicative administrative costs. Cost-sharing responsibilities are unclear. For example, providers would be held responsible for collecting payments for services they thought were authorized by one HMO but were part of the capitation for the other HMO.

The same client, served in two plans, is covered by two separate contracts, has two distinct and different grievance and appeals processes to follow, is contacted by two different entities to enroll in managed care, has two separate enrollee handbooks, and is subject to other confusion caused by two discrete plans.

If a state wished to avoid the confusion of two plan enrollment, it could elect to contract only with TEFRA HMOs for Medicaid services for its dual eligible population. However, coverage under TEFRA HMOs is not available in many areas. Further, those HMOs may not have clinical capacity or interest in serving frail, chronically ill clients, and cost-shifting can still occur. Two contracts, two enrollment mechanisms, two quality assurance and monitoring systems, and two sets of rates continue. Medicaid may anticipate cost savings from Medicare and attempt to discount its rates, but plans still can game costs between a Medicare rate and a Medicaid rate. Given the complexity of care required by at least some of the dually eligible, Medicaid may wish to share risks with plans and develop risk adjustments, but Medicare does not do so. In a TEFRA–based system, dually eligible beneficiaries can now at least apply to and be served by one plan, but separate processes still exist for Medicare and Medicaid. For example, a grievance made on a Medicare benefit may not even be known to Medicaid, although the complainant is a dual eligible and also receives Medicaid.

Conclusion

Two distinct sets of laws, rules, and administrative structures governing Medicare and Medicaid are in operation. The conflicts are real. For example:

—Different eligibility requirements exist for participating managed care organizations.

—The two programs have different requirements for rate setting, and while Medicare cannot share risk, Medicaid may.

—Medicare mandates freedom of choice of provider for beneficiaries; Medicaid allows states to require beneficiaries to enroll in managed care.

—Quality assurance systems are different, compounding confusion for consumers.

—Benefit design is different between the two programs.

—Accountability is divided and often unclear between the federal government and state governments.

Several managed care demonstrations are particularly notable: the Community Medical Alliance for people with acquired immune deficiency syndrome (AIDS) and Wisconsin's I–CARE. They are emerging examples of integration of acute and long-term care, but they are limited models.

To truly experiment with integration between acute and long-term care and to serve persons who are dually eligible requires much better coordination between Medicare and Medicaid. Additional demonstrations are now under way. HCFA has recently approved a demonstration in Minnesota to meld Medicare and Medicaid to experiment with integrated care. Arizona, Colorado, Wisconsin, and others wish to do the same. These experiments need to be encouraged to end cost-shifting and to improve continuity of care and consumer sensitive services for persons with disabilities.

Disability Policy in an Age of Reform
R. Alexander Vachon

How well are people with disabilities served by federal policies and programs? What might be done to make federal policies and programs more effective? Not only are these questions of intrinsic importance, but they also assume some urgency for at least three reasons.

First, despite substantial federal spending for people with disabilities, the outcomes of federal disability policies and programs are not heartening. In 1993, the federal government spent about $175 billion on programs for people with disabilities.[45] Given that total federal outlays in 1993 were $1.2 trillion (net of interest payments), about 15 percent of the federal budget was spent on people with disabilities.[46]

Nonetheless, on two of the most significant indicators of quality of life—employment and economic well-being—the situation is not good.[47] Sixty-nine

45. Scully and others (1995).
46. Office of Management and Budget (1996).
47. Vachon (1991a).

percent of working-age disabled adults are jobless—a historic high.[48] As one disability expert has stated, "Not working is perhaps the truest definition of what it means to be disabled in this country."[49] Joblessness is accompanied by a high poverty rate. About 28 percent of people with a disability live in poverty, compared with 11 percent of the total working-age population.[50] Fewer men with disabilities are the economic mainstays of their families, placing a greater burden on their spouses to make up lost income.[51]

Second, disability is changing—as evidenced by a growing disabled population, the increasing variety of disabilities, and heightened social expectations for people with disabilities. Although only limited information is available on the epidemiology of disability, the number of Americans with disabilities appears to be growing rapidly.[52] This trend is especially clear in federal cash assistance programs. For example, between 1980 and 1995, the number of disabled workers receiving Social Security disability insurance (DI) benefits grew 48 percent, and Social Security Administration (SSA) actuaries predict an 88 percent increase over the corresponding period of 1995 through 2010.[53]

Furthermore, over the past several decades, new disabling conditions have emerged. For example, people with quadriplegia are survivors of once-fatal injuries, albeit with lifelong disability. And learning disabilities, which have been widely recognized since only the 1960s, present a new challenge. Today about 5 percent of all school-age children are identified with a learning disability and comprise half of all special education students.[54] In the United States and similar societies, where even taking a bus requires minimal literacy, cognitive skills are increasingly essential to good jobs.[55] At the same time, a profound shift has occurred in expectations about people with disabilities—for example, people with developmental disabilities should live in the community instead of institutions—and about society's obligation to accommodate people with disabilities.[56]

Third, a heightened scrutiny of disability policies and programs, as with most federal programs, should be expected in "the new age of reform." Three events precipitated this age of reform. First, the end of the cold war weakened the rationale for the national security state, where considerable domestic

48. Harris (1994).
49. Harris (1986, p. 47).
50. Vachon (1991b).
51. Burkhauser, Haveman, and Wolfe (1990).
52. Pope and Tarlov (1991); and Vachon (1987).
53. Board of Trustees (1996).
54. Lyon (1996).
55. Vachon (1987).
56. Berkowitz (1987); Dole (1994); and West (1991).

spending—from education to highways—was justified on national security grounds. Second, the national security state reinforced, and was reinforced by, the broad expansion of federal authority initiated during the national economic emergency of the Great Depression in the 1930s. The enactment of welfare reform legislation in August 1996 is the symbolic end of that national emergency. Third, the federal budget crisis, with continuing deficits and huge long-term entitlement obligations, is placing enormous pressures on discretionary domestic spending.[57]

One indicator that these changes have affected disability policy thinking is the differing recommendations regarding reforms of the Supplemental Security Income (SSI) program from two expert panels. A 1992 review of the SSI program undertaken by SSA recommended increased SSI benefits and liberalized deeming and resource tests used to determine income eligibility and benefit amount.[58] Four years later, another blue-ribbon working group, organized by the National Academy of Social Insurance, was silent on raising benefit levels, emphasizing instead the frugal design of disability income benefit programs and the importance of removing barriers to work and increasing work incentives.[59]

The Ambivalence of Disability Policy

In their paper, Bruce Vladeck and his colleagues explore why the Medicaid and Medicare programs have not been fully responsive to the needs of people with disabilities, particularly in the areas of long-term care, mental health, and assistive technology. Vladeck offers six reasons for this ambivalence in disability policy, from outdated program priorities to structural problems inherent in disability policymaking by Congress and the executive branch. Vladeck offers provocative and original observations, although perhaps not always supported by the history he describes. For example, he writes, "Policymakers have been hesitant to enhance medical and social services for the disabled because the likelihood that they would use those services to achieve a level of rehabilitation that would allow them to return to work is thought to be slim," further noting that "Congress ended funding for [vocational] rehabilitation of SSI and DI beneficiaries in 1982."

However, Congress never ended funding for the vocational rehabilitation (VR) of SSI and DI beneficiaries. In the Omnibus Reconciliation Act of 1981,

57. Kerrey and Danforth (1995).
58. Social Security Administration (1992).
59. Mashaw and Reno (1996).

Congress replaced state grants for VR services to SSI and DI beneficiaries with a system of reimbursement of state VR agencies for successful rehabilitations. States had been receiving funds whether or not SSI or DI beneficiaries returned to work. Congress believed that a reimbursement-based system would provide state VR agencies with greater incentives to provide effective VR services.[60]

Nonetheless, federal disability policy has preferred income replacement to rehabilitation solutions, with unfortunate consequences.[61] Vladeck's key point that disability services could be improved can be easily accepted. However, to Vladeck's list of explanations of why more appropriate services are not available, another can be added: The kind of policy work that policymakers—Congress in particular—need is often lacking.

This point is illustrated by another example raised by Vladeck. He worries that reforms in eligibility for SSI benefits by drug addicts and alcoholics and by children contained in welfare reform legislation in the 104th Congress (and subsequently enacted) may signal a return to the "dark period" of the 1980s when "a public perception that disability rolls were swollen with thousands of undeserving individuals" led to hamfisted reviews of the continuing eligibility of DI beneficiaries.[62]

Regarding SSI benefits for individuals who are drug addicted or alcoholic, the debate has not been over whether these conditions are disabling but whether such individuals are well served by receiving SSI or DI cash benefits—or better served by treatment. Congress originally intended that SSI benefits be available to drug addicts or alcoholics only for a limited period while such individuals were in treatment. As the House Ways and Means Committee report on the bill creating the SSI program stated, the "committee believes that those people who are disabled, in whole or in part, as a result of the use of drugs or alcohol should not be entitled to benefits under this program unless they undergo appropriate, available treatment in an approved facility, and the bill so provides."[63] However, as implemented, drug addiction and alcoholism became eligible conditions for SSI benefits, and the treatment requirement was never enforced.[64]

---

60. For a review of VR services to SSI and DI beneficiaries, see Social Security Administration (1988).

61. Berkowitz (1987).

62. The history of those reviews is more complicated. For a revealing first-person account of the origins of the Carter administration policy, see Califano (1981).

63. U.S. House of Representatives (1971, p. 149).

64. U.S. General Accounting Office (1994b).

In 1996, with enactment of P.L. 104-121, Congress corrected this problem by ending SSI eligibility based solely on drug addiction or alcoholism. Witnesses before congressional committees reported that SSI payments were frequently used to subsidize continuing substance abuse and significantly complicated the treatment of individuals with both a serious mental illness and addiction.[65]

Is this change in policy a return to putative dark days? Hardly; it demonstrates how good intentions can have harmful consequences. Moreover, the failure of policy analysts to focus on this issue was a missed opportunity in another way.[66] If one feature of the new age of reform is a reordering of priorities within tight spending limits—that is, legislative initiatives must be paid for with either new revenues or, preferably, from savings in existing programs—then the estimated $3.1 billion in net savings over seven years from eliminating SSI eligibility solely on the basis of substance abuse might have been redirected for new initiatives to help SSI and DI beneficiaries, such as those proposed by the National Academy of Social Insurance.[67]

Children's SSI eligibility reforms provide another illustration of the complexities of disability policymaking. Growth in the children's SSI rolls has been impressive: In 1989, about 300,000 children were enrolled, at a annual cost of $1.1 billion. By February 1995, according to SSA, 927,000 children were enrolled, at an annual cost of $5 billion. In five years, SSI emerged as the largest program serving children with disabilities, spending more than all other such programs combined (excluding Medicaid).[68] This growth was caused by three factors: Congressionally mandated outreach to find disabled children eligible for SSI, revision of the eligibility regulations for mental impairments, and the addition of a new set of eligibility determination regulations called the individualized functional assessment (IFA).[69]

During Senate oversight of the children's SSI program, the IFA regulations quickly became a matter of close scrutiny. The IFA regulations were written by SSA following the 1991 Supreme Court decision in *Sullivan* v. *Zebley*.[70] In *Zebley,* the Court found that SSA had failed to properly implement statutory requirements for assessing child eligibility for SSI benefits in two respects. Under the SSI statute (Title XVI of the Social Security Act), SSA is required to

---

65. Shaner and others (1995). See also the accompanying commentary by Satel (1995).

66. See, for example, Social Security Administration (1992) and Disability Policy Panel (1996).

67. U.S. Senate (1995, p. 59); and Mashaw and Reno (1996).

68. Aron, Loprest, and Steuerle (1996); and Scully and others (1995).

69. Mashaw, Perrin, and Reno (1996).

70. 493 U.S. 521.

make eligible needy children who have disabilities of comparable severity to ones that would qualify adults for SSI benefits. In addition, SSA is required to consider the disabling effects of combinations of impairments where no single impairment would qualify an individual for SSI.

Regarding comparable severity, under SSA's regulations the Court identified two steps for evaluating adult SSI eligibility. An individual's impairment could (1) meet or equal a Listing of Impairments (a taxonomy of disabling conditions), or (2) result in that individual being unable to engage in any substantial gainful activity.[71] Generally, the second standard is less demanding than the first with regard to severity of disability.

With children, the Court found that SSA's Listing of Impairments were of comparable severity for both adults and children but that SSA had not established a comparable step beyond the listings. To implement this second step, SSA devised the IFA. The IFA is not a customized child assessment. In practice, consistent with the less demanding adult eligibility standard, the IFA regulations were to be met by less severe impairments.[72] For example, the standard diagnosis of mild mental retardation begins with an intelligence quotient (IQ) of 70 to 50, which is 2 standard deviations below the IQ population mean.[73] However, under the IFA, a moderate cognitive (intellectual) limitation would be an IQ one-and-a-half standard deviations below the mean.[74]

In revisiting children's SSI, Congress concluded that the program was intended for children with severe disabilities, following conventional definitions of disability, and therefore eliminated the IFA.[75] The eligibility standards for SSI, however, are inclusive. For example, children may qualify for mental retardation in six different ways, including children with mild mental retardation.[76] The elimination of the IFA was a bipartisan agreement in the Senate and was subsequently included in President Bill Clinton's legislative proposals to Congress.

While Congress was reviewing the children's SSI program, reports on the program were issued by two expert panels—the National Commission on Childhood Disability and a panel organized by the National Academy of Social Insurance.[77] Although both reports contained useful recommendations, some

71. 483 U.S. 521, 526.
72. U.S. General Accounting Office (1995b).
73. Terman and others (1996); and Matarazzo (1972).
74. Social Security Administration (1996, DI 25220.020).
75. U.S. House of Representatives (1996, pp. 327–28).
76. Social Security Administration (1996).
77. National Commission on Childhood Disability (1995); and Mashaw, Perrin, and Reno (1996).

important issues were not adequately addressed. For example, what is the psychological impact on children in providing cash benefits based on disability? The sensitivity of this issue was illustrated in a *New York Times* article, which also described aggressive efforts by New York City to enroll poor children into SSI to save city-funded welfare benefits:

> A Brooklyn parent, Blossom Richards, who had been fighting to get her son, Shawn, out of exclusively special-education classes, decided to battle the system when a caseworker told them to fill out some forms for Supplemental Security Income two years ago. Her son, then a senior at South Shore High School in Canarsie, was classified as emotionally disturbed. "He told me that Shawn would be getting SSI for the rest of his life," said Ms. Richards, a hotel housekeeper. "I told him that Shawn is not handicapped, that Shawn can work, but the guy said that doesn't matter. He could sit at home and get money and it would be increasing instead of decreasing."
>
> She said she later told the staff worker that they were not interested. "The caseworker said I was making a fool out of myself," she recalled. "But if I take something like that, it means I am telling them that I have a handicapped child."[78]

In other areas, these reports defined important issues but failed to address them thoroughly. For example, two key issues are whether cash benefits or services yield better child outcomes, and whether the amount of SSI benefit should be scaled in proportion to need and severity. Both reports answer "yes" on the first question and "no" to the second. Yet neither report explored the growing literature that in-kind programs produce bigger benefits for children.[79] Nor did either report address the data that perhaps two-thirds of families incur no extra costs for their disabled child on SSI, but perhaps 5 percent of children have enormous expenses.[80] Large costs or none, the SSI cash benefit can be identical.

The point is this: The ambivalence of disability policy identified by Vladeck is clearly evident in the reluctance of policy analysts to fully grapple with many issues.

78. Richardson (1996).
79. Currie (1996).
80. Maxfield and Kendall (1981).

Conclusion

If disability issues seem demanding today, an impending but nearly invisible disability crisis can easily be envisioned. Disability promises to become the number one health care and social welfare issue in the next decade. As a disability expert has stated bluntly, "We [in disability services] continue to plan for yesterday . . . to overcome the deficits of a decade ago."[81] Unfettered thinking and better ideas are needed. Here then lies the challenge for disability policymaking.

References

ACRM, Committee on Social, Ethical, and Environmental Aspects of Rehabilitation. 1993. "Addressing the Post-Rehabilitation Health Care Needs of Persons with Disabilities." *Archives of Physical Medicine and Rehabilitation* 74 (December): 8–14.

Aron, L. Y., P. Loprest, and C. E. Steuerle. 1996. *Serving Children with Disabilities: A Systematic Look at the Programs.* Washington: Urban Institute Press.

Berkowitz, E. D. 1987. *Disabled Policy: America's Programs for the Handicapped: A Twentieth Century Fund Report.* Cambridge University Press.

Board of Trustees, Federal Old-Age and Survivors Insurance and Disability Insurance Trust Funds. 1996. *1996 Annual Report of the Board of Trustees, Federal Old-Age and Survivors Insurance and Disability Insurance Trust Funds.* Washington.

Brown, Randall, and others. 1992. *The Impact of the Medicare Risk Contract Program on the Use of Services and Costs to Medicare.* Mathematica Policy Research (December 3).

Burkhauser, R. V., R. Haveman, and B. Wolfe. 1990. "The Changing Economic Condition of the Disabled: A Two Decade Review of Economic Well-Being." Paper prepared for the Writing National Policy on Work Disability symposium, National Disability Policy Center, Washington, November.

Califano, J. 1981. *Governing America: An Insider's Report from the White House and the Cabinet.* Simon and Schuster.

Cornes, P. 1984. *The Future of Work for People with Disabilities: A View from Great Britain.* New York: World Rehabilitation Fund.

Coughlin, T. A., L. Ku, J. Holahan. 1994. *Medicaid since 1980.* Urban Institute Press.

Currie, J. 1996. "The Effect of Welfare on Child Outcomes: What We Know and What We Need to Know." Paper prepared for a meeting on "The Effect of Welfare on the Family: What Do We Know?" National Academy of Sciences, June (revised).

Disabilities: The Challenge of Writing National Disability Policies." In *The Changing Nature of Work, Society, and Disability: The Impact on Rehabilitation Policy,* edited by D. E. Woods and D. Vandergoot, 19–45. New York: World Rehabilitation Fund.

81. N. Acton quoted in Cornes (1984).

——. 1996. *Findings and Recommendations*. Washington: National Academy of Social Insurance.

Dole, R. 1994. "Disability Future: A 25th Anniversary Statement." Statements on Introduced Bills and Joint Resolutions: National Commission on the Future of Disability Act. *Congressional Record,* April 14, S4334–36.

Fowles, Jinnet, Jonathan Weiner, and David Knudson. 1994. *A Comparison of Alternative Approaches to Risk Measurement*. Physician Payment Review Commission (December).

Fox, D. M. 1989. "Policy and Epidemiology: Financing Health Services for the Chronically Ill and Disabled, 1930–1990." *Milbank Quarterly* 67 (supplement 2, part 2): 257–87.

Goldman, H. H., and A. A. Gattozzi. 1988. "Balance of Powers: Social Security and the Mentally Disabled, 1980–1985." *Milbank Quarterly* 66 (3): 531–51.

Harris, Louis, and Associates, Inc. 1986. *The ICD Survey of Disabled Americans: Bringing Disabled Americans into the Mainstream*. New York.

——. 1994. *N. O. D./Harris Survey of Americans with Disabilities. New York.*

Health Care Financing Administration. 1992. *Medicaid and Institutions for Mental Diseases: Report to Congress*. HCFA Pub. No. 03339.

Hennessey J. C., and L. S. Muller. 1994. "Work Efforts of Disabled Worker Beneficiaries: Preliminary Findings from the New Beneficiary Follow-Up Survey." *Social Security Bulletin* 57 (3): 42–51.

Henry J. Kaiser Foundation. 1995. *Medicare Chart Book*. October.

Jackson, M. E., and others. 1992. "Eligibility for Publicly Financed Home Care." *American Journal of Public Health* 82 (6): 853–56.

Kerrey, J. R., and J. C. Danforth. *Bipartisan Commission on Entitlement and Tax Reform: Final Report*. Government Printing Office.

Lakin, K. C., B. Hill, and R. Bruininks, eds. 1985. *An Analysis of Medicaid's Intermediate Care Facilities for the Mentally Retarded (ICF/MR) Program*. University of Minnesota, Department of Educational Psychology.

Luft, Harold S. 1994. "Potential Methods to Reduce or Eliminate Risk Selection and Its Effects." Paper prepared for the Robert Wood Johnson Foundation Risk Selection in a Reformed Marketplace workshop, Alpha Center, October 6.

Lyon, G. Reid. 1996. "Learning Disabilities." *The Future of Children* 6 (1): 54–76.

Mashaw, J. L., J. M. Perrin, and V. P. Reno, eds. 1996. *Restructuring the SSI Disability Program for Children and Adolescents*. Report of the Committee on Childhood Disability to the Disability Policy Panel. Washington: National Academy of Social Insurance.

Mashaw, J. L., and V. P. Reno, eds. 1996. *Balancing Security and Opportunity: The Challenge of Disability Income Policy*. Final Report of the Disability Policy Panel. Washington: National Academy of Social Insurance.

Matarazzo, J. D. 1972. *Wechsler's Measurement and Appraisal of Adult Intelligence,* 5th ed. Baltimore: Williams and Wilkins Company.

Maxfield, M., and A. Kendall. 1981. *Disabled Children in the Supplemental Security Income Program*. Washington: Social and Scientific Systems, Inc., and Mathematica Policy Research, Inc.

National Commission on Childhood Disability. 1995. *Supplemental Security Income for Children with Disabilities: Report to Congress*. Washington.

Newhouse, Joseph P. 1994. "Patients at Risk: Health Reform and Risk Adjustment." *Health Affairs* (Spring).

Newhouse, Joseph P., and others. 1989. "Adjusted Contribution Rates Using Objective Health Measures and Prior Utilization." *Health Care Financing Review* 10 (3).

———. 1993. "Risk Adjustment for a Children's Capitation Rate." *Health Care Financing Review* (Fall).

Office of Management and Budget. 1996. *Budget of the United States Government, Fiscal Year 1996: Historical Tables*. Government Printing Office,.

Pope, A. M., and A. R. Tarlov. *Disability in America: Toward a National Agenda for Prevention*. Washington: National Academy Press.

Richardson, L. 1996. "Disability Benefits Encourage Poor Families to Keep Children in Special Education." *New York Times (Internet Edition),* April 6.

Robinson, James C. 1993. "A Payment Method for Health Insurance Purchasing Cooperatives." *Health Affairs* (Supplemental).

Robinson, James C., and others. 1991. "A Method for Risk Adjusting Contributions to Competing Health Insurance Plans." *INQUIRY* (Summer).

Satel, S. L. 1995. "When Disability Benefits Make Patients Sicker." *New England Journal of Medicine* 333: 794–96.

Scully, D. C., and others. 1995. *A Guide to Federal Programs for People with Disabilities*. Portland, Maine: National Academy for State Health Policy.

Shaner, A., and others. 1995. "Disabilty Income, Cocaine Use, and Repeated Hospitalization among Schizophrenic Cocaine Abusers." *New England Journal of Medicine* 333: 777–83.

Slesinger, Mark, and David Mechanic. 1993. "Challenges for Managed Competition from Chronic Illness." *Health Affairs* (Supplemental).

Social Security Administration. 1992. *Supplemental Security Income Modernization Project: Final Report of the Experts*. Baltimore.

———. 1988. *Report of the Disability Advisory Council*. Baltimore.

———.1996. "Listing of Impairments." Program Operations Manual System. *Social Security Administration CD-ROM Publications,* January.

Starfield, Barbara, and others. 1991. "Ambulatory Care Groups: A Categorization of Diagnoses for Research and Management." *Health Services Research 26 (1)*.

Starr, P. 1992. *Social Transformation of American Medicine*. Basic Books.

Stone, D. 1984. *The Disabled State*. Temple University Press.

Tannenbaum, S. 1986. *Engineering Disability*. Temple University Press.

Terman, D. L., and others. 1996. "Special Education for Students with Disabilities: Analysis and Recommendations." *The Future of Children* 6: 4–21.

U.S. Court of Appeals for the Third Circuit. 1995. *Opinion of the Court, Helen L., Beverly D., Florence H., Ilene F., Idell A., and American Disabled for Attendant Programs Today ("A.D.A.P.T") v. Karne F. Snider, Secretary, Pennsylvania Department of Public Works.* No. 94-1243, January 31.

U.S. General Accounting Office. 1992. *HCFA Criteria and Standard Forms Could Reduce Medicare Payments.* GAO/HRD-92-64.

——. 1994a. *Report to Congress on Medicare.* September.

——. 1994b. *Social Security: Major Changes Needed for Disability Benefits for Addicts.* GAO/HEHS-94-128.

——. 1995a. *Social Security: Federal Disability Payments Face Major Issues.* GAO/T-HEHS-95-97.

——. 1995b. *Social Security: New Functional Assessments for Children Raise Eligibility Questions.* GAO/HEHS-95-66.

U.S. House of Representatives. 1971. Report 92-231. 92 Con. 1 sess. Government Printing Office.

——. 1989. *The Federal Employees Health Benefits Program: Possible Strategies for Reform.* Prepared by the Congressional Research Service for the Committee on Post Office and Civil Service. Government Printing Office. May 24.

——. 1989. Report 101-391 (Part II). 101 Con. 1 sess. Government Printing Office.

——. 1990. Report 101-485 (Part III): 50. 101 Con. 2 sess. Government Printing Office.

——. 1994. *The Federal Employees Health Benefits Program.* Prepared by the Congressional Research Service for the Committee on Post Office and Civil Service. Government Printing Office. September.

——. 1996. Report 104-725. 104 Con. sess. Government Printing Office.

U.S. Senate. 1989. Report 101-116: 20. 101 Con. 1 sess. Government Printing Office.

——. 1995. Report 104-96. 104 Con. sess. Government Printing Office.

Vachon, R. A. "Inventing a Future for Individuals with Work

——. 1991a. "Has the Federal Government Failed People with Disabilities? The Promise of Vocational Rehabilitation to People with End-Stage Renal Disease." Paper prepared for the 14th Annual Renal Rehabilitation Conference, Department of Rehabilitation Medicine, Emory University.

——. 1991b. "Federal Coordination in the Prevention of Disabilities." Paper prepared for the plenary session of the National Conference on Prevention of Primary and Secondary Disabilities. National Council on Disability, the Centers for Disease Control and Prevention, and the Minority Health Professions Foundation, Atlanta, June.

West, J., ed. 1991. *The Americans with Disabilities Act: From Policy to Practice.* New York: Milbank Memorial Fund.

5

Workers' Compensation, Twenty-Four-Hour Coverage, and Managed Care

John F. Burton Jr.

THE GROWTH OF WORKERS' compensation costs has slowed in the 1990s to less than 3 percent a year, which is well below the rapid pace of cost increases in the 1984–90 period, when the annual rate of increase averaged more than 13 percent a year. While this deceleration in costs is a welcome development that has reduced much of the strain on the workers' compensation system, one factor of concern to many observers has continued into the 1990s, namely the tendency for medical benefits to grow more rapidly than cash benefits. This disparate growth of medical costs has led to efforts to control medical costs by various measures, including consolidating medical benefit delivery through twenty-four-hour coverage and introducing managed care into the system.[1]

Reasons for Recent Interest in Managed Care and Twenty-Four-Hour Coverage

The recent surge in interest in managed care and twenty-four-hour coverage in workers' compensation is driven by the growth in costs generally and the growth in medical costs in particular. Workers' compensation costs to employers have increased to $57.3 billion nationally in 1993, up from $2.1 billion in 1960.[2] The primary source of the higher costs to employers is the increasing benefits, both medical/hospitalization and cash, paid to injured workers. In each of the five subperiods spanning 1965 to 1990, medical benefits increased

---

1. This presentation is based in part on Burton (1996), which includes additional references. A more extended examination of medical benefits provided by the workers' compensation program is provided by Burton and Schmidle (1995). The Burton and Schmidle article in turn is largely based on *Twenty-Four-Hour Coverage: The Significance for the Workers' Compensation Program,* a report Schmidle and I are preparing for the Zenith Insurance Company.

2. Most of the data and discussion in this section are from Burton (1995a).

at least 10 percent a year.[3] And, except for the 1960–65 and 1971–79 sub-periods, medical benefits have increased more rapidly than cash benefits.

Medical benefits increased at a faster rate during 1984–90 than in any other subperiod since 1960, which helps explain the rapid annual rate of growth (13.3 percent) of employers' costs of the program during this period. And even though the annual increase in medical benefits was smaller in 1990–93 than that over the preceding three decades, the rate still exceeded the increase in cash benefits for those years. As a result, in 1993, medical benefits accounted for 41.9 percent of all workers' compensation benefits—the highest percentage for any year since 1960 (and probably for any year in the history of workers' compensation in the United States).

Workers' compensation medical care expenditures are not only increasing more rapidly than cash benefits, but until recently they were also rising faster than medical expenditures in the U.S. general health care system. The only good news—at least from the standpoint of workers' compensation—is that, between 1990 and 1993, workers' compensation health care expenditures grew more slowly than in the general health care system (4.9 percent compared with 8.3 percent).

Managed Care in Workers' Compensation

Since about 1990, concern was evident that the rapidly escalating medical costs in the workers' compensation program resulted, in part, from cost-shifting from the rest of the health care system as the rest of the health care system moved rapidly into managed care. Consequently, many states have recently introduced managed care into the workers' compensation system, either directly by the state or through statutes or regulations applicable to the private sector.

Cost containment mechanisms have been used to control the growth in medical care costs, such as medical fee schedules, utilization review, hospital prospective payment systems, limits on employees' choice of treating physician, and introduction of cost sharing by covered employees.

Strategies that Directly Regulate Prices

A medical fee schedule specifies maximum reimbursement rates for services supplied by hospitals, physicians, and other health care providers. The

---

3. The subperiods are 1960–65; 1965–69; 1969–71; 1971–79; 1979–84; and 1984–90. In the first, third, and fifth of these subperiods, the annual rate of increase in workers' compensation costs was less than 10 percent a year; in the other subperiods, costs increased by more than 10 percent a year.

most recent review conducted by the Workers Compensation Research Institute (WCRI) indicated that medical fee schedules were in effect in forty states as of early 1995.[4] Many such schedules have been adopted recently, with the number having increased from twenty-seven jurisdictions in 1991.

Fee schedules vary on several dimensions, including the scope of services covered; the basis of the fee schedule (actual dollar amounts or a relative value scale with dollar conversion factors); the factors used in creating the fee schedule (for example, workers' compensation or other payers' charge data; payment data from only the promulgating state or also from other states); who promulgates and enforces the schedule; the frequency with which the schedule is reviewed and revised; and the dispute resolution procedure for disagreements over charges (for example, mediation, arbitration, administrative review, hearings).[5]

Relative value scales are used in most jurisdictions with medical fee schedules. According to the WCRI survey data, twenty-eight states rely on the relative value system. Schedules with relative values specify an index number (instead of a dollar amount) for each medical procedure; the index number (unit value) reflects the relative value of the procedure. Fee levels are determined by multiplying unit values by a dollar value conversion factor.

Considerable interstate variation exists in fees. A WCRI summary of schedule fees for ten common workers' compensation procedures as of February 1994 revealed that the ratio of highest to lowest fee ranged from 2.63 (for an office visit, established patient, brief exam) to 4.87 (for a CAT scan, lumbar without contrast); the ratio was more than 2.75 for nine of the ten procedures.[6] These differences are not attributable to interstate differences in health care providers' costs (as proxied by state average weekly wages)—even though providers' charges and Medicare rates are highly correlated with wages—according to a WCRI analysis of fee schedules in effect as of January 1, 1992.[7]

Fee schedules are viewed as a vehicle for restricting health care providers' fees and making allowable charges more consistent. As reported by Stacey M. Eccleston, fee schedule advocates assert that "unregulated charge-based reimbursement systems are inherently inflationary" and that "fee schedules explic-

4. Eccleston (1995, p. 27).

5. The WCRI survey results indicated that, as of January 1995, "[m]edical, surgical, radiological, chiropractic, and physical and occupational therapy fees were covered in all states reporting, with the vast majority of schedules covering anesthesiology and pathology. About one-half of the states cover medical equipment and dental services. Coverage for prescriptions, home health care, and vocational rehabilitation are less common, varying between 43 percent and 28 percent of states surveyed." Eccleston (1995, p. 29).

6. Eccleston (1995, p. 37).

7. Eccleston, Grannemann, and Dunleavy (1993).

itly define the acceptable charge and minimize costly litigation over the issue."[8] John H. Lewis, however, cautions that:

there is also considerable suspicion that fee schedules which are low enough to have a substantial impact on system costs may drive quality providers out of the system, make access to quality care more difficult, and increase the proportion of providers who are willing to manipulate the system for their own financial well-being by increasing the number of services rendered, providing a greater number of higher cost services, and in general playing games with the fee schedule. Finally, there is always the possibility that the maximum fees established in a schedule are so high in relationship to usual and customary charges that they have virtually no cost-reduction potential. They may even increase costs when those who would normally charge less begin to increase their fees to the maximum permissible level.[9]

Despite the widespread use of medical fee schedules and divergent views about them in workers' compensation, relatively few studies have been conducted of the impact of these schedules.

An evaluation by the California Workers' Compensation Institute of the influence of the workers' compensation fee schedule in that state concluded that the schedule did "not effectively control medical provider costs in California's workers' compensation system." That study used 1990 and 1991 data from thirty-one workers' compensation insurers who accounted for 71 percent of the state's direct written premium.[10]

Recent research by William G. Johnson and others suggests that the California workers' compensation fee schedule may affect unit prices but not utilization.[11] Their analysis compared workers' compensation data provided by the Zenith Insurance Company on 36,134 workers with general health insurance data provided by Calfarm Life Insurance Company on 3,595 patients. The authors found that for three injury groups (back injuries; sprains, strains, and dislocations; inflammations, lacerations, and contusions), average unit charges for California health insurance cases exceeded the average unit charges for the California workers' compensation cases.[12] However, the average total charges

8. Eccleston (1995, p. 27).
9. Lewis (1992, pp. 106–07).
10. California Workers' Compensation Institute (1992, p. 1).
11. Johnson and others (1994).
12. The fourth injury group (fractures) was an exception; average unit charges for workers' compensation were greater than the average unit charges for health insurance.

for treating workers' compensation injuries in California were four times greater than the average total charges for treating comparable, non-work-related injuries. The authors observed:

> If fees per unit of service are fixed and the coverage of services is comprehensive, providers who seek to maximize their income have few alternatives other than to increase the quantity of services provided. In other words, overutilization becomes the strategy of choice in California [workers' compensation] because the fee schedule limits opportunities for price discrimination.[13]

Leslie I. Boden and Charles A. Fleischman found a low correlation between use of a fee schedule and annual growth in medical costs.[14] They computed the average annual growth rate in workers' compensation medical costs (1965–85) for forty-one states, twelve of which had a fee schedule in effect for at least fifteen years during this period and were thus deemed fee schedule states. Though the two jurisdictions with the slowest increase in workers' compensation medical costs (Massachusetts and New York) used fee schedules, the correlation was nonetheless very low (–0.08) between the presence of a fee schedule in a state and the annual average growth rate in workers' compensation medical costs.

David Durbin and David Appel specified several multivariate statistical models that assessed the effect of fee schedules; they used workers' compensation medical costs data from thirty-three states for the period 1964–84 and took into consideration a variety of other factors that may influence costs.[15] The fee schedule variable was statistically significant and (depending upon the model specification) reduced medical costs between 3.5 and 5.4 percent.

In another empirical analysis of the effect of medical fee schedules in workers' compensation, Silvana Pozzebon used information from more than 350,000 claims in the National Council on Compensation Insurance's Detailed Claim Information survey pertaining to workers who were injured between 1979 and 1987.[16] The data were from seventeen states, of which seven used fee schedules for all or some of this nine-year period. Pozzebon found that states with fee schedules had workers' compensation health care expenditures that were 3.8 percent lower, on average, than states that did not use this cost

13. Johnson and others (1994, p. 35).
14. Boden and Fleischman (1989).
15. Durbin and Appel (1991).
16. Pozzebon (1993).

containment policy. However, the effect varied from year to year, and average growth rates in medical expenses were not much higher in states without fee schedules (6.32 percent versus 5.64 percent in jurisdictions with fee schedules). The evidence from the most sophisticated statistical (or econometric) analyses concerning the effect of fee schedules on medical costs was inconclusive. Considering all the evidence, Pozzebon concluded that "the effect of fee schedules on moderating the rate of increase in medical prices is modest at best."[17]

Strategies that Directly Limit Utilization

Utilization review programs, according to Helen Halpin Schauffler and Tracy Rodriguez, "attempt to reduce unnecessary care and to educate patients and providers about appropriate care by establishing standards for care; scrutinizing the past, current, or intended provision of care; . . . and sometimes denying payment for care that does not meet established standards. In most utilization review programs, unnecessary or inappropriate care refers to care that has no clinical benefit or [that] could be provided in a lower-cost setting."[18] Utilization review can be provided prospectively, concurrently, or retrospectively, with varying effects.

States' workers' compensation laws may authorize, encourage, mandate, or prohibit utilization review. According to 1995 WCRI survey data, in thirty-three jurisdictions, workers' compensation statutes mandate some form of utilization review or management.[19] Prospective utilization (preauthorization) is prohibited by the Wisconsin statute, however.

Though numerous studies are available of the impact of utilization review in the general U.S. health care system, none includes an evaluation of utilization review programs in workers' compensation.

Hospital Prospective Payment Systems

Pozzebon also evaluated the effectiveness of another cost containment policy in workers' compensation: regulation of hospital expenditures. In three of the five states in her data set with such a policy, the mandatory hospital rate regulation systems applied to all payers, not just to payers in the workers'

17. Pozzebon (1993, p. 20).
18. Schauffler and Rodriguez (1993, p. 167).
19. Eccleston (1995, p. 75).

compensation system. Both simple averages and the statistical modeling found that states that regulate hospital expenditures had lower medical costs.

Her econometric analysis indicated that states with hospital rate regulation had costs that were 16 to 22 percent lower than states with no hospital rate regulation, after other factors affecting medical costs were considered. Pozzebon observed that the "fact that the policy applies to all payers in three of the five states that control hospital costs may also be a relevant consideration. It suggests that the success of a cost containment policy may lie in its universal application."[20]

The diagnostic-related group (DRG) system, which is used in the Medicare program, classifies a patient's condition into a specific diagnostic-related group for which the provider receives a preset, fixed reimbursement, irrespective of the actual expenditures incurred in the patient's treatment. A useful description is provided by Michael D. Reagan:

> The DRG system applies a fixed payment to the inpatient's diagnosed condition that corresponds to one of about 480 treatments and procedures. For example, DRG 79 is for respiratory infections, 103 is for a heart transplant, 134 is for hypertension, and 410 covers chemotherapy. The radical difference [from the fee-for-service approach] is that the payment is fixed by the diagnostic category rather than by how much time the patient spends in the hospital or which specific services or supplies are involved in an individual case. In other words, Medicare no longer pays on the retrospective basis of the detailed bill submitted by the hospital. Instead, it pays a prospectively set fee—one known in advance of the treatment—based on an analysis of typical hospitalization costs (especially average length of stay) involved in a particular diagnosis. (DRGs do not include physician's charges.)[21]

The WCRI survey indicated that workers' compensation programs in three states used DRGs in regulating inpatient hospital payments as of January 1995. Eccleston notes that a "DRG system is difficult to carry out in workers' compensation because only about twenty DRGs used by other payers are common in workers' compensation."[22] A Minnesota Department of Labor and Industry report offered the following observations of the applicability of DRGs to workers' compensation:

20. Pozzebon (1993, p. 21).
21. Reagan (1992, p. 24).
22. Eccleston (1995).

The limited use of the DRG system in workers' compensation systems suggests several conclusions. First, the development of a DRG system based solely on experience within a state's workers' compensation system is probably only feasible in a state with an exclusive state fund. . . .

Second, the New York experience indicates that a DRG system that applies to all payers in a state can be adapted to the workers' compensation system. . . . Third, . . . [t]he Medicare DRG system could be adapted for use in the workers' compensation system. However, the Medicare case load may differ from workers' compensation patients in terms of demographics or other factors that would influence the expected durations of hospitalization. As a consequence, the adaptation of the Medicare DRG system to workers' compensation may require extensive adjustments. Fourth, . . . there is little evidence concerning the effectiveness of the approach in containing hospital costs.[23]

Strategies that Limit Employee Choice of Providers

Insurers and employers assert that, absent restrictions on the employees' choice, injured workers may overutilize medical services or select physicians who prescribe excessive diagnoses and treatments.[24] Organized labor argues, however, that such restrictions have an adverse impact on the injured worker.[25]

Limits on the employee's choice of the treating physician may take a variety of forms, depending upon whether the employee's initial choice is limited to choosing within a managed care organization if one exists, or from a list of providers specified by a workers' compensation insurer or an employer; the employees' decision to switch providers is constrained (by requirements with respect to the possibility or frequency of such changes, and the need for approval from an employer, insurer, or workers' compensation agency for changes); the insurer or employer makes the initial choice of treating physician; and the employer or insurer can change providers without restriction.[26]

23. Minnesota Department of Labor and Industry (1990, pp. 77–78).

24. Eccleston (1995, p. 43).

25. Ellenberger (1992, p. 250–51) has stated the labor position effectively: "Unions have always been strong advocates for employee choice of physician in workers' compensation. Years of experience with company-dictated terms of employment and company doctors have underscored the difficulty of obtaining a good, independent, and objective medical opinion from a physician whose livelihood and support are dependent on the employer. . . . The issue of who chooses the treating physician is not, despite arguments to the contrary, an issue over the quality of medical care or even the cost of that medical care. It is purely and simply an argument over control. And control does indeed have an impact on costs, particularly when questions of the work-relatedness of the injury or illness or the extent of permanent impairment must be resolved."

26. Eccleston (1995, p. 44).

The WCRI survey indicated that, as of January 1995, workers' compensation programs in fourteen states gave employees an unrestricted initial choice of the treating provider. Four jurisdictions required employees to select from an insurer's or employer's list of providers, and thirteen required the employee to choose from within a managed care organization if one exists. Four states placed no restrictions on the employee's decision to change providers. The WCRI also noted that, in some jurisdictions that restrict the employee's choice of treating provider, an employer or insurer may nonetheless be required to pay for unauthorized care. The study concluded that:

the variation in administrative requirements [regarding choice of provider] reflects the conflict between the statutory requirement to provide all 'reasonably necessary treatment' and statutory provisions to limit the utilization of medical care. This underscores the inherent difficulty of containing costs by restricting utilization within the workers' compensation environment.[27]

Only a few empirical studies have investigated the cost-effectiveness of limiting the employees choice of physician. And the findings are inconsistent among studies.

Boden and Fleischman concluded that the employee choice of physician approach had no discernable effect on workers' compensation medical costs.[28] In contrast, two other studies found that limiting the employee's choice decreased medical costs in workers' compensation.[29] All these studies used state-level aggregated data, not data on individual claims.

The Pozzebon study, which used information on individual workers' compensation claims, included six states out of seventeen in the data set that limited the employee's initial choice of physician and eleven states that limited the employee's ability to change the treating physician. Both simple averages and the statistical modeling revealed that limits on the employee's choice of physician were associated with increased medical costs. The more sophisticated (statistical) analysis found that workers' compensation health benefit payments were 5 to 15 percent higher in states limiting initial choice of provider than they were in jurisdictions that do not impose such limits. Likewise, health care costs were 7 to 15 percent higher in states that restricted the employee's ability to change the treating provider.

27. Eccleston (1995, p. 53).
28. Boden and Fleischman (1989, p. 33).
29. Victor and Fleischman (1990); and Durbin and Appel (1991).

Strategies that Involve Cost-Sharing by Employees

Cost-sharing requires medical care beneficiaries to pay some of their medical costs out-of-pocket through the use of one or more of the following mechanisms: premium contributions by employees; coinsurance, whereby patients pay a percentage of the medical charges or a fixed fee each time they use certain medical services; and deductibles, in which patients pay 100 percent of the first portion of their medical costs up to a specified maximum. Cost-sharing is practically nonexistent in workers' compensation and is frequently prohibited by states workers' compensation laws.[30]

In principle, cost-sharing, such as the use of deductibles and coinsurance for patients, could be introduced into the workers' compensation program without involving the rest of the health care system. However, organized labor asserts that such cost-sharing devices are a serious violation of the fundamental principles of workers' compensation.[31] The only feasible way to make such devices politically acceptable may be to imbed them in a more general reform of the entire health care system, such as a national health insurance plan.

New Approaches for Workers' Compensation Cost Containment

In several states, workers' compensation programs have begun to use some of the cost containment approaches that have been widely used in the general health care system, including health maintenance organizations (HMOs) and preferred provider organizations (PPOs). Recent publications by the National Council on Compensation Insurance, as well as other articles, report on statutory and regulatory changes regarding workers' compensation managed care. While intensive activity was evident in this area throughout the early 1990s, little legislative activity occurred in 1995.[32] To date, little published research has evaluated the effectiveness of this wave of managed health care in workers' compensation.

One exception is the research on two managed care pilot projects authorized by 1990 workers' compensation legislation in Florida.[33] One project involved seventeen thousand state employees, half of whom had workers' compensation medical care provided under the traditional fee-for-service arrangement and

30. A national survey conducted for the Minnesota Department of Labor and Industry identified only one instance of cost-sharing. Washington state requires workers to pay part of the workers' compensation premium attributed to health care. Minnesota Department of Labor and Industry (1990, p. 80). See also, Eccleston (1995, p. 11).

31. Ellenberger (1990).

32. National Council on Compensation Insurance (1995); and Hughes (1995).

33. Borba, Appel, and Fung (1994).

half of whom had workers' compensation medical care provided by an HMO. The research findings indicated that, after taking into account the administrative fees for managed care, total direct claims costs for those covered by the HMO were, on average, 54 percent lower than were costs under the fee-for-service arrangement.

The second Florida pilot project involved seventy-five hundred private sector employees who received their workers' compensation medical care through a PPO network. The research findings revealed that, after taking into account the administrative fees for managed care as well as geographic factors, total direct claims costs for those covered by the PPO were, on average, 23 percent lower than were costs for the control (comparison) groups.

Overall Assessment of the Cost Containment Strategies

Efforts to control health care costs within the workers' compensation program have not been generally successful, as demonstrated by the generally higher growth rate of medical expenditures in workers' compensation than in the general health care system. The few research studies of traditional cost containments devices, such as fee schedules and limits on employee choice of physician, provide little support for the effectiveness of these approaches.

Perhaps the new approaches to cost containment in workers' compensation will be successful, although the favorable evidence from Florida's managed care pilot projects is the only rigorous study I have seen. In any case, the magnitude of the health care cost problem in workers' compensation, as well as a concern that cost containment solutions internal to the workers' compensation program may be ineffectual, has prompted a consideration of reforms involving both workers' compensation and other components of the health care system.

Twenty-four-hour coverage is one example of more inclusive reform and has been viewed by some as a possible way to limit the costs of medical care in the workers' compensation program. The possible advantages to workers' compensation from an integration of medical benefits include lower administrative costs resulting from a single delivery system; less opportunity for cost-shifting into (or even out of) the workers' compensation health care system; and better management of care if, for example, the same HMO provides medical benefits for both the work-related and non-work-related disabilities of workers covered by the plan. Before examining the recent developments in twenty-four-hour coverage, a clarification of what the concept entails is necessary.

The Components of the Disabled Workers' Benefits and Services System

A variety of benefits or services are available to disabled workers because of their status as employees. Some of these benefits and services are provided only if the injury or disease that causes the disability is work-related (see table 5-1). These benefits and services are contained in three main categories: medical benefits, including medical rehabilitation; income benefits; and disability management services, including an array of efforts designed to reduce the duration or extent of disability.

A number of benefits and services also are available to disabled workers because of their status as employees, which are provided if the injury or disease that causes the disability is not work-related or are available to disabled workers regardless of the origin of their injury or disease.[34] Some benefits or services, such as long-term disability (LTD) plans, appear in both the "work-related" and "other" columns because many employers have LTD plans that apply to all disabilities resulting from any source. Other benefits, such as group health plans, appear only in the "other" column of table 5-1 because typically workers are precluded from using these plans for treatment of work-related injuries or diseases.

The Definition of Twenty-Four-Hour Coverage

Twenty-four-hour coverage describes various efforts to reduce or eliminate the distinctions between benefits and services provided to disabled workers for work-related injuries and diseases, and benefits and services provided for non-work-related conditions. Twenty-four-hour coverage can involve standardization of the amount, quality, and price of the benefits or services provided for work-related and non-work-related disabilities. Twenty-four-hour coverage can also involve integration or coordination of the procedures used to provide benefits or services for work-related and non-work-related disabilities.[35]

34. Excluded from this discussion are programs available to workers regardless of their employment status, because these programs are available to all disabled persons. One example is the Supplemental Security Income program, which provides cash benefits to low-income disabled persons whether or not they have a prior work history.

35. Bateman (1995) offered this alternative definition of twenty-four-hour coverage: "As used most frequently today, the term refers to delivering workers' compensation and group health benefits through the same managed care networks, although the benefits remain different and the care may be delivered by a different set of providers."

Factors Influencing Recent Twenty-Four-Hour Coverage Developments

During 1993–94, considerable attention was focused on efforts to reform health care at the national level. The Clinton administration health care plan proposed a partial or total integration of the health care benefits for work-related disabilities into a general health care system. The motivation was in part a belief that savings could result from the integration that could be used to help finance the general health care system.

To counter the Clinton proposal, the insurance industry and employers argued that the medical benefits and cash benefits of the workers' compensation program were interrelated. If carriers lost the ability to use case management for the medical component of workers' compensation, the resulting increased expenditures on cash benefits that would more than offset any savings in medical benefits. Whatever the merits of this argument, it has shaped the discussion of twenty-four-hour coverage so that efforts to establish a separate health care system not intertwined with the cash benefits and disability management services for work-related disabilities would be suspect.

Efforts by states to integrate medical benefits for work-related and non-work-related disabilities have also been influenced by the perception—or reality—that the Employee Retirement Income Security Act of 1974 (ERISA) would preempt any state law that required employers to establish twenty-four-hour coverage plans.

The Four Primary Variants of Twenty-Four-Hour Coverage

Numerous variants of twenty-four-hour coverage have emerged in recent decades. No state or country has adopted a universal disability program (UDP), which totally eliminates the distinction between work-related and non-work-related sources of disability. The closest example is the New Zealand system, which provides benefits for injuries from all sources but only encompasses work-related diseases. Significant integration of benefits for work-related and non-work-related disabilities has also occurred in the Netherlands. Each of these examples has its critics, and the adoption of a UDP in any U.S. jurisdiction seems unlikely. In any case, the definition of twenty-four-hour coverage should not be confined to a UDP because a restrictive definition would exclude many important developments in the United States that meet the inclusive definition of twenty-four-hour coverage.

Four variants of twenty-four-hour coverage have emerged in recent years in the United States. They can be arrayed by the increasing complexity of the

Table 5-1. Voluntary and Mandatory Employment-Based Disability Benefits and Services for Injuries and Disabilities

Type of benefits or services	Definition	Source of benefits	
		Work-related illness or disability	*Other illness or disability*
		Medical benefit	
Medical	Medical care including rehabilitation	Workers' compensation	Group health plans
		Cash benefits	
Income	Cash benefits (or monetary awards) for lost wages and noneconomic losses; temporary and permanent periods of disability; and partial and total disability	Workers' compensation is primary source for replacement of lost wages; may be supplemented by other cash benefits (such as LTD benefits). Workers' compensation may be replaced at least in part by tort suits against third parties or (rarely) against the employer	Short-term: sick leave from employer; TDI benefits, which are mandatory in 5 states, voluntary in others
		Disability management services	
Prevention	Efforts to reduce number and severity of injuries and diseases	OSHA regulations and enforcement activities; workers' compensation experience rating; loss prevention activities by employers and carriers	Wellness plans voluntarily set up by employers

Managed medical care	Includes organizations that "seek to reduce costs by eliminating unnecessary services and ensuring the delivery of care in the most effective way . . . to prevent health problems that can be caused by excessive uncoordinated utilization of medication and radiology and other medical services," and to shorten the healing period so the worker can return to employment as soon as feasible[a]	HMOs, PPOs, utilization review, and so on under workers' compensation	HMOs, PPOs, and so on under group health plans
Vocational rehabilitation and return to work	Light duty or modified duty assignments and reasonable accommodation adjustments required by the Americans with Disabilities Act	Employers, workers' compensation carriers	Employers, LTD insurers
Case management	Efforts to direct medical care, vocational rehabilitation, and return-to-work programs to reduce duration or extent of disability	Employers, workers' compensation carriers, third-party administrators, or state agencies	Employers or insurers

Note: DI = Social Security disability insurance; HMO = health maintenance organization; LTD = long-term disability; OSHA = Occupational Safety and Health Administration; PPO = preferred provider organization; TDI = temporary disability insurance.

a. Eccleston (1995).

legal and regulatory environment in which they must operate. In general, the legal and regulatory issues that are applicable to the variants of twenty-four-hour coverage I discuss first also apply to the later variants.

Type A: Integration within Self-Insuring Employers

Typically, large self-insuring employers disperse responsibility among several departments for the various components of the disabled workers' benefits and services system. For example, administration of the sick leave plan might be with the employee benefits department, workers' compensation with the legal department or with the human resource management plant staff, and state short-term disability plans by whatever department has responsibility for unemployment insurance benefits. Coordination among these departments typically is limited, and disability policies often are inconsistent. Different definitions of disability are likely to be found in the sick leave plan, the workers' compensation program, the LTD plan, and the disability retirement option in the pension plan.

Increasingly, self-insuring employers recognize the value of coordinating administration of disability benefits. Sharon Kaleta described the experience at her former employer in establishing a disability management program whose mission was "to reduce the financial costs associated with all disabilities, while fostering an open, honest, non-adversarial environment of claims administration through the development of a coordinated disability management program with a focus on ability rather than disability."[36] The process included identifying the strategic targets, which included the medical/dental program, workers' compensation, life insurance, sick leave, the state short-term disability program, the employer's own short-term disability plan, the LTD plan, and the pension or retirement plan.[37] The process also involved all the principal parties, which included external organizations such as the workers' compensation carrier, the health care provider, third-party administrators, the life insurance carrier, the disability insurers, the managed care providers, and the union, as well as internal units, such as human resources, finance, risk management, safety, and operations.

The company established a team that was asked to establish a disability management program. The team helped develop a partnership among the internal and external parties that established a computer interface to share data, a coordinated approach to vocational rehabilitation regardless of the source of

36. Roberts (1995).
37. These state-mandated, short-term disability plans are found in five states.

the disability, a standardized medical exam for all disability programs, identical expiration dates for policies, and standardized protocols for medical treatment. The results, according to Kaleta, were not only reduced costs and greater administrative efficiency, but also improved employee morale.

No significant legal or regulatory limitations were placed on reorganizations that involve coordination of efforts or consolidation of responsibility within firms. Self-insuring firms nonetheless must adhere to procedures and benefits required by state workers' compensation laws; that is, the firms can neither unilaterally change the cash or medical benefits provided to workers as a result of work-related injuries or diseases, nor unilaterally abrogate the statutory procedures used to provide the benefits. Several recent developments should facilitate the coordination of workers' compensation benefits and benefits from other programs, however.

—As a result of statutory amendments in several states, unionized firms can negotiate procedures and standards that replace, but not diminish, the normal workers' compensation benefits and dispute resolution procedures.[38]

—Increasingly, states are authorizing employers to select the treating physician for workers' compensation cases. This will allow employers to establish HMOs or other networks of health care providers to which workers can be directed for both work-related and non-work-related disabilities.[39] The employees cannot be required to pay for that part of their medical care resulting from work-related injuries and diseases, but advantages arguably still exist in having the same health care providers treat all the medical problems of a worker.

A legal obstacle to establishing of managed care for both work-related and non-work-related disabilities is the "any willing provider" provision in some state laws. These laws require managed care networks to accept all health care providers who indicate their willingness to abide by the managed care rates and rules. These laws are being supported by some health care providers and are generally resisted by managed care organizations.

Type B: Integration of Benefits and Services in Insurance Policies

Insurance carriers, teams of carriers, and health care providers may offer insurance arrangements or plans that combine cash benefits for work-related disabilities (that is, workers' compensation benefits) with medical benefits and disability management services for both work-related and non-work-related disabilities. Because of state laws or regulations, separate policies for the

38. Lewis (1995).
39. Hughes (1995).

individual insurance lines are still required, although the goal is to have the employer view the plan as a single policy.

Some individual carriers have the capability to offer such plans because they offer both workers' compensation and group health care benefits. Other carriers had to develop the capability to offer twenty-four-hour coverage policies. For example, Blue Cross of California created Wellpoint (a for-profit subsidiary for group health care) and purchased Unicare (a workers' compensation company) to offer a twenty-four-hour coverage product in California. It has announced plans to move toward a similar strategy nationwide.

Another approach to offering a twenty-four-hour coverage product involves cooperative arrangements among independent companies. In California, Pacificare, a health care provider, has formed an alliance with Liberty Mutual, a workers' compensation insurer, to offer such a product.

While most of the twenty-four-hour coverage products have involved cash benefits for work-related disabilities, medical care for all sources of disabilities, and disability management services, at least one alliance has added LTD to the product. SinglePoint is an alliance among UNUM (an LTD carrier), Zenith (a workers' compensation carrier), and Sharp (a health care provider) that is offering their variant of a twenty-four-hour coverage policies in the San Diego area.

Because the separate lines of insurance are maintained (at least below the surface of the plan offered to the employer), dual licensure for workers' compensation and health care is probably required in most states. However, the states can make the integration of the work-related and non-work-related medical care much easier by allowing the employer to control the initial choice of physician.

Type C: Integration of Benefits and Services by Expanding Workers' Compensation

Several states have enacted laws authorizing various types of twenty-four-hour coverage by using workers' compensation benefits as the nucleus of the plan and then adding medical or cash benefits. Most of this legislation involves pilot programs. Florida, which was the first state to authorize twenty-four-hour coverage in 1990, initially allowed all employers to establish twenty-four-hour coverage plans for medical care. The employer was authorized to use deductibles and coinsurance for all medical care, including benefits for work-related disabilities. However, the employer was required to pay the entire premium for the twenty-four-hour coverage plan, including the portion of the premium for the non-work-related medical care. The Florida plan was subsequently amended to allow pilot programs that would include cash benefits that were less than the normal workers' compensation benefits but that would be identical for work-related and non-work-related disabilities. These latter pilots have not yet been established in Florida but apparently soon will be.

Nine state laws now authorize twenty-four-hour coverage pilots.[40] The general characteristics of the laws are as follows:

—They all authorize pilots that require prior approval by a state agency, instead of allowing any interested employer or carrier to establish a twenty-four-hour coverage plan.

—Most are for limited duration and require reports on cost savings and other outcomes.

—Most prohibit the use of coinsurance and deductibles for medical care, although several states authorize at least nominal payments by workers.

—The primary focus is on medical benefits, but several states permit or encourage twenty-four-hour coverage plans involving cash benefits.

The major obstacle to the enactment of state laws that mandate integration of benefits and services is ERISA.[41] It preempts most state regulation of employee benefit plans, such as group health insurance, as well as indirect regulation of these plans under the guise of regulating the workers' compensation program. Thus, a state could not expand the medical benefits portion of a workers' compensation statute to require employers to provide medical benefits for non-work-related injuries or diseases. To avoid the ERISA preemption threat, the state laws establishing pilots have made the programs voluntary and often require the participating employers to waive any right to challenge the plans under ERISA.

Some have argued that twenty-four-hour coverage plans that reduce preexisting workers' compensation benefits, such as plans that allow the use of deductibles and coinsurance for medical benefits, may represent a threat to the exclusive remedy feature of workers' compensation. Under the exclusive remedy concept, employer-financed workers' compensation benefits are provided to injured workers without requiring a finding that the employer was at fault. In exchange, workers accept the workers' compensation benefits as the exclusive remedy for the work-related injury. They forgo any tort remedy against employers. The argument asserts that, because deductibles and coinsurance reduce benefits, the employer may lose its immunity to tort suits. However, the

40. Additional information on the nine state laws that authorize twenty-four-hour coverage pilots is included in tables 3.1 to 3.9 of Burton (1995b).

41. ERISA sets federal standards for employer-provided pension plans and welfare plans. Welfare plans include health insurance, disability insurance, prepaid legal services, and most other types of benefits provided by employers. States are permitted under ERISA to regulate workers' compensation programs but may not regulate other programs encompassed by ERISA.

argument would seem to have little merit, given that the cash benefits in workers' compensation already contain a deductible, in the form of a waiting period, and also use coinsurance, in the form of a benefit formula that typically only replaces two-thirds of the worker's lost wages. Regardless of the merits of the argument, some states have dealt directly with this issue by including in the statute a provision that the twenty-four-hour coverage pilot does not denigrate the exclusive remedy provision.

A series of legal issues arises because of the different eligibility rules and underwriting obligations for workers' compensation and group health benefits. For example, what happens if a worker has a preexisting condition that is excluded from coverage in the group health plan but that is aggravated by a work injury? Presumably, the medical benefits will be paid, but at a minimum the origin of the injury will have to be determined, perhaps in litigation.

Type D: Integration of Benefits and Services through General Health Care Reform

A final variant of twenty-four-hour coverage that has received much discussion and some action involves the integration of benefits and services for work-related and non-work-related injuries and diseases by starting with general health care reform and expanding the scope of the reform to include the medical benefits traditionally offered by the workers' compensation program. The difference between this variant of twenty-four-hour coverage and the integration of benefits and services by expanding workers' compensation is that the type C of twenty-four-hour coverage begins with workers' compensation and expands outward, while the type D variant is motivated by general health care reform for which workers' compensation becomes a possible target for inclusion.

The Clinton health care reform proposal is an example of this approach. The appropriate outcome for health care benefits for work-related injuries was widely debated during consideration of the Clinton health care reform proposal. The issues are now largely moot. Meanwhile, several states—including Washington, Minnesota, and Kentucky—have proposed or enacted general health care that would at least encourage integration of medical benefits for work-related and non-work-related disabilities.

The legal issues for this variant of twenty-four-hour coverage include the limitations on state action because of the ERISA preemption threat and the possible threat to the exclusive remedy principle if workers are required to pay for a portion of their medical care for work-related injuries through the imposition of deductibles and coinsurance.

Conclusion

Workers' compensation is in a period of great experimentation, with a rapid onset of managed medical care in most states. Twenty-four-hour coverage has also spread rapidly, primarily in terms of the first two types of integration that depend on voluntary action, by employers or insurers, not state mandates. Because they are voluntary, they have not been significantly deterred by the threat of ERISA preemption.

Distinguishing among the four types of twenty-four-hour coverage is important. Not only are different legal issues involved (such as the ERISA preemption possibility), but the chance of adopting the four types of integration also varies among companies by size. Only a large self-insuring firm is likely to benefit from the types A, C, or D integration, while potentially almost any size employer could purchase an insurance policy utilizing the type B approach to twenty-four-hour coverage.

The primary focus so far has been on the integration of medical benefits for non-work-related injuries and diseases with workers' compensation medical benefits. Not much interest has been expressed in developing identical cash benefits for work-related and non-work-related disabilities, in part because of a fear of the cost and litigation consequences of introducing permanent partial disability benefits for non-work-related disabilities.[42]

Careful studies of the effect of twenty-four-hour coverage are needed, including the impact on the costs of medical and cash benefits, as well as on the quality of the medical care provided to workers. I am concerned about the lack of careful examination of the consequences of managed care in workers' compensation. Insufficient evidence is available to warrant all the effort that has gone into the adoption of managed care in most U.S. workers' compensation jurisdictions. Most of the laws establishing twenty-four-hour coverage pilots mandate studies of those experiments, but sophisticated analysis is needed to clearly demonstrate the accomplishments (or lack thereof) from twenty-four-hour coverage plans. As a long-time supporter of the notion that twenty-four-hour coverage deserves a chance to demonstrate its virtues and defects, I am encouraged by current endeavors, though apprehensive that this may be another area of workers' compensation in which reform is based more on fad than fact.

---

42. One possibility would be to combine short-term disability programs for work-related and non-work-related disabilities and to leave separate programs for disabilities that continue for more than six months after the date of injury. If this integrated short-term disability program were combined with identical medical benefits for all sources of injuries and diseases, the need to litigate the work-related test would be eliminated for the substantial majority of cases that now are handled by the workers' compensation program.

Comment by Bruce Barge

I want to begin by examining some historical evidence that shows the difficulty of making true change in a complex system such as disability management. Jack Worrell at Rutgers University and his colleague Dick Butler did research on the workers' compensation system back in the 1980s. They noted that, as state legislatures went about making changes in the workers' compensation system, lawmakers would make a certain modification intended to produce a certain kind of behavior. The modification would begin to change behavior for a period of time, perhaps six months or a year. Then the lawyers and the employees and all the people who are using the system would figure out an angle to get around that change, and soon the system would be subverted back to where it was before. In thinking about making systemic change to twenty-four-hour coverage, attention must be given to the dynamics and organizations that are driving change and that will determine whether these changes will work or not.

I would like to focus on the concept of twenty-four-hour management, not twenty-four-hour coverage, defined by four key characteristics. First is a focus on total cost, not just the narrow cost of a program but the total cost to the organization. Second is a focus on customer, who, in the case of disability management, is the individual disabled worker. Third is a focus on reengineering the internal systems at the employer level, which encompasses the changes that employers can make in their organizations to support a more effective delivery of value to that customer. And, fourth is a focus on active operational management on a day-to-day basis. The four characteristics define what has to happen in the day-to-day management of health and disability in organizations so that twenty-four-hour coverage and twenty-four-hour management become a reality for disabled people.

Total Cost

Oftentimes when people think about health and disability, they think about the cost of their workers' compensation premium. They think about the cost of their health care premium, short-term disability premium, long-term disability premium, and so forth. Perhaps, they think about the administrative costs. The human resources department, the risk-management department, and so forth must be paid for. That is about as far as most organizations think. However, they should be thinking much more broadly than that because, as Monroe

Berkowitz says, the real subject is productivity. Productivity has far more financial impact on organizations than the out-of-pocket costs for administration or premiums. That is true not only for self-insured employer but also for small employers.

In addition, the impact of health on the work force in general must not be overlooked. What is more important to people than the health of themselves and their family? What is more important in retaining key employees, keeping up morale, fostering a sense of loyalty and commitment to the organization than delivering excellent health and disability programs? They provide a way for an organization to differentiate itself from its competitors and to attract key people into its company and win in the marketplace.

The total cost requires consideration of premiums, as well as the big picture in terms of business competitiveness. It is a new way of thinking about health and disability that can be very effective.

Customer

The customer is the person who got hurt and who gets the value out of the system. As a result, changes in the system should be made to provide customers with faster cycle time, higher quality products and services, and better value. Adopting this mindset can drive a much different way of configuring the system.

The discipline of quality improvement is widely used in organizations today to study and improve work systems. Such an analysis would be broader than a demographic analysis alone. The problem should be studied in terms of qualitative data to gain an understanding of what the experience is like for a person in the health and disability system. Focus groups could be held with customers, and the factors that motivate their behavior and those that de-motivate their behavior could be identified. The goal is to achieve a richness of understanding of the customer, looking at the system from the customer's perspective. From there, conclusions can be reached about how to reconfigure that system to deliver customers better value.

This is the way manufacturing and every other part of the business operates. Health and disability should, too.

Reengineering Internal Systems

The companies on the cutting edge of disability management include General Electric, L. L. Bean, California/Edison, and Corning. A number of small companies also are doing some innovative things to bring these systems together. For example, one of the first things that they do is try to create a shared vision across all the partners in the system; that is, bring together the provider community, the carrier community, the internal people in human resources or risk management or safety, and people from the line. Their perspectives are heard, and then a vision of what an effective system would be can start to be built.

Once that vision is secured, customer data are gathered. Process mapping is done, for example, on what happens when a person gets hurt. That person gets hurt and then goes to the supervisor, who fills out a form. The procedure is displayed on a flip chart for all to study. From there, a fundamental understanding can be reached of how the system works and where the bottlenecks and redundancies are. The system then can be transformed into something that can deliver value more effectively.

Operational Management

The companies that are doing disability management effectively have built it into the way that employees and managers think about their jobs. It is a key part of how they do business. For example, DuPont is America's leader in safety. DuPont's safety experience is fifteen hundred times better than the national average. At DuPont, every time a management meeting opens, the first five minutes are devoted to safety. This is true for a meeting of the board of directors, a meeting to talk about the budget, or a meeting to consider a new product. Safety is deeply ingrained into the company's culture. Managers are compensated on the basis of workers' compensation experience, and costs are then charged back. DuPont is not alone, however. At Weyerhauser and other companies, for example, line managers have been trained to think about the health and the safety of their people as being a legitimate productivity expense and an element of competitiveness.

Conclusion

An opportunity exists with twenty-four-hour coverage and twenty-four-hour management to transform the health and disability system in the United States. The task is not going to be easy. Many challenges are ahead—changing mindsets and skills at the supervisor level, at the employee level, and at the manager level within organizations.

In considering whether this can be done, the example of productivity and quality in American industry should be examined. Ten or fifteen years ago, the United States was outpaced by international competitors who had figured out what they had to do to perform faster, cheaper, and better to compete in the marketplace. American industry has come back and is experiencing greater market share in those target markets. The same sort of thing can be done in health and disability, and in so doing, better value could be delivered to the employee—in this case, the disabled employee—who is the customer of the system.

Comment by James N. Ellenberger

Workers' compensation is the oldest social insurance system in the United States, dating back about eighty-five years. After the signing of the Occupational Safety and Health Act in 1970, President Richard Nixon had the good sense to appoint John F. Burton, Jr., as the chair of the National Commission on State Workmen's Compensation Laws. That commission was extremely important in bringing about an examination of the health and viability of the nation's workers' compensation system. The National Academy of Social Insurance's Disability Policy Panel looked at the commission's work to gain information and knowledge for its deliberations—particularly for how to present its findings and recommendations.

The workers' compensation commission's eighty-four recommendations were a tribute to Burton's stewardship and leadership. These recommendations were unanimously adopted by a panel that was diverse, with representatives of employers, workers, insurance companies, the medical profession, lawyers, and the academic community. Nineteen recommendations were said by the commission to be essential to the future of the state-based workers' compensation system. Furthermore, in its unanimous message to Congress and the president, the commission recommended that unless the states adopted these nineteen essential recommendations within two years, Congress should intervene and establish federal standards. Now—nearly twenty-four years after the issuance of the report—the record of compliance by the states with those nineteen recommendations is a paltry 65 percent.

States such as Georgia have a maximum benefit, if an injury occurs on the job, of $275 a week. That is less than the federal poverty level for a family of four. Regrettably, the situation is not much better in states that are thought of as more progressive. For example, in New York, the maximum benefit is $400 a week; in California, $406 a week. The average weekly wage is $655 and $578, respectively.

Who Pays for Job Injuries and Illnesses?

John Burton and his colleague at Rutgers University James R. Chelius have done important work about who pays for workers' compensation.[43] Significant evidence exists that workers actually pay for the costs of job injury and illness.

There were 6.8 million injuries and illnesses arising out of and in the course of employment in 1994, and between sixty-eight hundred and more than fifty thousand fatalities, depending on whether deaths from occupational diseases are included. Workers pay in blood and in pain, and their work injury has severe consequences on their families. The cost of job injuries and illnesses is not only lost wages, but also the loss of accrual to retirement plans and Social Security deposits and health care insurance for workers and for their dependents. And all of that happens before the costs of workers' compensation are added up.

Workers' Compensation and Disability Policy

The Academy's Panel was charged with looking at Social Security disability insurance (DI) and Supplemental Security Income (SSI). In reality, however, a number of other elements help constitute the national disability policy system. Workers' compensation exists in every state, although in three states it is still voluntary. The Federal Employee's Compensation Act pertains to federal workers; the Longshore and Harbor Workers Act, inland waterway workers, workers in shipyards, and longshoremen; and a separate quasi-tort-based system for railroad workers under the Federal Employers Liability Act and a similar one for seafarers under the Jones Act. Temporary disability insurance programs have been set up in five states as well as a similar federal program for railroad workers. There also are private long-term disability insurance programs and private short-term disability insurance programs. And automobile insurance provides indemnity insurance and medical coverage arising from injuries suffered in auto accidents.

Despite all these systems, some people fall through the cracks. On December 13, 1995, a twenty-four-year-old worker went to work on a farm in Idaho. While using a tractor-driven post hole digger, he suffered a horrendous accident and lost both arms and one leg. This worker has a seventeen-year-old wife and a young child. He, unfortunately, was not covered by Idaho's workers'

43. Chelius and Burton (1994).

compensation law. Fourteen states do not cover agricultural workers, despite the Burton commission's recommendation that all states adopt coverage for farm workers. If anything good can come out of a tragedy such as the one that occurred in Idaho, it is that the governor, who is a rancher, and other political forces in the state have finally come out—after being embarrassed—in favor of extending workers' compensation coverage to farm workers in Idaho. Similar coverage should be extended to farm workers in the thirteen other states that currently exclude them.

The Idaho case underlines the importance of medical coverage, disability insurance, and workers' compensation. The worker in Idaho has nothing: His employer did not have workers' compensation; he did not have enough earnings to qualify for DI; and, because he is an alien, he is not eligible for the means-tested SSI program. His medical expenses will be paid by donations or, as in so many other cases, absorbed by health providers and their institutions. In all likelihood, this disabled worker will be a lifelong candidate for welfare, public assistance, and charity.

Twenty-Four-Hour Coverage

The promise of twenty-four-hour coverage is that it is efficient, will save money, is easier to understand, and is sensible. In the context of workers' compensation, a complete twenty-four-hour coverage program would include medical and disability benefits for all diseases and injuries without regard to the source or cause of the condition. In other words, no distinction would be made between occupational and nonoccupational injuries and illnesses. If an individual needed medical treatment, he or she would be covered; if an individual suffered a loss of income as a result of such illness or injury, he or she would receive disability indemnity benefits until the return to work.

Many variants of twenty-four-hour coverage involve schemes that fall short of complete coverage—particularly in regard to indemnity benefits. Most are directed at merging, in some fashion, the medical portion of workers' compensation with whatever health care coverage the worker has for conditions not caused on the job. This can simply mean integrating the management of two different insurance policies (workers' compensation and group health) or combining the medical coverage for all of a worker's injuries and illnesses into a single policy. Virtually all variants would restrict the right of workers to choose their own doctor and would introduce copayments or deductibles for medical treatment for work-related conditions.

Why the Interest in Twenty-Four-Hour Coverage?

Some scholars and policymakers have argued that the interest in twenty-four-hour coverage is driven by market forces. They claim that employers are seeking cost savings that can be achieved through the merger of two health policies and administrative networks into one. The reality is that employers are not seeking to expand coverage for their employees but to reduce it. While twenty-four-hour coverage is being sold to employers by insurers as a method of reducing costs, it is less an issue of controlling costs than of retaining or gaining market share, dictating choice of physician, and shifting costs onto the backs of workers.

John Burton, not long ago, encouraged policymakers in Florida to adopt a provision that gave employers the option of providing a twenty-four-hour health insurance policy with deductibles and coinsurance that would supplant the medical benefits otherwise required by workers' compensation law. The idea was to encourage employers to extend regular health insurance to their employees by giving them the opportunity to shift some of the costs of medical coverage under workers' compensation to their employees. In other words, employers opting for this twenty-four-hour coverage option could shift some of the costs of medical treatment for work-related conditions from themselves to injured workers.

The clear trend in the economy is in the direction of declining health care coverage—not its expansion. Florida employers are unlikely to offer health insurance when they did not in the past. On the contrary, a number of employers who already provide health insurance benefits will simply use the twenty-four-hour coverage option to shift some of the burden and risks of work injury and illness to their employees.

Market Share

As a result of President Bill Clinton's support for managed competition in the health care reform effort, group health insurers rushed to position themselves for managed health care. Workers' compensation insurers, not wanting to lose their market share to group health insurers, became the most vocal advocates of managed care in workers' compensation while organizing their own managed care networks.

Choice of Physician

The carriers knew that managed care offered a way to override the historic legislative battles over who has the right to choose the treating physician—the employee or the employer. Simply providing by statute the right of the employer or insurer to designate medical treatment through a managed care arrangement has decided this issue in favor of the employer or insurer. Twenty of the twenty-eight employee-choice states now provide for managed care in workers' compensation.

In some contexts, managed care is advocated as a means to improve the quality and control the cost of medical care. But, in workers' compensation, treating doctors make important determinations that have nothing to do with quality or cost of medical care. These determinations are critical to questions of compensability (Is the condition work-related?); they are pivotal in deciding the amount of benefits to be paid (What is the degree or extent of impairment?); and they are crucial to decisions about return to work (Under what conditions or restrictions can the individual resume work?). Controlling choice of treating physician is directly related to efforts by insurers and employers to influence the decisions made by health care providers that have important financial consequences in workers' compensation.

Cost Shifting to Injured Workers

Workers' compensation has historically operated on the principle that the employer would provide health care for work-related conditions at no expense to workers.

The focus on the escalation of medical costs encouraged workers' compensation insurers to examine the cost containment methods used by group health insurers. Much of this containment involved cost-shifting from insurers to health care users through copayments or deductibles. Costs to employers for workers' compensation insurance, they argued, could be brought down by having workers participate in the payment for health care for work-related conditions. According to this scenario, indirect savings also would accrue to insurers and employers as workers would reduce their utilization of medical care under workers' compensation if they were subject to deductibles or copayments.

Problems with Twenty-Four-Hour Coverage

The elimination of artificial and frequently irrational distinctions between occupational and nonoccupational disabilities is one of the great attractions of twenty-four-hour coverage. That appeal has been weakened by several factors. One is that coordination or integration of cash or wage-replacement benefits has been ignored by virtually all twenty-four-hour coverage proposals. Another is that merging medical benefits would inevitably be accomplished by introducing limits, restrictions, and cost-shifting arrangements that exist in group health plans to the otherwise higher standards and conditions that exist in workers' compensation coverage. Conflict with other laws and the erosion of exclusive remedy remain serious stumbling blocks for advocates of twenty-four-hour coverage.

ERISA

The Employee Retirement Income Security Act (ERISA) preempts most state laws or regulations dealing with employee benefit plans. A specific exclusion exists for such plans "maintained solely for the purpose of complying with applicable workmen's compensation laws or unemployment compensation or disability insurance laws." The twenty-four-hour pilot projects, which contemplate provisions beyond simple compliance with workers' compensation laws, have thus far been made voluntary to avoid the preemption issue.

Shifting Costs to Workers yet Retaining Exclusive Remedy for Employers

Shifting costs to workers through copayments or deductibles would alter the historic trade-off that gave employers immunity from lawsuits under the principle of exclusive remedy. That is, employers may not be able to claim exclusive remedy if workers have to pay for medical treatment for injuries or illnesses that arise out of and in the course of employment.

Some insurers and scholars have argued that copayments and deductibles in medical benefits would not denigrate the exclusive remedy protections accorded to employers because cash indemnity payments under workers' compensation already contain a deductible, in the form of a waiting period, and a copayment, in that lost wages are only partially replaced. In addition, they have argued that workers in the state of Washington already pay 50 percent of the medical premium in that state's workers' compensation program.

In answer to these arguments, the following should be noted:

—While labor has always opposed waiting periods, their use is common because most short-term lost time resulting from work injuries or illnesses is covered by employer sick-leave plans. Employers find covering short-term lost time administratively cheaper than processing workers' compensation indemnity payments. And, in every state, after the passage of a specific period of time out of work, benefits are paid retroactive to the first day of lost time.

—Among the reasons workers' compensation benefits only partially replace lost wages is that benefits are tax free. Others argue that benefits should be partial to provide a return-to-work incentive to the injured worker and that expenses are less for individuals who are not working.

—In the state of Washington, commercial insurers are not allowed to write workers' compensation. Washington labor has fought hard to preserve the exclusive state fund and furthermore agreed to coinsurance in the medical aid premium (which is different from copayments or deductibles) to have a stake in the administration of that fund. Self-insured employers are prohibited from charging their employees any amount of money (whether it is coinsurance, copayments, or deductibles) for medical treatment for work conditions.

New Benefit Cuts and Limitations

Combining the medical portion of workers' compensation with group health implies a coordination of benefits, limits, and other conditions so that the differences between policies would be removed. Workers' compensation medical coverage (first dollar coverage and unlimited necessary treatment) will always be brought down to coordinate or merge it with group health. In addition to copayments and deductibles, workers could expect to see the medical portion of workers' compensation adjusted to accommodate the introduction of waiting periods for eligibility, caps or maximums for certain medical procedures or treatments, and exclusions for preexisting conditions among other things.

Combining Different Types of Insurance

Folding together the medical portion of workers' compensation with group health insurance in the context of insurance provided by private carriers will be a nightmare. Workers' compensation is a statutory obligation, with a long tail (for those injuries or diseases that go beyond the year in which the incident occurred). Group health insurance is a contractual obligation that only obligates insurers or self-insured employers for a specific period. Workers' compensation covers workers; typically, group health insurance covers workers and their dependents.

Assessment of Disabilities still Required

Even if medical treatment is provided without regard to the source of the condition—whether occupational or nonoccupational—the traditional dilemma in workers' compensation remains: Disabilities must be assessed and those assessments translate into the amount of cash benefits the injured worker receives. Most workers' compensation systems rely heavily on the opinion of the treating physician, and twenty-four-hour coverage will ensure that employers and insurers are able to choose the health care provider who will influence that determination.

Conclusion

The AFL-CIO remains convinced that the medical portion of workers' compensation can and should be integrated into a national health care system. The failure of President Clinton's initiative has made it unlikely that national health care reform will emerge as a serious consideration in the near future. States that have adopted pilot projects or other efforts to encourage twenty-four-hour coverage, or those that are considering such action, should:

—Prohibit copayments and deductibles. The pilot programs in California, Kentucky, Louisiana, and Oregon have such language.

—Mandate that selection of the health care provider of twenty-four-hour coverage be chosen through collective bargaining in organized workplaces or be based upon agreement of the employees in nonorganized workplaces.

—Require that any pilot project be thoroughly evaluated by an appropriate academic program.

—Provide sunset clauses that terminate all pilot programs or experiments in twenty-four-hour coverage after an appropriate period of time.

References

Bateman, Keith T. 1995. "Twenty-Four-Hour Coverage: Magic or Myth?" Paper prepared for the Integrating Health, Workers' Compensation, and Disability Benefits conference, Global Business Research, Chicago, September 27.

Boden, Leslie I., and Charles A. Fleischman. 1989. *Medical Costs in Workers' Compensation: Trends and Interstate Comparisons.* Cambridge, Mass.: Workers Compensation Research Institute.

Borba, Philip S., David Appel, and Matthew Fung. 1994. *Florida Managed Care Pilot Program: July 1994 Final Report.* Prepared for the Florida Department of Insurance. Milliman & Robertson.

Burton, John F., Jr. 1995a. "Workers' Compensation Benefits and Costs: Significant Developments in the Early 1990s." In *1996 Workers' Compensation Year Book,* edited by John F. Burton, Jr., and Timothy P. Schmidle, I-1–I-13. Horsham, Pa.: LRP Publications.

———. 1995b. "Workers' Compensation and 24-Hour Coverage: The Legal and Regulatory Environment." In *1996 Workers' Compensation Year Book,* edited by John

F. Burton, Jr., and Timothy P. Schmidle, I-96–I-103. Horsham, Pa.: LRP Publications.

———. 1996. "Workers' Compensation, 24-Hour Coverage, and Managed Care." *Workers' Compensation Monitor* 9 (1): 11–22.

Burton, John F., Jr., and Timothy P. Schmidle. 1995. "The Current Interest in 24-Hour Coverage for Medical Care." In *1996 Workers' Compensation Year Book,* edited by John F. Burton, Jr., and Timothy P. Schmidle, I-88–I-95. Horsham, Pa.: LRP Publications.

California Workers' Compensation Institute. 1992. "Physician Costs under the Official Medical Fee Schedule: Unit Price vs. Utilization." *CWCI Research Update.*

Chelius, James R., and John F. Burton, Jr. 1994. "Who Actually Pays for Workers' Compensation?: The Empirical Evidence." *Workers' Compensation Monitor* 7 (6): 20–27.

Durbin, David, and David Appel. 1991. "The Impact of Fee Schedules and Employer Choice of Physician." *NCCI Digest* 6 (3): 45–47.

Eccleston, Stacey M. 1995. *Managed Care and Medical Cost Containment in Workers' Compensation: A National Inventory, 1995-1996.* Cambridge, Mass.: Workers Compensation Research Institute.

Eccleston, Stacey M., Thomas W. Grannemann, and James F. Dunleavy. 1993. *Benchmarks for Designing Workers' Compensation Medical Fee Schedules.* Cambridge, Mass.: Workers Compensation Research Institute.

Ellenberger, James N. 1990. "Medical Cost Containment in Workers' Compensation." *Workers' Compensation Monitor* 3 (4): 15–16.

———. 1992. "Labor's Perspective on Health Care Cost Reform." In *Workers' Compensation Health Care Cost Containment,* edited by Judith Greenwood and Alfred Taricco. Horsham, Pa.: LRP Publications.

Hughes, Carol. 1995. "The Future of Workers' Compensation Is Managed Care: And the Future Is Now." *Workers' Compensation Monitor* 8 (5): 13–21.

Johnson, William G., and others. 1994. *The Excess Costs of Health Care for Work Related Injuries.* Report No. 1. Zenith Project. Reprinted in John F. Burton, Jr., and Timothy P. Schmidle, eds. 1995. *1996 Workers' Compensation Year Book,* I-79–I-82. Horsham, Pa.: LRP Publications.

Lewis, John H. 1992. "Legislative Reform Efforts and the Medical Benefit." In *Workers' Compensation Health Care Cost Containment,* edited by Judith Greewood and Alfred Taricco, 106–07. Horsham, Pa.: LRP Publications.

———. 1995. "Improving Workers' Compensation through Collective Bargaining." In *1996 Workers' Compensation Year Book,* edited by John F. Burton, Jr., and Timothy P. Schmidle, I-131–I-136. Horsham, Pa.: LRP Publications.

Minnesota Department of Labor and Industry. 1990. *Report to the Legislature on Health Care Costs and Cost Containment in Minnesota Workers' Compensation.*

National Council on Compensation Insurance. 1995. *Compendium of Workers Compensation Managed Care Statutes and Regulations.* Boca Raton, Fla.

Pozzebon, Silvana. 1993. "Do Traditional Health Care Cost Containment Practices Really Work?" *Workers' Compensation Monitor* 6 (3): 17–22.

Reagan, Michael D. 1992. *Curing the Crisis: Options for America's Health Care.* Boulder, Colo.: Westview Press.

Roberts, Sally. 1995. "A Better Way to Manage Disabilities: Integrating These Benefits, Work Is Hard But Worthwhile." *Business Insurance* 29 (May 1): 20.

Schauffler, Helen Halpin, and Tracy Rodriguez. 1993. "Managed Care for Preventive Services: A Review of Policy Options." *Medical Care Review* 50 (2).

Victor, Richard B., and Charles A. Fleischman. 1990. *How Choice of Provider and Recessions Affect Medical Costs in Workers' Compensation.* Cambridge, Mass.: Workers Compensation Research Institute.

6

Alternatives to Income Support: Where Are the Jobs?

VARIOUS PERSPECTIVES ARE OFFERED in this chapter on the state of the labor market and the prospects for employment for the disabled and other recipients of social services benefits.

How Will Labor Market Trends Affect People with Disabilities?
Alan B. Krueger

WHAT WILL THE LABOR MARKET of the future be like? Will it be more or less hospitable to people with disabilities? If government transfers to people with disabilities decline in the future, will the private sector generate sufficient employment demand? Forecasting labor market trends is hazardous business. Predicting the future course of jobs is a little like predicting the future course of the weather: One can do a reasonably good job with short-run trends, but long run-trends are much more difficult to predict. Moreover, as in weather forecasting, recent trends probably provide the best insight into short-run movements in job growth.

A good deal of evidence suggests that recent trends have caused a substantial shift in labor demand toward higher skilled workers relative to lower skilled workers. For example, the employment-to-population rate for college graduates increased slightly between 1979 and 1994 (by 1 percent), while it fell for high school graduates (–3 percent) and for high school dropouts (–10 percent).[1] Further evidence of an increase in demand comes from wage trends. The relative increase in employment for college graduates was accompanied

1. These statistics pertain to workers age twenty-five and older and are from the *Current Population Survey*.

by a sharp increase in relative earnings for college graduates and rising wage inequality, which suggest an increase in relative demand for skilled workers instead of an increase in supply of skilled labor.

Unfortunately, the causes of this shift in demand for skilled workers are unclear. The primary suspects include technological change and increased international competition.[2] A recent survey found that a large majority (71 percent) of labor economists listed technological change as the leading cause of rising income inequality in the United States.[3] Although the evidence is still incomplete, some evidence does support a major role for technological change. For example, Claudia Goldin and Lawrence Katz find that capital-skill complementarity in the manufacturing sector was at a relatively high level by historical standards in the 1980s.[4]

What aspect of technology has changed in recent years? The most obvious candidate is the proliferation of computers. In 1984, one quarter of the work force in the United States reported hands-on computer use at work. By 1993, nearly half of the work force directly used a computer.

The computer revolution has the potential to greatly expand employment for people with disabilities. Computer technology can compensate for the physical limitations inherent in many disabilities. For example, deaf people can use e-mail and voice-recognition programs; mobility-limited people can use computer-operated machines or telecommute (with puff keyboards, if necessary); and blind people can read touch screens. Are disabled people more or less likely to use computers? Has the spread of computers raised employment rates for disabled workers? Little is known about these questions. To provide some evidence on these issues, in 1994, Doug Kruse and I conducted a survey of New Jersey residents who suffered spinal cord injuries (SCIs) in the preceding ten years and a matched set of individuals without SCIs.[5] The results are not very encouraging. The great potential of computers has not been realized by most people with SCIs.

Only about 30 percent of those with an SCI were working in the week they were surveyed, and only 20 percent worked full time. Individuals with an SCI are somewhat less likely to use computers at home or at work than are equally educated individuals without an SCI (41 versus 54 percent). Those who work after suffering an SCI, however, are much more likely to use computers at work

---

2. Institutional changes, including the decline in unions and the fall in the real value of the minimum wage, may also have affected the wage structure. See DiNardo, Fortin, and Lemieux (1994); and Card (1995).

3. Whapples (1994).

4. Goldin and Katz (1995).

5. Krueger and Kruse (1995); and Krueger, Kruse, and Drastal (1995).

than are non–SCI workers with similar characteristics (61 versus 48 percent). The main reason SCI individuals are less likely to use computers appears to be that they are less likely to work, and most people learn how to use computers at work. The subsample of SCI individuals who worked are also much more likely to hold white-collar jobs than non–SCI individuals (83 versus 65 percent). Moreover, having used a computer at work before an injury is associated with a quicker return to work, and with substantially higher pay, among those with an SCI. People with SCIs who use a computer at work earn just as much per week as non–SCI individuals who use a computer at work, whereas SCI people who hold jobs that do not involve computer use earn 35 percent less per week than comparable non–SCI individuals.

The likely continued growth in jobs that require some facility with computers may open up more job opportunities for individuals with severe disabilities, such as SCIs. However, unless people with these disabilities have greater access to computer skills, they may not be able to realize these opportunities.

Workers with less severe injuries have a different occupational distribution than those with severe disabilities (such as SCIs), so the computer revolution may hold out less promise for these workers. A tabulation of occupational status presented below for those who report a disability that limits the amount or kind of work that they can do from the March 1994 *Current Population Survey* (CPS) shows that workers who report such a disability are more likely to be employed in blue-collar jobs than both the general population and those with SCIs. Thus, for the disability population at large, the shift in demand against less skilled workers may well have negative consequences.

The Next Decade

In the United States, technological change has not meant a decline in aggregate employment. Employment has grown significantly since the advent of computers. Relative to population, employment growth was almost as great in the sixteen years between 1979 (approximately the beginning of personal computer revolution) and 1995 as it was in the sixteen years before 1979.[6] Employment seems to be determined largely by the supply of available workers in the United States, which suggests that jobs will be available for many more disabled workers if they seek them (even if many of the jobs do not pay

6. The fraction of people of working age who were employed was 55.4 percent in 1963, 59.9 percent in 1979, and 63 percent in October 1995. Between 1963 and 1979, employment increased by 33 million nonagricultural jobs; and between 1979 and October 1995, employment increased by 28 million.

well). While many European nations have experienced anemic job growth, especially in the private sector, the U.S. jobs machine keeps humming along. Although the same ailments that afflict European job growth may eventually affect U.S. job growth, a safe prediction is that aggregate employment will continue to grow in the United States over the long run. But employment growth is expected to slow down along with the projected slow down in the growth of the working-age population in the next decade.

A much more difficult forecast concerns the composition of job growth. For several decades, the Bureau of Labor Statistics (BLS) has prepared projections of employment for the U.S. economy. Although the BLS track record is not perfect, for major occupations the BLS projections are reasonably correlated with actual employment growth. For example, the correlation between actual and projected employment growth between 1980 and 1990 was 0.62 for major occupations.[7] Notably, the BLS underestimated employment growth in professional jobs and overestimated it in blue-collar jobs. Nevertheless, the BLS projection for aggregate employment growth was only 0.9 percent less than actual growth between 1980 and 1990.

The data in table 6-1 include 1983 and 1994 employment and the latest employment projections for the year 2005 for major occupations.[8] The BLS projects that employment growth rates will be greatest in the professional and service occupations and lowest in blue-collar and agricultural occupations.

The occupational distribution for those who report a work disability is shown in column 6 and for those who do not report a work disability in column 7. Those with self-reported work disabilities are more concentrated in blue-collar and service jobs than are those without disabilities. As is well known, this mode of determining disability status is fraught with problems. For example, comparing two individuals with identical disabilities, the one with a more stressful job is probably more likely to answer that he or she has a work disability that restricts his or her work. Thus, blue-collar workers may be more likely to report disabilities than white-collar workers because their work is more physically demanding. However, disabilities may be more common among blue-collar jobs because work-related injuries are higher and because

---

7. This correlation is based on data reported in Rosenthal (1992). Bishop and Carter (1991) conclude that the BLS occupational projections are prone to greater inaccuracy than the 0.62 correlation would indicate. Their evaluation compares the BLS projections with employment growth based on household-reported occupational status from the CPS, whereas the projections and correlation cited above are based on employment growth derived from the Occupational Employment Statistics survey, which is an establishment-based survey.

8. Kutscher (1995, table 5).

Table 6-1. Actual and Projected Employment Growth and Occupational Distribution for Disabled and Nondisabled Workers

Occupation	Employment (thousands)			Proportionate employment growth		Occupational distribution (1993)	
	Actual 1983 (1)	Actual 1994 (2)	Projected 2005 (3)	1983–94 (4)	1994–2005 (5)	Disabled (percent) (6)	Nondisabled (percent) (7)
Executive and managerial	9,591	12,903	15,071	0.35	0.17	8.6	12.9
Professional	12,639	17,314	22,387	0.37	0.29	8.8	13.9
Technical and support	3,409	4,439	5,316	0.30	0.20	2.3	3.5
Marketing and sales	10,497	13,990	16,502	0.33	0.18	11.0	12.0
Administrative support	18,874	23,178	24,172	0.23	0.04	13.3	15.4
Services	15,577	20,239	24,832	0.30	0.23	21.8	13.8
Agricultural	3,712	3,762	3,650	0.01	-0.03	3.9	2.7
Precision production	12,731	14,047	14,880	0.10	0.06	11.0	11.1
Operators, fabricators, and laborers	15,374	17,142	17,898	0.11	0.04	19.3	14.7
All occupations	102,404	127,014	144,708	0.24	0.14	100	100

Sources: Columns 1–5 are U.S. Bureau of Labor Statistics projections and actual employment reported in Kutscher (1995). Columns 6–7 are the author's tabulations based on weighted counts of the March 1994 *Current Population Survey*.

the characteristics of workers that are associated with blue-collar work are also associated with a higher incidence of disability.

To quantify the impact of the projected occupational shifts on employment for the self-reported disabled and nondisabled samples, I calculated the employment-weighted average of occupational growth rates using either the disabled or nondisabled occupational distributions as employment weights. That is, I calculated $\Sum_i f_i g_i$, where f_i is the percentage of workers in major occupation i (for either the disabled or nondisabled samples in 1993) and g_i is the BLS projection of employment growth for occupation i. Between 1994 and 2005, this calculation predicts slightly less job growth for workers with disabilities than for workers without disabilities: 13.4 versus 14.1 percent. When I performed the same calculation for 1983–94 using actual employment growth, I also found that job growth was shifting slightly against disabled workers, with 23.6 percent growth using the occupational distribution of disabled workers and 25.2 percent growth using the distribution of nondisabled workers.

A related question concerns the educational demands of the labor market of the future. As mentioned, employment growth in the last decade has been strongest in sectors that tend to employ more highly educated workers. The BLS projections indicate that employment growth will be greatest for occupations that tend to require some postsecondary education. Several studies have found that workers who have a disability are less well educated, on average, than workers who do not have a disability. For example, my tabulations with the March 1994 CPS data indicate that one-fifth of workers who report a disability have a two-year college degree or higher, compared with one-third of workers who do not report a work disability. Less well educated workers may be more likely to suffer from disabilities for a host of reasons, including participation in more risky behaviors (such as smoking), less access to health care, and more dangerous work. But if employers continue to demand more highly educated workers, many of those with disabilities are likely to face a more difficult labor market.

Conclusion

Labor market trends offer reasons for both pessimism and cautious optimism for the future employment of workers with disabilities. The main reason for pessimism is that employment has shifted away from jobs that tend to employ disabled workers, and this trend is projected to continue. A reason for optimism is that the continued spread of computers and other forms of technological change means that many more jobs will be accessible to people with severe disabilities. But the scattered evidence available suggests that so far only a minority of severely disabled workers have taken advantage of technological change that is transforming work.

Inner-City Labor Markets: Where the Jobs Are Not
Katherine S. Newman

I SPENT THREE YEARS studying the working poor in central Harlem, a community plagued by high levels of unemployment and poverty. At first glance, this might appear to be far afield as a topic of discussion for a volume on disability. Yet, when one focuses on the problem of jobs, and even more on proposed changes in federal policy toward either the nation's poor or its disabled, some common problems emerge.

Poverty and Disability

First, the poor and the disabled are not entirely strangers to one another. Poor people commonly lack access to medical care and are exposed to unhealthy living conditions that subject them to far higher rates of chronic disease than those who are better off. Asthma, diabetes, tuberculosis—these are diseases of poverty. These disabling conditions afflict millions of the poorest citizens. Between 1980 and 1993, asthma rates more than doubled. More than 5 million children annually are diagnosed with this potentially deadly disease, with African Americans suffering at far higher rates than the rest of the American public. Many of those children are going to end up disabled adults by virtue of this and other deadly diseases. In this land of plenty, the situation is a national scandal.

Poor people are therefore more likely to find themselves among the disabled than are others. And in this sense the two populations overlap to a degree not commonly credited.

Second, the nonworking poor and the disabled are on the receiving end of government regulation because they depend upon benefits administered by the states and the federal government to a greater degree than the nonpoor. They live administered lives by virtue of the labyrinthian regulations that both protect them and control them, the only medium through which they can receive Aid to Families with Dependent Children (AFDC), Supplemental Security Income (SSI), Medicaid, housing assistance, home health aids, and a host of other critical resources. One could spend a great deal of time discussing the consequences of having to live with a bureaucratic regime that is often frustrating, hidebound, and demeaning, even as many of its employees attempt to be helpful, sympathetic, and enabling. For the moment, however, I make the point about administered lives because on either side of the poverty and disability line winds of change are blowing through those federal agencies that have similar premises and may have similar effects on the communities of interest here.

Bruce C. Vladeck notes that skepticism is rising over the legitimacy of claims for disability coverage. As budgets tighten around the country, so, too, does conservative ire grow about whether adults and children claiming SSI are truly disabled, or whether a plague exists of dishonest people attempting to game the system to the detriment of the hardworking taxpayer. The occasional case of abuse is magnified into a major epidemic of fraud and used to fuel attacks on the entire system that allocates resources to the disabled. These attacks usually result in increasing regulatory restrictions and higher thresholds of qualification for the benefits that disabled people are legally entitled to by virtue of federal legislation. The number of recipients shrinks by administrative fiat—simply by making it harder to claim benefits—as the cost of supporting them grows in a country preoccupied by deficits, the need to provide tax breaks, and the like.

The same kind of sentiment is growing, and has grown wildly, toward populations that are involved in the welfare system. Hence, welfare reform has tightened eligibility, cut funds for legal immigrants, created hopelessly unrealistic time limits, and devolved responsibility to the states with insufficient funds to cover the cost. Welfare legislation will eject millions of people from the rolls and put them into the labor market where they reportedly will find refuge. The assumption underlying these reforms is that no one need worry too much about where those jobs are going to come from. Being forced into the labor market will be good medicine for the population under welfare regulation.

Once the perverse incentives that have made being on welfare so comfortable are disbanded, recipients are expected to straighten up and fly right into the labor market where jobs abound. And, it is general knowledge that there are plenty of jobs, because lots of help wanted signs are displayed in windows of places such as suburban fast food restaurants. Elected leaders claim that unschooled immigrants are snapping up jobs, and that is proof, again, that plenty of employment is available. The success of many immigrants is taken as evidence for the supposed retreat of the native-born poor from the world of work. Inner-city residents, such as those in central Harlem, no longer try to find work because their values have been warped living so easily on welfare—or so it is said.

The Working Poor in Harlem

I want to challenge some of those assumptions by examining the findings of a three-year study of African Americans, Dominican immigrants, and Puerto Ricans who work at the bottom of New York's service sector. These people live and work in some of the poorest, roughest neighborhoods of New York City, where unemployment, officially, crests over 18 percent and the poverty rate is about 40 percent. In central Harlem, about 29 percent of the households are on public assistance, unemployment is very high, and the underground economy is flourishing. Many long-term welfare recipients live in these kinds of neighborhoods because, with the resources that they have, they cannot afford to live anywhere else. Furthermore, if the safety net does disappear, many of these people will have to look for work there.

But these job seekers are in good company because, although the community is very poor, some 67 percent of the households in central Harlem have at least one full-time worker in them. About a quarter of these workers are employed in the service sector industries, the sector that has been the focus of my research. Specifically, I concentrated on workers in the fast food industry, the entry way into the formal labor market for millions of minority teens in the United States.

The public perception is that getting a "McJob" is easy. The pay is minimum wage, and entry-level employment is often deemed to be skill-free and therefore available to anyone who wants a job. However, a study of rejected applicants—people who were looking for these minimum-wage jobs who did not get them—in central Harlem suggests that, although finding such employment may be easy in the suburbs, it is not so easy in the inner city.

Rejected Applicants

To understand the challenge of finding work in the ghetto, I interviewed a random sample of about one hundred people who had applied for a fast food job in central Harlem over a five-month period. Most of these job seekers were experienced workers. The average number of jobs they had held before this application was about three, with the average rising to four with older age groups. Nonetheless, these people were turned back for $4.25 an hour fast food jobs. About 73 percent of the people in this reject pool were still unemployed a year after they began searching or after they applied for this minimum-wage job; and this was not for lack of trying. Even the youngest people in the applicant pool—sixteen to eighteen years old—had applied for four or five other positions before they went to seek this $4.25 an hour fast food job.

Some suggest that inner-city unemployment is high because the population has an inflated expectation about what they will find in the way of wages in the labor market and refrain from searching for anything that falls short. Yet unsuccessful job hunters in Harlem are stark realists. Both the wages they were looking for and those they would have accepted hovered right around the minimum wage.

Imagining a human face attached to these kinds of numbers can be helpful. For example, Mary is a thirty-four-year-old African American mother of three teenage children, a real jobseeker in central Harlem. Mary has an eleventh grade education. She has applied for fifteen jobs that she can remember, since she was sixteen years old. She was rejected for about half of them, but she landed the other half. In total, Mary has had about six years of work experience. But she did not get the fast food job she applied for in 1993 and still had not found a job when she was interviewed a year later.

George is a twenty-year-old African American who graduated from high school and has had one year of college. George has worked on and off since he was sixteen years old. He has worked in the summertime. He worked for a year as a cook and as a cashier and delivery person. All of his jobs were at or around the minimum wage. He can remember sixteen jobs that he has applied for and was rejected for twelve of them. He was also rejected for a fast food job, and he, too, had been unable to find work a year later.

These two cases are presented to illustrate what kinds of people are out there pounding the pavement already in central Harlem. These are the kinds of people who are standing in line ahead of the welfare recipients and, perhaps, many disabled people, as well, whom the government is proposing to terminate from their benefits with the expectations that they will find jobs.

Mary and George are far better qualified, in terms of prior work experience and education, than many of the nation's long-term welfare recipients. However, they have not been able to find a fast food job. Is it realistic to expect that welfare mothers, for example, with young children to look after are going to beat out the Marys and Georges? It is not.

Too Few Jobs

The reason that so many people remain unemployed in the inner city is that too many people are chasing too few job opportunities. For every opening in these inner-city restaurants, fourteen applicants were submitted. The oversupply is dramatic and is reflected in a form of creeping credentialism.

What are the characteristics that seem to make a difference? First, older people are preferred over younger people. What used to be a youth labor market niche in the inner city is no longer in this neighborhood.

Second, African Americans are having a more difficult time finding jobs than anyone else, even in neighborhoods that are very nearly 100 percent African American in their residential population. Many do find employment, but African Americans are rejected at a much higher rate than are their principal competitors in Harlem, especially Dominicans and Puerto Ricans. Latino applicants are enjoying an advantage in these black ghettos.

Third, outsiders, people who do not live in the neighborhood, are favored over insiders or locals. Employers favor people who live farther away over people who were right around the corner, controlling for all their human capital characteristics.

Fourth, people with contacts in the restaurants were preferred over people who took any other job-search route. In high-skill occupations, finding a job requires that the applicant know someone. Contrary to received wisdom, the same principle holds at the bottom of the low-wage labor market. Many restaurants in New York City, including the most profitable, never advertise or hire from the walk-in trade. All recruiting is done by personal contacts of the work force in place. This practice has ensured a mono-ethnic population employed in these restaurants without a single African American among them.

This suggests further research prospects. Social networks make a big difference in the hiring process. How are those networks affected by disability? Are newly disabled people able to remain effective members of the networks that control access to jobs, even low-wage jobs? And for those who have been disabled for some time, what kinds of new networks spring up to which they can be attached? Or are they excluded from the connections that everyone needs to find work? These empirical questions have not been examined.

Finally, immigrants were doing better than the native-born in Harlem's low-wage labor market, and this was true even among black immigrants. The longer people had resided in the United States, the harder it was to get a minimum-wage job.

In sum, employers in the inner-city neighborhood of central Harlem were drawing on a set of preferences that disadvantaged African Americans, local residents in the inner-city ghetto, young people, the native-born, high school dropouts, and those who lacked contacts to somebody who is already on the job.

Why did job hunters in Harlem not hop a bus and find a job in some other neighborhood? Inner-city jobhunters do not restrict their searches to the immediate area, although teenagers often do stay closer to home than adults. For the most part, however, jobs searches extend all over the city. They do not tend to do well, however, in more upscale neighborhoods such as midtown Manhattan. First, they often lack the links necessary to get a job in more affluent zones. Second, skill requirements are often higher in the areas dominated by white-collar employment, so those who have only a high school diploma or who lack prior experience find obtaining a job more difficult.

National Findings

My findings parallel national studies. Harry Holtzer at Michigan State University surveyed more than three thousand employers in four cities across the country for his book *What Employers Want.*[9] Holtzer asked this random sample of employers about the skill demands they have for jobs that do not require a college education. He found that skill requirements for noncollege jobs were surprisingly high. About 55 percent of the noncollege jobs require reading skills, arithmetic calculations, dealing with customers, and the use of computers. Only 5 to 10 percent of the available jobs required none of these tasks.

About 70 percent of the employers in Holtzer's study require that applicants have specific forms of work experience. Almost half of them issue a job test. Less than half of the employers say that they would hire someone with only short-term or part-time job experience, and these requirements turn out to be more pronounced in central cities than in the suburbs.

Holtzer also concludes that minorities are much less likely to be hired where skill needs and hiring criteria are more substantial. What this means for the people of Harlem is that an imbalance already exists between the job requirements and the personal skills of job applicants in central city areas. Jobs that represent realistic possibilities are already heavily oversubscribed.

Conclusion

AFDC recipients constitute about 20 to 25 percent of the households in some of the nation's central cities, such as New York and Detroit. These people are going to have a hard time being absorbed into the available jobs, even if they were phased into the job market. As the current welfare reform policies become a reality, a growing queue of people will not be absorbed into the low-wage economy. This is already the case in central Harlem among people

9. Holtzer (1996).

who are, on average, better qualified than the long-term welfare recipients who are the target of these reforms.

Political leaders and others must recognize the realities of these low-wage labor markets and the kind of desperation that job seekers feel when they are turned down for work despite the effort they have put into pounding the pavement. Believing that welfare recipients will do much better is sheer folly.

Inflamatory pronouncements to the contrary, the jobs problem is not a matter of values, either among the inner-city poor or the disabled. The problem is an economy that is no longer generating enough decent jobs, or even enough bad jobs in depressed communities.

A View from Business
Van Doorn Ooms

KATHERINE S. NEWMAN says that not enough jobs are available in the inner cities—that a genuine lack of demand exists, at least in this part of the labor market. However, Alan B. Krueger says that employment in the United States is fundamentally determined in the long term by labor supply, because the labor market will adjust through wage changes and other mechanisms to bring the demand for labor in line with labor supply. The discrepancy between these assertions is more apparent than real. The labor market has always contained submarkets, partly insulated by geographic and skill differences, that are unlike the typical market characterized by the aggregate data. However, the two characterizations do highlight the contrast between the bright and dark sides of the labor market, which have become sharper in recent years.

In the aggregate, the labor market looks very good. The total unemployment rate has remained in a narrow range around 5.5 percent for nearly two years, and the economy has created nearly 9 million new jobs during this expansion, since the end of the last recession in the spring of 1991. In Europe, where labor markets are less flexible and more regulated, private sector job creation is anemic, and double-digit unemployment is the norm. From that perspective, the recent U.S. performance is regarded as an extraordinary success.

But the bad news is that, within this overall picture, serious problems have arisen in particular labor markets, both geographically as illustrated by many urban labor markets and in terms of the markets for different levels and kinds of education and skill. Some of those problems will probably get worse before they get better. The shift in labor demand toward more skilled and educated workers has implications for the disabled.

First, an important change in the economy underlies these labor market changes: Most sectors of the economy are becoming increasingly competitive. Under this more intense competitive pressure, firms have made dramatic technological improvements that have reduced their costs and raised their productivity.

In economics, the term "satisficing" described the behavior of managers who did not try to maximize profits and who often did not have to minimize costs. They simply muddled through, relatively inefficiently, passing on unnecessarily high costs to consumers, and their competitors did likewise. Often they were protected from vigorous competition by trade barriers, regulatory constraints, transportation costs, economies of scale, or other barriers to entry and competition. "Satisficers" do not last long in the present American economy. Cost efficiency and productivity improvements are now imperative for most larger American companies. They are matters of survival for many firms, and the forces that produce them are continuing and relentless.

This new competitive environment has brought both good and bad news. The good news is that the competition drives efficiency and innovation, producing productivity changes that will raise the incomes of most Americans over the longer term. As a matter of economic and social policy, giving up these developments would be ill advised. But doing so would not be possible, even if desired, because competition is now global.

The bad news is that this more intense competition has brought a less forgiving world. There are many new opportunities, but also much higher risks. Many of those risks are now borne by workers in ways that they were not in the old economy where firms were more paternalistic.

Second, the growing use of information technologies, and computers in particular, is a central feature of the new economy. The nature of work has already been fundamentally altered for many Americans, and the end of this process is by no means in sight. These changes began in manufacturing, are moving through the service sector, and, undoubtedly, will become the standard for most of the economy before long.

But the introduction of the new information technology is a complex process and has profound effects on labor demand. These changes should not be considered as simply displacing labor with machines, which is the way that many think about this problem.

The direct displacement is visible and compelling. The automatic teller machine (ATM) directly displaces bank tellers; many fewer telephone operators are employed now than a few years ago; gas station attendants are rapidly disappearing. However, at the same time that the new technology displaces some workers, the demand for others increases, expanding job opportunities and raising wages of those workers that complement the new technology because they can use it effectively or learn to use it quickly. Auto mechanics who can understand a car's computer chips are rare and well compensated, as are the managers who can effectively integrate the more autonomous teams that characterize modern production.

Furthermore, workers at the low end of the scale are not the only ones being displaced, although many of them may be. Design artists are being displaced by computer graphics. Bank and insurance agents, with specialized skills, are being displaced by computer software packages. The *Wall Street Journal* recently described the competitive threat to second-tier medical diagnostic organizations from the preeminent diagnostic centers. Some doctors can now do much of their work at a distance from their patients.

A primary effect of these shifts has been an increased demand for labor with specific skills using the technology. But, the data on employment growth by occupation also show a bulge at the bottom. While rapid employment growth is evident in occupations at the top pay and skill levels, employment growth in some low-paying service occupations—such as retail sales, food preparation and service, child care, and cleaning—has increased quickly, too. A spillover of labor supply into these occupations has occurred, with some tendency toward a dual economy based on skill differentials.

These shifting demands show up not only in employment changes, but also as increasing wage premiums for training, education, and for many character-istics that cannot be readily identified. Both the employment and relative wage changes fall hard on those without skills at the bottom of the labor market.

Imbalances between demand and supply for less skilled labor can be re-solved, in principle, in one of two ways. Unemployment may rise as a result of excess supply if wages cannot fall (for instance, because they are regulated, as in some European countries) or if for some reason employers are unwilling to hire these workers, even at lower wages. Alternatively, employment may increase at lower wages, often in jobs that turn over rapidly. Newman's data may describe higher permanent unemployment, but they may also describe increased job instability among the unskilled, which may present similar prob-lems.

Whatever the case, the lower end of the labor market experienced an enormous amount of adjustment. It shows up vividly in the employment and wage data. Large numbers of less skilled people are employed, but they are employed at low wages. The drop in real wages at the bottom of the wage distribution has been extraordinary. The real earnings of year-round, full-time male workers in the lowest 5 to 10 percent of the distribution have fallen on the order of 25 to 30 percent over the last two decades. That is an enormous change, indicating that the labor market is working, but in ways that radically change relative opportunities and rewards in society.

This raises a fundamental social problem. Historically, education—and especially pubic education—has been a great equalizing force in American society. Education has been the door through which those who began life with meager assets but strong backs or strong motivation could march to join the more fortunate. It has been the major avenue for social and economic mobility.

However, some danger exists, as labor demand shifts toward higher skills, that education might have the opposite effect. It could impede rather than facilitate mobility, so that those already well endowed with skills accumulate more of them and those that start off with few skills gain relatively few and fall further behind. Whether this happens in practice depends on how investments in human capital are distributed within the society, and how effective those investments are. The shift in labor demand, however, provides a prima facie case for a reexamination and possible readjustment of the distribution of those investments. The rationale for public education in the United States is that a society does not trust entirely in the market and the existing structure of income and wealth to generate an appropriate distribution of human capital. The current distribution of resources within the public school systems and, more important, the effectiveness with which those resources are applied, become critical, and the current situation is not encouraging.

Two additional points need to be made with respect to the impact of these labor market changes on the disabled specifically. First, labor markets will adjust to changes in the incidence of disability, but these adjustments will take time. Large increases will occur in the proportion of disabled workers in the labor force, not in the immediate future, but ten to twenty years down the road. The labor force will age, and more elderly and disabled will be working. These changes will result both from simple demography and from medical technology that will lengthen productive work lives in spite of disabilities.

In facilitating adjustment, intensified competition is a double-edged sword. On one hand, it means that many firms will have a smaller margin of benevolence in which they can make accommodations for disabled workers that do not produce economic returns. This would be most true of smaller firms. On the other hand, as skills become more valuable, the costs of discrimination against skilled disabled workers become higher. Therefore, that type of discrimination should diminish, albeit slowly, as it has for other groups in the society that have been subject to job discrimination.

Second, as the demand for skills increases—as human capital becomes more valuable—firms will develop stronger incentives to protect that human capital. This also is a double-edged sword. Firms will try harder, and invest more, to keep valued workers, whether disabled or not. Many corporations appear to be attempting to do that now. Safety and wellness initiatives, employee assistance programs, return-to-work policies, and similar measures should become more common and more important in the future.

Conversely, however, as less skilled workers become relatively less valuable, the incentives for accommodation of their disabilities diminish. A careful distinction must be made between disabled workers who have skill deficits and disabled workers who do not when discussing these issues.

The coincidence between disabilities and skill deficits is very high, placing many workers in double jeopardy in a skill-demanding labor market. The interaction between the lack of skills and disability may make the obstacles more than additive. For instance, increasing job stability among the unskilled raises the cost of accommodating disabilities among such workers. The chances of employment for a disabled, unskilled worker, therefore, would be less than that suggested by the employability of average unskilled and disabled workers considered separately.

In summary, the enhanced value of skills in the new economy appears problematic for the disabled. While resistance to economic change is hardly a viable option, little in the historical record suggests that the private labor market offers an adequate solution in itself, without substantial policy interventions.

The Clash between Advocacy and Implementation
Leslie J. Scallet

MY EXPERIENCE AS A LAWYER and public interest advocate includes many years in patients' rights in the disability field, primarily in mental health. This conference has highlighted the impact of mental illness as a disability on the social insurance programs. Over the past twenty years, a major reform movement to deinstitutionalize care for people with mental disabilities has fostered goals of liberty, better choice for people, self-reliance and individual responsibility, and reducing public costs. Not all of those goals have been shared by everyone advocating deinstitutionalization, but when combined, the result has been to shift a large number of people out of institutional care and into the mainstream.

When people with mental health problems and mental illnesses did enter the mainstream, conflicts became apparent. The biggest one was that the cost often was more, at least at the beginning, instead of less, as advocates had promised. And the savings often accrued in one place while the costs accrued elsewhere.

Those conflicts broke apart the coalition that had promoted deinstitutionalization and made the promise of deinstitutionization and mainstreaming more difficult to realize. The advocates got what they wanted. People came out of institutions and into the community. Legislation outlawed discrimination. But the results for many people suffering from mental illnesses were not necessarily what was anticipated or desired.

For many individuals who left institutions, deinstitutionalization was a great boon. They melted back into the community and their families, and they no longer constituted a problem for society. But others who emerged from hospitals, or who no longer entered them in the first place, had a far different experience. Many could not cope with community or family life. Many simply had no place else to go. Few community-based facilities were set up, and few jobs were available to these individuals.

One result has been a rise in the costs of Social Security disability insurance (DI), and particularly Supplemental Security Income (SSI). Without SSI, DI, and Medicaid, no deinstitutionalization could have occurred. Those programs provided the basic income and services that enabled public systems to accomplish the shift from institution to community.

The Americans with Disabilities Act (ADA), for which advocates also fought long and hard, is designed to make it possible for people who have mental, as well as physical, disabilities to participate in the labor force and particularly in competitive employment. Competitive employment is the gold standard, the ultimate mark of success for all the policy goals. However, again the result was not wholly desirable.

Confessions of a Well-Meaning Employer

As an employer beginning about eight years ago in a small not-for-profit organization concerned with mental health—the Mental Health Policy Resource Center—I was motivated to be nondiscriminatory, to include everyone in my work force. All the values that I had espoused as an advocate could be implemented in this new role. But the goal has not been as easy to realize as I would have hoped.

As an employer, I have a number of responsibilities. One set concerns encouraging and increasing the diversity of the work force. Work involving mental health policy is facilitated by a diverse work force, including people who have disabilities. An understanding must be reached of the perspectives, talents, and skills of various people so that they can be incorporated into the job to be done. Having consistent values—feeling that the values that are espoused are being applied in the conduct of business—is highly beneficial.

Another set of responsibilities centers around performance. Clients and grantors provide funding, and they have expectations about the work produced—that it be of high quality, efficiently performed on a timely basis, and so forth.

A basic responsibility is to show a profit. The center is a not-for-profit organization, and the profit does not accrue to any individual. But if a profit is not made, then the organization has no working capital. If the next grant does not come through, the center is in trouble. So, for the sake of survival, enough profit must be made to plow back into the organization.

Another set of responsibilities is to workers who have disabilities and must, in accordance with the ADA, be reasonably accommodated. The organization sought to implement that standard before the ADA became law. In fulfilling this responsibility, however, the center responds to the same incentives as anyone in the private sector, to ensure that individuals who have a high level of skills are retained or returned to work as soon as possible. Those incentives do not necessarily apply for employees with fewer skills.

A difference in timing also exists. When someone is being hired, one set of incentives is in operation. For example, the current labor market discourages hiring people who are going to be difficult in any way. The particulars—a disability or some other factor—does not matter, but disability can be seen as adding complexity or administrative time, which costs money. When trying to retain an employee, another set of incentives kicks in. Almost any hiring is more costly than retaining an experienced employee, so the incentive is to help people to stay on the job.

For example, an individual who has a high level of analytic skills develops a mental health problem while on the job. The not-for-profit employer has bent over backwards to keep that person on the payroll and has tried not only to reasonably accommodate but also to go beyond what would be required under the ADA's mandate. This person has been given extra time off and has not been held to the same standard as other employees. The incentive is that this tactic is much easier and less costly (up to a point) than is replacing this person. So, this set of responsibilities for workers with disabilities who are already employed is a legal mandate and a good business decision, as well as part of the organization's value structure.

However, an employer also has responsibilities to workers who do not have disabilities. Among the problems that have arisen is a sense among some of those workers that their colleagues who have disabilities are the subject of favoritism. They are the ones who get some kind of accommodation. Sometimes a question arises about whether these individuals need accommodation or whether they feel that they have the right to demand accommodation because they are disabled in one fashion or another. The other people in the office feel that this is unfair, and the employer wants to retain them, too. They also have valuable skills. The organization also has a responsibility to them.

A second issue that arises is the added responsibilities that many of the nondisabled coworkers face. With a staff of fifteen, if any one person is not performing adequately—no matter what their level of skills—the burden falls on others. With a staff of one hundred, perhaps, the responsibilities could be spread around more, but the same principle would apply.

In the past, when the work force and labor market were different, the employer might simply hire another person. Today's labor market will not allow that. For the organization to survive, everyone has to pull his or her own weight. If he or she does not—for whatever reason, including disability— justifying keeping him or her is difficult. Relieving one staff member from responsibilities and handing off those responsibilities to other members of the staff is untenable. They resent it, as they should.

The third area is the added stress and pressure of the current work environment. This is a concern both for workers with and without disabilities.

Ultimately, the question is: Who is supposed to pay the price for the changes that policy has wrought? The answer is that the people who have the least power are the ones who always bear the cost.

Under deinstitutionalization, the people who paid the price were those patients who were discharged into the mainstream without the help they needed. Some became homeless, and many others who are less visible did not receive adequate treatment. Being in institutions also extracts a cost, but the same people pay the highest price. And those with disabilities will pay the price when pressure comes to the work environment.

Troublesome Implications

What are some of the implications of current trends? Here are some observations.

The general employment trends—the downsizing and uncertainty—are occurring in all sectors of the economy. More flexibility is required, and employees must be jacks of all trades. Instead of having two or three employees, only one may be hired, who is expected to have the skills, the time, and the organizational ability to perform all the different roles needed.

Many problems result, especially for people who have mental disabilities. Individuals with mental disabilities who are in the work force, particularly those with severe disabilities, may have a harder time being as flexible as this kind of environment requires. The demand for higher productivity may be more difficult for them to meet.

Many of these individuals will not have the technical skills and education that the labor market demands, and gaining those skills may not be possible. Mental illness often strikes in the late teens, when people would be in school. Recouping that loss is extremely difficult. These individuals are often vulnerable to high stress, so that the present labor situation is especially challenging for them.

Employers cannot be as benevolent toward their employees as they would like while ensuring the survival of their company or organization.

Many individuals who have returned to the work force—particularly those with a mental illness—have come not to the private sector but into public or nonprofit employment. Aside from the trends in the private sector that are discussed widely, enormous budgetary and downsizing pressure has been felt on public employment and on nonprofit organizations.

Much of the progress in employing people with mental disabilities may be lost, not because specific programs for them will be terminated (although that is happening) but because success has been in a semi-sheltered environment. And unless other forms of semi-shelter are provided, these individuals will face the extreme risk of being relegated back onto social insurance programs for life. That assumes the programs will be open to them.

Enough has been heard about the pressures on these programs to fear, realistically, that many more individuals will be pushed into gaping cracks in the system. In reforming SSI and DI, such considerations must be addressed.

References

Bishop, John, and Shani Carter. 1991. "How Accurate Are Recent BLS Occupational Projections?" *Monthly Labor Review* 114 (10): 37–43.

DiNardo, John, Nicole Fortin, and Thomas Lemieux. 1994. "Labor Market Institutions and the Distribution of Wages, 1973-92: A Semiparametric Approach." University of Montreal.

Card, David. 1995. "The Effect of Unions on the Structure of Wages: A Longitudinal Analysis." Princeton University.

Goldin, Claudia, and Lawrence Katz. 1995. "Technology, Human Capital, and the Wage Structure: Learning about the Future from the Past." Harvard University.

Holtzer, Harry. 1996. *What Employers Want.* New York: Russell Sage Foundation.

Krueger, Alan, and Douglas Kruse. 1995. "Labor Market Effects of Spinal Cord Injuries in the Dawn of the Computer Age." Working Paper. Cambridge, Mass.: National Bureau of Economic Research.

Krueger, Alan, Douglas Kruse, and Susan Drastal. 1995. "Computer Use, Computer Training, and Employment Outcomes among People with Spinal Cord Injuries." *Spine.*

Kutscher, Ronald. 1995. "Summary of BLS Projections to 2005." *Monthly Labor Review* 118 (1): 3–8.

Rosenthal, Neal. 1992. "Evaluating the 1990 Projections of Occupational Employment." *Monthly Labor Review* 115 (8): 32–48.

Whapples, Robert. 1994. "Where Is There Consensus among American Labor Economists?" Unpublished manuscript.

7

Is Cash Benefit Policy in Conflict with the ADA?

Lex Frieden

I BECAME INTERESTED IN DISABILITY policy about thirty years ago when I broke my neck in a car accident. I was not driving, but I was drinking and so was the driver. No one had seat belts on, and I was the only one seriously hurt. I could not get out of the car under my own steam, and I went through months of rehabilitation.

After about a year and a half of this rehabilitation, I got a letter from Robert M. Ball, commissioner of Social Security. He sent a check with the letter. It was a small check, but a check, nonetheless. The letter said that I had been deemed eligible for Social Security disability insurance, based on a finding that I was permanently disabled and unable to work in the economy.

The next important thing that happened—about two days later—was that I got a phone call from the college that I had applied to. I was told that my application had been denied. I could not understand that. I had done well on the exams. The college also knew that I had a scholarship. This was Oral Roberts University, and Oral Roberts had just become a Methodist minister. So I asked if the letter of recommendation from my Methodist minister had been received, and I was told, "Yes, you did very well in Sunday School." I then was told that my application was denied because I used a wheelchair for mobility and had so indicated on my application.

This was my first experience with discrimination. The letter granting me disability benefits and the phone call denying me admission to college, coming one after the other, left me with some serious introspection to do. Talking about how I felt was difficult then. Talking about discrimination is still hard. If a person has not experienced it, he or she does not know what it is; and if it has been experienced, describing the feeling is not easy. Whatever the basis for discrimination—ethnicity, gender, or personal characteristics such as disability—when somebody tells you that you cannot do something because of conditions over which you have no control, your response is gut-wrenching.

Counselors told me that I could not do what I had planned to do before I got disabled because those things required mobility. Fortunately, I found a school that admitted me, and I studied like many people with disabilities did then and still do because there is nothing else to do: I went to school without a career goal, and I received a degree.

The only reason I went to work was because I found something that I enjoyed doing. Then I got a paycheck, and the paycheck was about three times the size of that check I was getting from Commissioner Ball. So, I wrote a letter saying, "Thanks, but I will take this job instead of your check. I appreciate it and I hope you still have money in the program if I should become disabled again someday."

Social Security and the Americans with Disabilities Act

The Americans with Disabilities Act of 1990 (ADA) and the Social Security disability insurance program are two different programs, conceived at different times with different objectives and different philosophical bases, and designed to solve different problems. These programs do not exist on a one-dimensional continuum. They are part of the loosely connected, multi-dimensional fabric of social policy, educational policy, employment policy, and disability policy.

Civil rights do not guarantee work, and social insurance does not guarantee work. As long as discrimination exists, then civil rights protection is necessary; and as long as people cannot provide for themselves and their families, then a comprehensive social welfare strategy must be available that includes provisions for assisting people who cannot work either because of personal characteristics, absence of work, or absence of needed infrastructure and environmental support in the community.

When I became disabled, was receiving a Social Security check, and was facing discrimination, I did not see any relationship between those experiences. Later on, I thought that civil rights was a progressive, employment-oriented strategy for the problems faced by people with disabilities in society. Now I see that employment promotion, civil rights, and accommodation must be the predominant strategy to attack the problems of disability in the United States. At the same time, disability insurance and Supplemental Security Income (SSI) are part of the safety net. The safety net existed before the nondiscrimination strategy.

Now a strategy has been devised with only part of the safety net intact. That is the problem in disability policy today. Experts discuss the ADA civil rights strategy versus the income maintenance strategy of the past, Social Security disability insurance, as if they were playing a zero-sum game. The fact is that the approaches are both effective solutions. The real problem is not a conflict between these two approaches, but a lack of other disability policies to talk about in this country.

Gaps in the Patchwork Quilt

Many open spaces exist in the patchwork quilt of disability policy and social policy. Health care for people with disabilities has not been effectively dealt with. Health care for people with disabilities is attached to the income support programs: Medicare for those receiving Social Security disability insurance, and Medicaid for those receiving SSI. Eligibility for health care should not depend on eligibility for a cash benefit program. Everyone needs health care. And people with disabilities need it whether or not they work. The Disability Policy Panel has made some recommendations to continue Medicare for beneficiaries who return to work. They represent a limited solution to a much larger problem.

The issue of personal assistance for people who want to work also must be addressed. Most personal assistance programs today drop their benefits when the recipient gets a job. That does not make any sense. When a disabled person takes a job, is he or she expected to pay for everything else other workers pay for and to pay for personal assistance, also? The Panel recommends a tax credit to ease the burden of paying for personal assistance when people go to work and leave public programs.

Environmental supports that people with disabilities need to work, vocational rehabilitation, and education and training must also be examined.

Furthermore, people with disabilities make up a large portion of the impoverished in the nation. It is hard to say whether people are poor because they are disabled or whether they are disabled because they are poor. But, because they are poor, many people with disabilities are much more concerned about clothing, food, and shelter than they are about work, education, and enjoyment.

A more systems-oriented view of the world must be taken. The focus cannot be solely on the ADA in the context of civil rights policy or the Social Security disability programs in the context of income policy. The patchwork quilt must be inspected to find the open spaces, so that programs can be woven effectively into those spaces. Then the question of money must be confronted.

How to Pay?

In the battle over the ADA, the question of funding was dealt with by the notion that, whatever it costs, it costs more not to do it. Many programs have been discarded because this question of who is going to pay could not be adequately answered. The only way these programs are going work is to weave them together and coordinate them. Sometimes programs do not seem to make sense, not because they did not originally make sense but because they are dealt with as distinct, segregated efforts. Threads must be woven between programs.

Managing Programs: Self-Determination

In times of fiscal constraints, programs that do work for people with disabilities must be defended. These programs need to be managed responsibly. The task should be delegated to program administrators as well as to people with disabilities. People with disabilities need to learn what their rights and benefits are and how they can control the transition from one program to another. People are needed to teach those with disabilities and to make information available in a form that can be followed without having to sort through law books and regulations.

Program administrators in Washington, D.C., or in the various state capitals are obligated to those with disabilities to give them the opportunity to manage their own lives by giving them the information needed in a form that is useful. And programs need to follow through with their side of the rules. In addition, many people with disabilities are afraid to get off Social Security despite provisions that allow them to get back on. They are afraid because they do not trust the government program to keep its side of the bargain. Beneficiaries' trust is vital for these programs to be able to effectively transition people to work.

Finally, frugality must rule the use of available resources. But efforts should not be stopped by those who say the money is not there. If a program is necessary and is going to save money in the long run, then the money must be found to see it through.

8

The Unfinished Business of
Disability Policy

Jerry L. Mashaw

A T THE BROADCAST LEVEL, the purpose of disability policy is to integrate persons with disabilities into full
participation in American society. The specific policy goals with regard to
disability and work are twofold. The first is to provide interventions that
maximize employment among those who have the capacity to work. The
second is to provide income and other supports that are adequate for those who
cannot work or whose ability to work is limited.

This conference considered how these goals are played out in three major
policy domains: in the labor market, in health care policy, and in income
policy. Various remedies were discussed for assisting people to be self-
supporting, to return to partial work, or to avoid work disability in the first
place. Policies can be designed to intervene on either the supply side or the
demand side of the labor market. On the supply side, the focus often is on a
broad range of potential interventions to increase people's work incentives,
facilitate their ability to get to workplaces, provide them with the skills that
they need to compete in the economy, and so on.

The demand side of the labor market is focused on much less. One of the
major proposals that the Disability Policy Panel has put forward—the disabled
worker tax credit—works at least partially on the demand side of the market by
subsidizing wages. The demand side should be emphasized, because the tendency is to focus on supply even when supply-side remedies may be of limited
effectiveness given the realities of the demand that is being expressed in the
labor market.

This imbalance in conventional policy discussion is illustrated by an alle-
gorical story that was suggested by a labor economist. He calls it the "dog-bone
economy." Imagine, he says, that ten dogs are kept in a pen, and every day
somebody shows up and throws nine bones into the pen. After a week or so,
one dog is looking a little weak and sluggish. So a multi-disciplinary panel of

veterinarians, doggy sociologists, and so forth are called in to observe, and they decide that the dog needs some services. They take the dog out of the pen, give him Alpo, and fatten him up. They give him exercise, aggressiveness training, and so on, and then they put him back in the pen. The dog-bone economy continues. Nine bones a day go into the pen, and a week or so later another dog is becoming weak and sluggish. The same group is called in, and they provide the same prescription: This dog needs services.

The point is that thought needs to focus more clearly on ways in which demand can be restructured so that the labor market has jobs for many more of the people that have severe obstacles to employment in today's market.

Health policy is also crucially important to people with disabilities. On the Disability Policy Panel, Gerben de Jong was constantly saying, "It is the health policy, stupid." And so, in many ways, it is.

Even the programs that are linked to disability cash benefit programs—Medicare and Medicaid—have great difficulty in supplying services that are adequate to meet the needs of persons with disabilities, as Bruce Vladeck and Patricia Riley discuss. In the private sector, the situation is even more difficult. Stan Jones is both concise and eloquent in pointing out the ways in which market pressures on private plans make it extremely difficult not to engage in a form of risk selection that severely disadvantages people with chronic conditions.

When payment for employees' health care coverage is discretionary, as it is for American employers, these same pressures weaken incentives to provide employment-based health insurance at all. As Dallas Salisbury notes, the number of workers who have employment-based health insurance coverage continues to decline. And employee cost-sharing has become the rule, not the exception, in health insurance plans that employers offer to workers and their families.

In brief, huge unfinished business exists in addressing labor market structures and access to health care as they relate to people with disabilities.

Unfinished business also remains in disability income policy, particularly in forms other than the two large programs—Social Security disability insurance (DI) and Supplemental Security Income (SSI).

Recent attempts to control costs in workers' compensation have been detailed by John Burton's comprehensive review of research and new developments in this area. Changes also have occurred or are being contemplated in other domains of income policy—the unemployment insurance system and the retirement benefit system. In some cases, these other programs can alleviate pressure on DI and SSI. Meanwhile, retrenchment in these systems increases demands placed on the disability income systems.

Workers' compensation covers work-based injuries and some work-based health problems from occupational diseases as well. But Jim Ellenberger notes that not all workers are covered by workers' compensation, and in some jurisdictions benefits are very low. Furthermore, cost containment efforts here can increase pressures elsewhere. In some cases, determining whether or not a particular impairment is work-related is not a black and white issue but involves shades of gray when chronic health conditions are exacerbated by both the toll of physically demanding work and the aging process itself. Rigorous cost containment in workers' compensation, therefore, is likely to increase demands on the universal, public disability systems.

The number of unemployed people who are eligible for unemployment insurance benefits has declined radically over the last several decades. Today, only about one-third to one-half of workers who are officially counted as unemployed are receiving unemployment insurance. While a more seamless system of unemployment protection might have supported impaired workers while they sought work they might be able to do or could be accommodated to do, gaps in the unemployment system tend to push unemployed workers with disabilities toward long-term disability benefits.

Some proposals to improve the long-term financing of the Social Security retirement system would further raise the retirement age at which full benefits are paid. Other changes are contemplated that would reduce the future cost of old-age benefits. Once again, those kinds of changes are going to put pressure on disability programs, particularly as the baby boomers move through the disability-prone ages and into retirement.

So, what is the situation? First, people are already concerned about the size of the beneficiary populations of the disability programs. After examining the changes contemplated in other income support programs, the declining demand in the labor market for low-skilled and disadvantaged workers, and the growing gaps in health care protection for workers, thinking that demands on the disability systems are going to decline through a strategy of benign neglect is not plausible. So, there remains a great deal of unfinished business.

Moreover, this unfinished business will confront some extremely difficult barriers to effective reform. The first obstacle to addressing these challenges is fiscal constraints, which prevent investment either in the human capital of the people that require help or in the administrative resources necessary to make programs work well. As disability policy is developed in the spheres of income, health care, and employment policy over the next decade or so, careful consideration must be given to the propensity of the policy process to promote short-term savings at the risk of long-term losses. Lex Frieden reiterates the importance of estimating the cost of doing nothing as well as the cost of any particular intervention.

A second obstacle is the risk that political ideology, and fighting amongst political factions, will triumph over hard facts and prudent judgment. This is a constant threat in the politics of the United States and the politics of any other collectivity.

As Bill Gradison pointed out in opening this conference, American political debate is going through a particularly fractious time. As sharp ideological divisions are confronted, efforts must be made to temper extremes in either direction. On the one hand, concerns should be raised about an ideology that places exclusive reliance on the individual and, thus, clouds judgment about what individuals with major disadvantages can realistically accomplish in the competitive job market without reasonable supports. This sort of ideology is skeptical of collective action of any sort and tends to miss the basic point of social insurance—that it secures, not only individuals, but also the underlying fabric of the society at large.

On the other hand, an ideology that suggests that entitlements in existing programs can never be changed is untenable. A distinction should be drawn that is important in understanding what "entitlement" means in the social insurance context. In the budget-driven policy debate, the term has been used in a perjorative way to suggest that collective commitments have been made that are beyond the control of policymakers or of the collective capacity for change. But the essential feature of entitlements, such as those conferred through social insurance, is that the benefits they confer are spelled out in law. The alternatives to this concept of entitlement would be to allocate benefits either at the discretion of government caseworkers or according to where one stands in the queue of supplicants for public relief. Given these alternatives, statutory entitlements have obvious virtues.

The point is that entitlements conferred by law can be changed by law. But the changes in these laws need to be made judiciously, after thoughtful study of their long-term consequences.

Bill Gradison's reminder is heartening that political debates have not always been so fractious and need not remain so in the indefinite future. From his legislative experience on the House Ways and Means Committee and the House Budget Committee and with the National Commission on Social Security Reform in the early 1980s, he relates how bipartisan efforts in the past have forged difficult compromises when they were needed to maintain the social insurance systems on a prudent and secure course. In programs with such important, long-term consequences for all Americans, thoughtful, periodic adjustments are inevitable as well as desirable.

As fiscal, ideological, and political constraints interfere with the kinds of sound policy analysis and civil dialogue that is needed to address these serious issues of public policy, one important development provides encouragement. The National Academy of Social Insurance, which conducted its eighth annual conference in 1996, provides a refuge where people of very different perspectives and persuasions can inform each other through solid facts and analysis and argue civilly with each other. As one surveys the world of public policymaking for promising developments, this is an institutional virtue to be cherished and defended.

Contributors

Bruce Barge is vice president of corporate quality at the St. Paul Companies and coauthor of *The Executive's Guide to Controlling Health Care and Disability Costs,* published by John Wiley & Sons.

Monroe Berkowitz is professor emeritus of economics at Rutgers University and a member of the Disability Policy Panel of the National Academy of Social Insurance.

Richard V. Burkhauser is professor of economics at the Center for Policy Research, the Maxwell School, Syracuse University, and a member of the Disability Policy Panel of the National Academy of Social Insurance.

John F. Burton, Jr., is dean of the School of Management and Labor Relations, Rutgers University.

Steven Clauser is director of the Office of Beneficiary and Program Research and Demonstrations at the Health Care Financing Administration.

Philip R. de Jong is professor of economics of Social Security at Erasmus University, Rotterdam, and fellow at the Institute for Law and Public Policy, Leiden University, the Netherlands.

James N. Ellenberger is assistant director of the Department of Occupational Safety and Health, AFL-CIO, and a member of the Disability Policy Panel of the National Academy of Social Insurance.

Lex Frieden is senior vice president at the Institute for Rehabilitation and Research and a member of the Disability Policy Panel of the National Academy of Social Insurance.

Andrew J. Glenn is an assistant professor in the Department of Economics and Finance, University of Central Arkansas.

Michael J. Graetz is Justus S. Hotchkiss professor of law at Yale University.

Thomas Hoyer is director of the Office of Chronic Care and Insurance Policy at the Health Care Financing Administration.

William G. Johnson is professor of health economics at the School of Health Administration and Policy and the Department of Economics, Arizona State University.

Stanley B. Jones is director of the Health Insurance Reform Project, George Washington University.

Alan B. Krueger is Bendheim professor of economics and public affairs at Princeton University and a research associate of the National Bureau of Economic Research.

Jerry L. Mashaw is Sterling professor of Yale University and chair of the Disability Policy Panel of the National Academy of Social Insurance.

Katherine S. Newman is professor of public policy at the John F. Kennedy School of Goverment, Harvard University.

Ellen O'Brien is a research analyst in the Office of Research and Demonstrations at the Heath Care Financing Administration.

Van Doorn Ooms is senior vice president and director of research for the Committee for Economic Development.

Virginia P. Reno is director of research at the National Academy of Social Insurance.

Patricia Riley is executive director of the National Academy for State Health Policy.

Dallas Salisbury is president of the Employee Benefit Research Institute.

Leslie J. Scallet is director of the Mental Health Policy Resource Center.

R. Alexander Vachon is a professional staff member of the Senate Committee on Finance.

Bruce C. Vladeck is administrator of the Health Care Financing Administration.

David C. Wittenburg is a doctoral candidate in economics and a graduate associate in the Center for Policy Research, Maxwell School, Syracuse University.

Tony Young is a policy analyst at the United Cerebral Palsy Association. At the time of the conference, he was director of residential and community support government relations at the American Rehabilitation Association.

Index